C000021997

A
HISTORY
OF
MALMESBURY

JANE FREEMAN
and
AELRED WATKIN

with contributions by
H. F. CHETTLE, ELIZABETH CRITTALL,
and D. A. CROWLEY

WILTSHIRE COUNTY COUNCIL
AND THE
WARDEN AND FREEMEN OF MALMESBURY
1999

The text, illustrations, and maps in this volume have been reset and reprinted from A History of Wiltshire, volume III, edited by R. B. Pugh and Elizabeth Crittall, 1956, and A History of Wiltshire, volume XIV, edited by D. A. Crowley, 1991 (The Victoria History of the Counties of England; Oxford University Press for the University of London Institute of Historical Research).

© University of London, 1956, 1991, 1999

All rights reserved. No part of this publication may be reproduced, stored in a retrieval system, or transmitted, in any form or by any means, electronic, mechanical, photocopying, recording, or otherwise, without the prior permission of Oxford University Press.

First published in this edition in 1999 by
Wiltshire County Council, Libraries and Heritage,
Bythesea Road, Trowbridge, Wiltshire BA14 8BS,
in conjunction with the Warden and Freemen of Malmesbury

ISBN 0 86080 444 5

Typeset in 11/12.5 Bembo
Typesetting and design by John Chandler
Printed by Wiltshire County Council

CONTENTS

EDITORIAL NOTE

Apart from the addition of the note on the bird's eye view of Malmesbury, the text presented here, including the numbering of the footnotes, remains unchanged from when it was first published in the *Victoria History of Wiltshire* series in 1956 (Malmesbury Abbey and Hospitals), and 1991 (Malmesbury and Westport). The format and pagination, however, are different, and in consequence a new index has been prepared based on the original indexes. A few footnotes have been amended to take account of the new pagination and the placing of maps and illustrations in the present edition. The footnotes and, to a lesser extent, the text include abbreviations employed according to the *Victoria History's* editorial conventions. While the meaning of most will be self-evident, some abbreviated references to documentary sources may cause difficulty, and readers are advised to consult the detailed lists of abbreviations and classes of public records used, which are prefaced to the original 1956 and 1991 publications. Among the most frequently used abbreviations are the following: B.L. (British Library); P.R.O. (Public Record Office); *V.C.H.* (*Victoria County History*); *W.A.M.* (*Wiltshire Archaeological and Natural History Magazine*); W.A.S. (Wiltshire Archaeological and Natural History Society); W.R.O. (Wiltshire and Swindon Record Office); W.R.S. (Wiltshire Record Society).

LIST OF ILLUSTRATIONS AND MAPS

ILLUSTRATIONS

v

MAPS

NOTE ON THE BIRD'S EYE VIEW
OF MALMESBURY

The bird's eye view of Malmesbury printed on the covers of this volume depicts the town as it was on 23 October 1646. The original drawing is on vellum, measures 44 cm. by 77 cm., and was done with a pen and coloured inks, and with watercolour. It bears a legend which reads (with modernized spelling, punctuation, and capitalization) 'The description of Malmesbury, or firstly Madalfsbury, a borough of north Wiltshire both ancient and famous, now in the possession and sole jurisdiction of a family of antiquity and honour, viz. Sir John Danvers of Dauntsey House, knight, a member of the House of Commons this parliament 1647. Which place is not only renowned for its natural strength, seated on a steep hill (unwinable by reason of the many rocks), extending unto, or containing, no more ground than what it standeth on, and (within less than pistol shot) surrounded with unfordable rivers, but also for its unconquered strength, and victory against the Danes after a long siege for Athelstan, a Saxon king, shut up within it: manifest by his charter extant there, who, for its services and fidelity, bestowed, besides several other privileges and immunities, very fair lands, which to this day it enjoyeth, and where, in testimony of his affection to so great a favour, his body at his desire was entombed. This shows the direct figure of the borough or garrison as it stood fortified the 23 of October 1646, the day it was demolished by the parliament's order, the whole kingdom being a little before reduced; when it had stood a firm garrison for the parliament of England under the commanding of Colonel Nicholas Devereux 2 years, 4 months, and odd weeks. Which description or draft, as proper, unto the said Sir John Danvers, the sole lord and owner of it together with the coat of arms of his family, the said colonel presented, as an acknowledgement of his many noble favours, this 10th of April 1648.' The legend indicates that the view was drawn between October 1646 and April 1648; the name of the draftsman is not recorded. The ownership and whereabouts of the view from 1648 to 1994 have not been traced. In 1994 it was offered for sale at Messrs. Sotheby's, New Bond Street, London, bought privately, and afterwards sold to the warden and freemen of the Old Corporation of Malmesbury. Its existence was not known to the authors and editors of the *Victoria History of Wiltshire* when the article on Malmesbury, now reprinted, was prepared in the late 1980s.

The view may have been commissioned by Col. Devereux, the commander of the parliamentary garrison at Malmesbury from the summer of 1644 until it was disbanded in 1646, and was presented by him to Sir John Danvers on 10 April 1648. Danvers was described as the sole lord and owner of Malmesbury borough and the head of the Danvers family. The borough had been held until his death in 1644 by Danvers's brother Henry, earl of Danby, who devised it to Danvers's son Henry. Lord Danby was a royalist, and after his death the disposition of his estates was in question until in 1644 the House of Commons resolved that they should pass to Henry (born 1633): in 1648 Danvers presumably held the borough in his son's right.

Malmesbury is seen in the view from the west or south-west with hills to the north and north-east. The view was designed as a record of the town when garrisoned by the parliamentary forces and shows it surrounded by walls and by the two branches of the river Avon. The legend lays great emphasis on the natural defensive strength of its position and makes reference to a tradition of a Saxon victory there over the Danes. In the first Civil War the town changed hands several times before being captured for parliament in May 1644 by Col. Edward Massey. Thereafter it accommodated a parliamentary garrison until 1646. Much of the detail shown in the view is military. The ancient walls had clearly been rebuilt and earth had apparently been banked steeply against them. At intervals around them there were watch towers and ordnance, and at the river crossings north-east and south-east of the town Holloway bridge and St. John's bridge were drawbridges. The heaviest fortifications, including two other drawbridges and two hornworks, platforms bearing cannon, were at the west end of the town where it was vulnerable to attack along the causeway from Westport. That area was further defended by a gun mounted high on the ruins at the west end of the abbey. On 14 August 1646 parliament ordered that the garrison should be slighted, and, the bird's eye view having been completed, the order was carried out on 23 October.

The layout of the streets within the walls is largely recognizable as that of the modern town. One marked difference is that in 1646 there were houses within Cross Hayes, an area later open and used as a market place. Most street names recorded in the view survived in the 20th century; one name or description which did not was 'the shambles called Carfax' applied to the area immediately north or north-west of the market cross. The complexity of the western fortifications makes it difficult to identify what is now Abbey Row and the east end of Westport suburb which both lay outside the walls.

Within the walls some of the houses had extensive areas of garden, and there were apparently some orchards. Two gardens or orchards enclosed by walls lay south of Abbey House. Perhaps surprisingly, gardens behind houses on the west side of High Street, in the foreground of the bird's eye view, included some of formal design with parterres. The houses in Burnivale, outside the wall on the west side of the town, had gardens running down to the river. A building at the south end of Burnivale, in 1646 called the old chapel, was probably that called the Hermitage in the 19th century. Apart from those in Westport and Burnivale, most buildings standing outside the town wall were mills scattered along the two branches of the Avon. To the north a farmhouse had been attached to the tower and steeple of the former church at Whitchurch.

The great extent to which both the individual buildings and the modern layout of Malmesbury can be recognized suggests that the bird's eye view provides a very accurate guide to the town as it was in the mid 17th century. Its evidence falls between that of a late 13th- or early 14th-century rental, which records the extent of the walls and the names of the main streets in the town, and the town plans which survive from the mid 19th century and record its expansion in the last 150 years.

Malmesbury: air view from the south in 1975

MALMESBURY

THE TOWN of Malmesbury stands on a steep hill almost encircled by the Tetbury and Sherston branches of the Bristol Avon.[32] The streams, flowing eastwards, come within 200 m. of each other at the town's north-western corner, diverge, and meet at its southern end.[33] The word Malmesbury was perhaps derived from the name of Mailduib, an Irish monk or hermit who may have settled on or near the town's site in the mid 7th century. Mailduib is said to have gathered around him a school which became the nucleus of the monastery later known as Malmesbury abbey.[34] A tradition was current in the abbey in the 14th century that Mailduib's settlement lay beneath a fortified place, called either Bladon or by the Saxon name Ingelbourne, which had been constructed by a heathen British king, had once been a thriving town, but was in Mailduib's time little frequented.[35] Malmesbury's naturally defensible site may have been that of a stronghold in an earlier period, but the tradition cannot be substantiated. Between the 7th century and the 11th the abbey was granted many estates near Malmesbury, including the lands, surrounding the town, which became Malmesbury and Westport parishes.[36] The two parishes may have been formed early: there was a church at Westport in the late Saxon period and the site of St. Paul's, the medieval parish church of Malmesbury, in or adjacent to the abbey precinct perhaps indicates a similarly early origin. The parishes were closely associated: the settlement called Westport formed a suburb of the town, and what became Malmesbury borough included part of that settlement and had most of its common land in Westport parish.[37]

32 See illus. on facing page.
33 This article was written in 1987–9. Maps used include O.S. Maps 1/50,000, sheet 173 (1974 edn.); 1/25,000, ST 88, ST 98–9 (1958 edns.); 6", Wilts.VIII, XIII (1888–9 and later edns.).
34 The hist. of Malmesbury abbey is related in *V.C.H. Wilts.* iii. 210 (reprinted below, pp. 147–99.   35 *Eulogium Hist.* (Rolls Ser.), i. 225–6.
36 Finberg, *Early Wessex Chart.* pp. 70–3, 100, 105–6; above, Brokenborough, introduction; below, manors; below, Westport, manors.
37 Below, Westport, introduction, econ. hist., church.

I

MALMESBURY c.1840

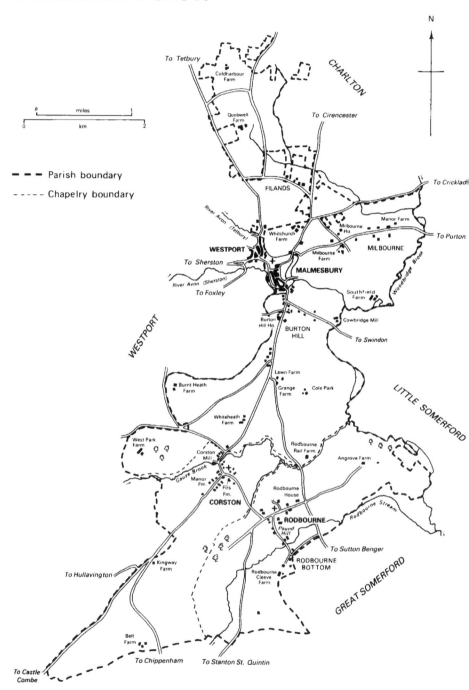

N

To Tetbury

Coldharbour Farm

CHARLTON

miles

km

To Cirencester

Quobwell Farm

Parish boundary

Chapelry boundary

To Cricklade

FILANDS

River Avon (Tetbury)

Milbourne Ho

Manor Farm

To Purton

Whitchurch Farm

WESTPORT

MILBOURNE

Milbourne Farm

To Sherston

MALMESBURY

River Avon (Sherston)

To Foxley

Southfield Farm

Woodbridge Brook

Burton Hill Ho

BURTON HILL

Cowbridge Mill

To Swindon

WESTPORT

Lawn Farm

Burnt Heath Farm

Grange Farm

Cole Park

LITTLE SOMERFORD

Whiteheath Farm

West Park Farm

Corston Mill

Rodbourne Rail Farm

Angrove Farm

Gauze Brook

Manor Fm.

Firs Fm.

Rodbourne House

CORSTON

RODBOURNE

Rodbourne Stream

Pound Hill

To Sutton Benger

Kingway Farm

RODBOURNE BOTTOM

To Hullavington

Rodbourne Cleeve Farm

GREAT SOMERFORD

Bell Farm

To Castle Combe

To Chippenham

To Stanton St. Quintin

Malmesbury parish comprised most of the town, but not the abbey precinct and the part in Westport parish, and lands north, east, and south of it. Within the parish were the villages or hamlets of Milbourne, Whitchurch, and Blick's Hill to the east, Burton Hill immediately south of the town, and Corston and Rodbourne further south. A settlement called Filands, north of the town, lay mainly in Westport parish.[38] The name of another, Walcot, in either Westport or Malmesbury parish may indicate an early settlement site or proximity to the town walls; the only references to it are from the late 13th century.[39] From the 14th century or earlier there was a chapel, dependent on St. Paul's church, at Corston and another at Rodbourne.[40] Each chapelry was a tithing: although neither relieved its own poor, both Corston and Rodbourne were thus separate from Malmesbury in some ecclesiastical and administrative matters. The main part of the following article deals with all Malmesbury parish except Corston and Rodbourne, with the abbey precinct which was apparently considered extraparochial until the 18th century when it relieved its own poor,[41] and with the history of the town including some aspects of that part of it which lay in Westport parish. Corston and Rodbourne are dealt with in separate accounts at the end of the article.

Malmesbury parish, including the abbey precinct, Corston, and Rodbourne, measured 10 km. from north to south and at its widest, south of the town, 5 km. from east to west. It narrowed where crossed by the two branches of the Avon, and 360 a. to the north were attached to the rest of the parish by a neck of land north-east of the town. Further north again *c.* 20 a. in two parcels were detached, one surrounded by lands of Brokenborough parish and one between Brokenborough and Charlton; north of Milbourne village were *c.* 10 a., parcels of Westport and Charlton parishes, enclosed by Malmesbury lands.[42] The boundary of the 360 a. with Charlton was marked by a stream, but the boundaries with Brokenborough and Westport were irregular: that irregularity, and the existence of islands of other parishes in Malmesbury and of Malmesbury in other parishes, may be the result of inclosure and allotment of land shared by several parishes, of basing parish boundaries on the ownership of land with which tithes were merged after the Reformation,

38 Below, Westport, introduction.
39 *Reg. Malm.* ii. 120–1, 358–9; *P.N. Wilts.* (E.P.N.S.), 277.
40 Below, Corston, church; Rodbourne, church.
41 Ibid. local govt. (par. govt.).
42 W.R.O., tithe award.

or of both. Further south the parish's eastern boundary was marked by the Avon, its tributary Woodbridge brook, and another tributary, while a tributary of the Sherston Avon marked part of the western boundary. Elsewhere the parish boundary was marked by few natural features, but on the western side of the town it may have followed part of the town wall and in other places was marked by roads. The boundaries of Rodbourne and Corston were surveyed in the late 11th century or early 12th when the road dividing Corston and Hullavington was mentioned and the Avon was Rodbourne's boundary with Little Somerford.[43] That last boundary was diverted west from the Avon, its natural line, at an agreed inclosure in 1281.[44] In the early 1630s, after the disafforestation of Braydon forest in 1630 and disputes with other landowners, the lord of Whitchurch and Milbourne manor was allotted 104 a. of the purlieus c. 6 km. east of the parish:[45] that allotment, Milbourne common, was part of Malmesbury parish in 1839.[46]

In the period 1882–4 the detached parts of Malmesbury parish to the north were transferred to Brokenborough, Milbourne common was transferred to Brinkworth, and the detached parts of Westport and Charlton embraced by Malmesbury parish were transferred to Malmesbury; north of the town there were also small changes to the boundaries with Westport and Charlton.[47] In 1885, after losing c. 100 a. in the changes of 1882–4, Malmesbury parish measured 5,333 a. (2,160 ha.), of which Corston and Rodbourne were a total of c. 2,500 a.[48] In 1886 Malmesbury municipal borough was created; it contained 178 a. formerly part of Malmesbury, Westport, and Brokenborough parishes.[49] In 1894 the reduced Malmesbury parish was renamed St. Paul Malmesbury Without parish; to it was added in 1896 all Westport parish outside the borough.[50] In 1981 it measured 2,903 ha. (7,173 a.).[51] In 1984 small areas were exchanged between that parish and Brokenborough, and some land was transferred from it to Malmesbury parish.[52] Thereafter St. Paul Malmesbury Without measured 2,699 ha. (6,669 a.).[53]

43 Arch. Jnl. lxxvii. 43–6, 88–90.
44 Reg. Malm. ii. 219–20.
45 V.C.H. Wilts. iv. 406; W.R.O., EA/34; ibid. 88/10/52.
46 W.R.O., tithe award.   47 Census, 1891.
48 O.S. Maps 6", Wilts. VIII, XIII (1888–9 edns.); W.R.O., tithe award.
49 W.R.O., F 2/141.   50 Census, 1901.
51 Ibid. 1981.   52 For Malmesbury par. in 1984, below.
53 Inf. from Chief Assistant (Environment), Dept. of Planning and Highways, Co. Hall, Trowbridge.

From the confluence of its Sherston and Tetbury branches the Avon flows south-east across the old Malmesbury parish, turning south near the eastern boundary. The name Ingelbourne was applied to the Tetbury branch in the 11th or 12th century and in the later 15th, and to the Sherston branch in the later 13th; it may also have been used for a stream rising south-west of the town.[54] Most of the tributary streams cross the parish from west to east. Gauze brook flows north-east across the southern half of the parish to join the Avon on the eastern boundary, and further south is a parallel stream, formerly called the Rodbourne; the names were in use c. 1100, when both streams were boundaries of Rodbourne, and perhaps much earlier.[55] The town stands on a steep sided outcrop of Cornbrash, above 76 m. Elsewhere the steepest slopes in the parish are around Rodbourne village. Nowhere does the land rise much above 90 m. and in the north and south-west it flattens out at that height. Kellaways Clay outcrops over most of the parish and there are small areas of Oxford Clay. Kellaways Sand outcrops near Rodbourne, and there are outcrops of clay of the Forest Marble beside the Avon and in the extreme north. In the lower parts of the parish, especially between the town and Corston village, Cornbrash outcrops. Alluvium has been deposited by the Avon and its main tributaries, and deposits of sand and gravel are in several places north of the town.[56]

Although the well watered clay soils favour pasture rather than tillage, open fields on the clay lay south of Milbourne village and in the north. The Cornbrash favours arable and the open fields near Corston village were on both the Cornbrash and clay. Most of the land between Gauze brook and the town was pasture and parkland from an early date. What became Cole park, beside the Avon south of the town, was wooded in the Middle Ages, but later there was little woodland in the parish. In the 19th century and the 20th there were quarries near Corston village and on the outskirts of the town, and the clay in the southern part of the parish was used for making bricks.[57] From 1935 the plateau in the south-western corner has been part of R.A.F. Hullavington.[58]

---

54   Arch. Jnl. lxxvii. 46; P.N. Wilts. (E.P.N.S.), 51; Reg. Malm. i. 122; W.R.O. 88/1/16.
55   Arch. Jnl. lxxvii. 88, 90; P.N. Wilts. (E.P.N.S.), 7, 51–2.
56   Geol. Surv. Maps 1", solid and drift, sheets 251 (1970 edn.), 252 (1974 edn.).
57   Below, agric.; ibid. Corston, econ. hist.; Rodbourne, econ. hist.
58   Inf. from Defence Land Agent, Durrington.

In the later 17th century the Oxford–Bristol road ran east and west through Milbourne village, Malmesbury, and Foxley crossing the Tetbury Avon by a stone bridge at the town's north-east corner.[59] The main road south from the town has always been that through Corston to Chippenham, called Kingway c. 1100 when it may have been on roughly its present course.[60] To the north the Tetbury (Glos.) road also served until 1778 as a link from Cirencester (Glos.) to Malmesbury and Chippenham, before 1743 via the Foss Way, thereafter alternatively on a turnpike road to Tetbury.[61] In 1756 the Tetbury–Malmesbury and Malmesbury–Chippenham roads were turnpiked to complete a Chippenham–Cirencester turnpike road via Tetbury. By then the Oxford–Bristol road may already have declined in importance and, east of the town, the more northerly Cricklade–Malmesbury road and, west of the town, the more northerly Malmesbury–Sherston road were turnpiked.[62] The road through Milbourne remained in use as a minor road. A more direct Cirencester–Malmesbury road was completed across Hankerton parish and turnpiked in 1778.[63] Another road, which left the Chippenham road south-east of the town, crossed the Avon by Cow bridge, and led to Wootton Bassett and Swindon, was in use in 1773 and turnpiked in 1809.[64] The Chippenham, Cirencester, and Tetbury roads were disturnpiked in 1874, the Cricklade, Swindon, and Sherston roads in 1876.[65] In 1973 the Cirencester–Chippenham road was diverted to bypass the town to the east.[66] There were few minor roads in the north part of the parish in the late 18th century. One, linking the Tetbury and Cirencester roads, was still in use in the late 20th century; since 1973 it has assumed greater importance by taking Chippenham–Tetbury traffic away from the town. Another, running north-west from the linking road east of and parallel with the Tetbury road,[67] was in use in 1842 but not in 1885.[68] South of the town in the late 18th century lanes led east

---

59 J. Ogilby, *Brit.* (1675), pl. 79.
60 *Arch. Jnl.* lxxv. 74.
61 *Andrews and Dury, Map* (W.R.S. viii), pls. 16–17; *V. C. H. Wilts.* iv. 257, 268; *L.J.* xxvi. 241.
62 *V.C.H. Wilts.* iv. 257, 269; *L.J.* xxviii. 526, 581.
63 Above, Hankerton, introduction.
64 *Andrews and Dury, Map* (W.R.S. viii), pl. 16; *L.J.* xlvii. 581.
65 *V.C.H. Wilts.* iv. 269, 271; 36 & 37 Vic. c. 90.
66 Inf. from Chief Assistant (Environment), Dept. of Planning and Highways.
67 *Andrews and Dury, Map* (W.R.S. viii), pl. 16.
68 W.R.O., tithe award; O.S. Map 6", Wilts. VIII (1889 edn.).

and south-east from the Chippenham road to Sutton Benger, to Rodbourne village, and to a road between Rodbourne and Stanton St. Quintin; they were crossed by others running north-east and south-west. Lanes led south-west from the Chippenham road 1 km. south of the town and west from it at the north end of Corston village to Malmesbury common in Westport parish, and further south one led west to Hullavington and another south-west along the parish boundary towards Castle Combe.[69] The road towards Castle Combe went out of use in the 19th century after a road through Hullavington village was turnpiked, but the road to Hullavington, part of that turnpike road, remains in use.[70] In the late 20th century the Sutton Benger road and that leading to it from Corston village were the only public metalled roads east of the Chippenham road, and Common Road, leading west from the north end of Corston village, was the principal route to Malmesbury common.

A canal between Bristol and Cricklade passing south-east of the town was planned in the late 18th century but not built.[71] A railway line through Malmesbury was proposed in 1864 but there was no service to the town until 1877 when a branch from the G.W.R. line at Dauntsey was opened. The new line skirted the town to the north-east, a tunnel was made under Holloway, and a small station was built east of the Tetbury Avon north of the abbey church. Part of the Bristol & South Wales railway was built across the south part of the parish in 1903, and in 1933 a spur was built to connect the Malmesbury branch to that line at Little Somerford; the southern half of the branch was then closed. Passenger services to Malmesbury ceased in 1951,[72] and goods services in 1963 when the station was closed.[73]

Despite the literary tradition of early settlement within the parish, little archaeological evidence of human activity in prehistoric times has been found. Some artifacts of the Iron Age and later have been found in the town and in the south part of the parish. On Cam's Hill south-east of the town are rectangular and circular prehistoric enclosures measuring 0.5 ha. and 0.25 ha. respectively.[74]

69 *Andrews and Dury, Map* (W.R.S. viii), pls. 13–14.
70 Above, Hullavington, introduction.
71 *W.A.M.* xlii. 399.
72 *V.C.H. Wilts.* iv. 281, 288.
73 C. R. Clinker, *Clinker's Reg. Closed Passenger Sta. 1830–1980,* p. 92; see below, illus. on p. 8.
74 *V.C.H. Wilts.* i (1), 84, 100, 269; *W.A.M.* lxviii. 138–9.

The railway station in 1966

In 1377 a total of 556 poll-tax payers lived in Malmesbury, in other villages in the parish, and, probably, in the suburb of Westport.[75] The population of the parish was 1,571 in 1801. Between then and 1851 it increased steadily to reach a peak of 2,581, and between 1851 and 1891 it declined. The sharpest fall, from 2,543 in 1861 to 2,306 in 1871, was ascribed to the emigration of labourers to work in the oilfields of Ohio (U.S.A.). In 1891, the last date for which figures are available, 2,263 people lived in what had been Malmesbury parish.[76] In 1981 the population of Malmesbury St. Paul Without parish was 1,993.[77] In 1773 and 1842, as presumably earlier, settlement was concentrated in the town and in Milbourne, Corston, and Rodbourne villages. There was a group of buildings at Burton Hill and scattered farmsteads in most parts of the parish.[78] The histories of the villages, hamlets, and farmsteads in the parish, apart from those of Corston and Rodbourne, which are dealt with separately, are described below after the account of the town.

75 V.C.H. Wilts. iv. 309.
76 Ibid. 324, 352–3.
77 Census, 1981.
78 Andrews and Dury, Map (W.R.S. viii), pls. 13, 16–17; W.R.O., tithe award.

TOWN HISTORY. The town which grew up around Malmesbury abbey had probably become a local trading centre by the late 9th century. At about that time it was included with three other places in Wiltshire in the list of fortified centres known as the Burghal Hidage: 1,200 hides were assigned to defend the fort which may therefore have had 1,650 yd. of wall. Moneyers worked at Malmesbury from the mid 10th century and coin evidence suggests that the town was one of the most important in the county in the early 11th. Its eminence was confirmed by Domesday Book, in which it was referred to as a borough, placed at the head of the entry for Wiltshire, and described in more detail than any other borough in the county, although it was not necessarily the largest or most prosperous. Within the borough in 1086 the king had 26 *masurae hospitate*, possibly houses let at rent, and 25 *masurae* exempt from geld, perhaps occupied by the king's servants; each *masura* may have consisted of more than one house. A further 22¾ *masurae* were held by other lords; in addition 8 or 11 burgesses of Malmesbury and 5½ houses in the borough were mentioned elsewhere in the survey as appurtenant to rural estates. Thus, although smaller than many others, the borough may have had in it 100 or more households. The mint in Malmesbury was the only one of perhaps five in Wiltshire to be mentioned in Domesday Book.[79] Between the 11th and the 16th centuries Malmesbury's importance in the county declined, although it was still highly assessed for tax in 1334 and was apparently populous in 1377.[80] In the later Middle Ages it was notable chiefly for its abbey and for its cloth industry, which was to remain a source of its prosperity until the mid 18th century. From the 18th century it was principally a local centre for commerce, manufacture, and administration.[81]

Before the Conquest Malmesbury was required to give to the king 20*s.* for his fleet when he went on an expedition by sea or a man for each five of its hides, probably three men, when he went on an expedition by land. Such a requirement suggests that Malmesbury was already a privileged borough.[82] A guild merchant had rights and lands and presumably played some part in the town's government in the 13th century. The burgesses' privileges, including exemption from certain dues, and lands, later called King's Heath or Malmesbury common, were

79 *V.C.H. Wilts.* ii, pp. 15–23, 113–25.
80 Ibid. iv. 296, 309.
81 Below, trade and ind.
82 *V.C.H. Wilts.* ii, pp. 22–3.

MALMESBURY AND
WESTPORT c.1845

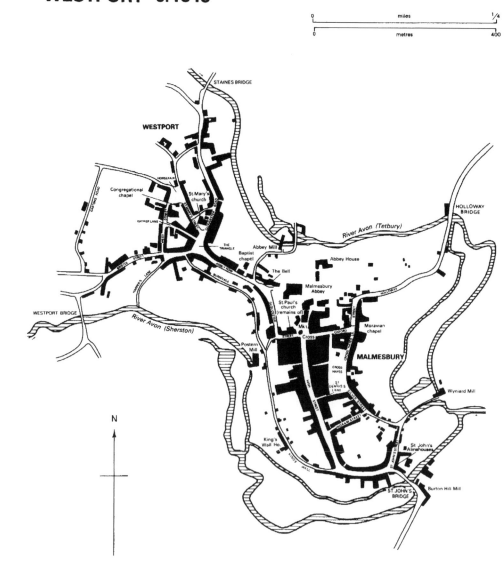

confirmed in 1381 when the burgesses made the implausible claim that they had been granted by King Athelstan. The governing body was known from the 16th century or earlier as the alderman and burgesses.[83] In the 16th century the borough presumably included all the land within the town walls, except that within the abbey precinct, and an area in Westport beyond the walls. The extension of the borough boundary across the neck of land linking Malmesbury and Westport may have been to bring within the borough the markets and settlements which had grown up outside the confined area of the town; a Thursday market granted in 1252 was for Westport, and both the Triangle and Horsefair in Westport, within the borough boundary, may have been the sites of markets or fairs.[84] In the late 13th century the walled part of the town within Malmesbury parish was called Bynport to distinguish it from Westport: the name was still in use in the 16th century.[85] The alderman and burgesses may have exercised rights over the abbey site from the Dissolution, but the precinct was not formally included in the borough until 1685.[86] The earliest map showing the borough boundary is of 1831. The east, south, and south-west boundaries were the two branches of the Avon, and the north was a ditch then called Warditch. The north-western, between the Tetbury road and the Sherston Avon and taking in part of Westport, was in places marked by streets but followed an indirect line and for much of its distance no prominent feature. Approximately a third of the borough lay in Westport parish.[87]

In 1831 it was proposed to extend the borough boundary where each of four main roads entered the town. There is no evidence that extensions were made, but the urban sanitary district formed in 1872 took in an area greater than the 1831 borough, and its boundaries were those of the municipal borough created in 1886.[88] In 1894 the municipal borough was divided into the civil parishes of the Abbey, Malmesbury St. Paul Within, Westport St. Mary Within, and Brokenborough Within. The Abbey and Malmesbury St. Paul Within included the parts of the town formerly in Malmesbury parish. The other two were those parts of

---

83 Below, local govt. (boro. govt.).
84 Ibid. trade and ind. (mkts. and fairs).
85 *Reg. Malm.* i. 121; *L. & P. Hen. VIII*, xix (2), p. 414; *Eng. P. N. Elements* (E.P.N.S .), i. 36.
86 *Cal. S.P. Dom.* 1685, p. 54.
87 S. Hudson, *Hill Top Town*, 119–21; Soc. Antiq. MS. 817, ix, f. 1.
88 *V.C.H. Wilts.* iv. 352; v. 258; O.S. Maps 6", Wilts. VIII, XIII (1888–9 and later edns.); Soc. Antiq. MS. 817, ix, f. 1.

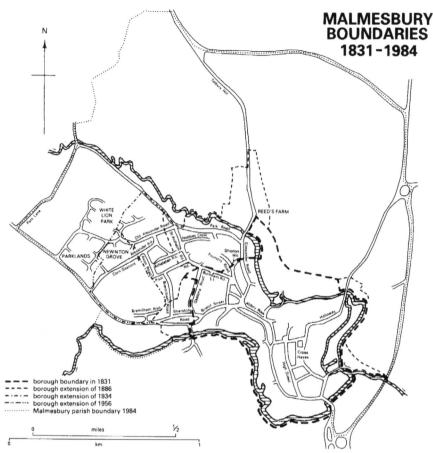

WHITE
LION
PARK

REED'S FARM

Park Road

Hobbes Close

NEWNTON
GROVE

Shipton
Hill

PARKLANDS

Corn Gastons

Athelstan Rd.

Foundry

Burnham Rd.

Bremilham Rise

Sherston

Bristol Street

Abbey Row

Holloway

Road

Cross
Hayes

High Street

- - -   borough boundary in 1831
- - -   borough extension of 1886
- · - ·   borough extension of 1934
- ·· - ··   borough extension of 1956
··········   Malmesbury parish boundary 1984

| 0 | | miles | | ½ |

| 0 | | km | | 1 |

Westport and Brokenborough parishes brought into the urban sanitary
district in 1872: they were merged as Westport St. Mary Within in 1897.[89]
In 1934 a further 25 a. of Brokenborough parish on the west side of the
town were added to the borough. The three civil parishes within the
borough were then merged as a new Malmesbury parish,[90] to which
was added in 1956 part of a built up area in Brokenborough and St. Paul
Malmesbury Without.[91] In 1974 Malmesbury lost its borough status,[92]
and in 1984 Malmesbury parish was extended west, north, and east,
bringing more housing within it and increasing its area from 93 ha. (230
a.) to 283 ha. (699 a.).[93]

89 *Census*, 1901.
90 Ibid. 1931; *V.C.H. Wilts.* iv. 352.
91 *Census*, 1951; 1961.
92 *Local Govt. in Eng. and Wales* (H.M.S.O. 1974), 117.
93 Inf. from Chief Assistant (Environment), Dept. of Planning and Highways.

In 1547 the adult population of the town of Malmesbury, presumably including its suburbs, was estimated at 860, the third largest total for a town in Wiltshire.[94] In 1801 the population of the town, apparently defined as the borough, was 1,107. It rose steadily to 1,624 in 1861, and in 1891 the municipal borough had 2,964 inhabitants, of whom 1,348 lived in that part of it which had been in the old Malmesbury parish. Numbers fell until 1931, when the borough had 2,334 inhabitants. The population of the enlarged borough was 2,510 in 1951;[95] in 1971, after further enlargement, it was no more than 2,610 and in 1981 Malmesbury parish had a population of 2,591.[96]

The chief buildings of the town stood in Malmesbury parish on the peninsula formed by the two branches of the Avon. At the northern end, on the highest ground, was the abbey. In the 1130s, when he held Malmesbury abbey and a lease of the borough from the Crown, Roger, bishop of Salisbury, built at Malmesbury a castle which reportedly encroached on a graveyard within a stone's throw of the abbey church.[97] Its site was probably west of the church, either that occupied in the late 20th century by the eastern range of the Old Bell hotel, formerly called Castle House,[98] or further west, beyond the lane which bounded the hotel. Another suggested site, east of the abbey church and encroaching on the monks' graveyard,[99] offered little command of the western approach to the town where the natural barriers were weakest. In 1215 the Crown granted the keeping of the castle to Malmesbury abbey, which in 1216 was licensed to demolish it and build on its site.[1] A document, apparently compiled by the abbey in the later 13th century, lists obligations to repair 26 sections of the town's wall, presumably its whole length. Those required to repair the wall, including the abbey itself in eight sections, were apparently the owners of the plots in the borough adjoining the respective sections. The correlation between the owners and the holders of the *masurae* listed in Domesday Book has given rise to the suggestion that the walls and the obligation existed in 1086, but it has been more plausibly suggested that although the wall was referred to in

94 *W.A.M.* vii. 3.
95 *V.C.H. Wilts.* iv. 352–3.
96 *Census*, 1971; 1981.
97 Wm. of Malmesbury, *Gesta Regum Angl.* (Rolls Ser.), ii. 484; below, manors.
98 *W.A.M.* li. 187.
99 *Memorials of Old Wilts.* ed. A. Dryden, 148.
 1 *Rot. Chart.* (Rec. Com.), 213, 222.

the document as the king's wall the obligations were imposed or defined
only after the abbey acquired the castle. The stone wall may therefore
also have been built by Roger in the 1130s.[2] Roughly parallel with the
rivers, it may have followed the lines of earlier defences, possibly those
of the later 9th century. The wall was still standing in the earlier 16th
century but was then said to be very feeble.[3] It probably suffered further
damage during the Civil War[4] and by c. 1800 had largely disappeared.[5]
The eastern and south-eastern line of the wall was marked in the later
20th century by the boundaries of the plots behind Cross Hayes Lane,
Silver Street, and Ingram Street, and the western by paths parallel with
and above the lanes called Burnivale and King's Wall. To the north the
wall may survive as the garden wall of the Old Bell; east of the Old Bell
the town wall was the outer wall of the abbey buildings which extended
to the edge of the steep slope above the river. In the late 13th century
there were at least four gates; the east gate was across the Oxford road,
there called Holloway; Wyniard gate was a little gate at the south end of
what became Silver Street; the south gate was at the southern end of
High Street; and the postern gate was at the junction of King's Wall and
Burnivale. A fifth, west, gate was mentioned in the earlier 13th century
and may be identified with the bar in Westport recorded later in the
century. It was presumably across what became Abbey Row, at or near
the castle site, and foundations opposite nos. 31 and 33 Abbey Row
have been identified as those of the gate. The gates were all ruinous in
the early 16th century. The east gate and the postern gate were not,
however, removed until the late 18th century.[6] In the late 20th century
one jamb of the east gate survived in Holloway, and the rounded plan of
the house at the junction of King's Wall and High Street may have
reflected that of the west side of the south gate.

The plan of the town within the walls had largely been established
by the late 13th century and had changed little by the late 20th. The
extent of the abbey precinct was marked by the southward diversion of
the old Oxford–Bristol road around three sides of a rectangle, near the
south-western corner of which stood St. Paul's church. The precinct

2 *E.H.R.* xxi. 98–105, 713–23.
3 Leland, *Itin.* ed. Toulmin Smith, i. 131.
4 Below.
5 J. M. Moffatt, *Hist. Malm.* 100–1.
6 *W.A.M.* li. 187–90; *Reg. Malm.* i. 118, 121, 127, 129; ii. 71; inf. from Mr. M. Green,
   English Heritage, Fortress Ho., 23 Savile Row, Lond.

may have been extended south to those boundaries either in the 12th century, when the abbey church was rebuilt, or by William of Colerne, abbot from 1260, in whose time the abbey buildings were much enlarged.[7] Apart from the abbey church and the undercroft of Abbey House, the most substantial monastic building surviving in the late 20th century

The north part of High Street

was the central east–west range of the Old Bell hotel. The range, of two storeys each divided into two rooms by a central chimney stack, was probably built in the 13th century to incorporate the abbot's lodging. The names of streets in the town are recorded in a rental of the late 13th century or the early 14th. High Street, called *magna strata*, presumably then as later formed the town's spine, running south from the abbey to the confluence of the two branches of the Avon; East Street was probably a parallel street following the line of the later Cross Hayes Lane and Silver Street. The streets were joined by lanes running east and west; Philip's Lane may have been the eastern part of the Oxford–Bristol road which skirted the abbey precinct, known from the 17th century as Oxford Street, and Griffin's Lane further south apparently became St. Dennis's

7 *V.C.H. Wilts.* iii. 220; below, churches.

Lane. The name of Ingram's Lane survives as Ingram Street. A market place adjacent to High Street may have been that within the abbey precinct, opposite the north end of High Street, where an octagonal vaulted market cross was built in the 15th century, or Cross Hayes which was mentioned in the rental and was presumably then as later an open space. King's Wall lay along the outside of the west part of the wall; further north a chapel, which became known as the Hermitage and was demolished in the early 19th century, stood in Westport parish between the lane later called Burnivale and the town wall. In the late 13th century the name Burnivale was apparently used for all or some of that part of the town which lay within Westport parish. At the southern end of the town Nethewall was the area between the wall and the lower parts of High Street and Silver Street,[8] below which Mill or St. John's bridge carried the Chippenham road across the river. St. John's hospital[9] had been built there by the 13th century; a blocked doorway of *c.* 1200 and other medieval stonework were incorporated into the south-west front when the hospital was rebuilt as almshouses probably in the 17th century.[10] Other buildings of medieval origin which survived in the late 20th century stood on or near the boundary of the abbey precinct. A building which became the Green Dragon inn, north-west of the market cross, incorporated a stairway perhaps of the 14th century; near the south-eastern corner of the precinct Tower House, which was extended in the 17th century and later, incorporated a later medieval roof with arch-braced collars; no. 8 Gloucester Street, formerly the White Lion inn, had a courtyard plan and may be of 16th-century origin. Mills were built beside the rivers on the outskirts of the town; in the later Middle Ages they occupied sites north of the abbey, below the postern gate, and beside Mill bridge and Wyniard, later Goose, bridge. In the late 13th century or the early 14th the Tetbury Avon was crossed by the Oxford–Bristol road over St. Leonard's, later Holloway, bridge and by the Tetbury road over Theyn, later Staines, bridge.[11]

The abbey church survived the Dissolution and replaced the ruined St. Paul's as the parish church of Malmesbury.[12] Other monastic buildings

8 *Reg. Malm.* i. 117–33; *P. N. Wilts.* (E.P.N.S.), 49; below, Westport, church. For High Street, see above, illus. on p. 15; below, illus. on p. 19. For the mkt. cross and Cross Hayes, see below, illus. on pp. 21, 60.
9 See illus. on p. 200.
10 *V.C.H. Wilts.* iii. 340–1.
11 *Reg. Malm.* ii, p. xxxiii; below, trade and ind. (mills).   12 Below, churches.

were used as workshops in the 1540s,[13] but most were probably demolished in the mid or late 16th century. In 1561 buildings in the borough were said to be in great decay;[14] the description presumably refers to the former abbey. A proposal by William Stumpe, the purchaser of the abbey site, to build a row or rows of weavers' houses north-east of the abbey church[15] apparently came to nothing. In the later 16th century, however, Stumpe's son Sir James built Abbey House there.[16] The house has a half **H** plan with two storeys and gabled attics: its central, northern, range is over a 13th-century undercroft, and it has short wings to the south. The undercroft, the vaulted roof of which was demolished, was partly filled to form a basement. There was a hall on the ground floor of the central range, in the east wing were parlours, and in the west wing kitchens and service rooms. A turret, housing a newel stair, was built in the angle between the hall and the east wing, and the main south front had a low porch bearing the arms of Stumpe and his wife Isabel Baynton.[17] There was probably a walled forecourt south of the house, and a re-used 12th-century arch, which survived in the late 20th century, was incorporated in the south part of the wall in line with the porch. In the early 19th century a low wing extended eastwards from the house and a long two-storeyed range ran south from the west wing; both were probably of 17th-century origin.[18] The western extension was demolished, probably in the early 20th century when the eastern extension was replaced by a two-storeyed wing with attics similar in style to the original building. In 1636 there were *c.* 60 houses within the former precinct and most of the inhabitants were poor.[19]

Abbey House is the only large house to have survived from the late 16th century or the early 17th. No. 9 Oxford Street is a gabled house of stone with a late 16th-century roof and is said to have been used as a guildhall.[20] Partly timber-framed buildings with jettied first floors survive at nos. 6 and 10 Gloucester Street, no. 9 High Street, and in the gabled southern wing of the King's Arms in High Street. No. 6 Oxford Street, sometimes called Manor House, has an elaborate early

13 Leland, *Itin.* ed. Toulmin Smith, i. 132.
14 P.R.O., E 301/26/153, no. 40.
15 Leland, *Itin.* ed. Toulmin Smith, i. 132.
16 See illus. on p. 18.
17 *W.N. & Q.* viii. 444–5.
18 J. Buckler, watercolour in W.A.S. Libr., vol. vi. 36.
19 *Wilts. Q. Sess. Rec.* ed. Cunnington, 117–18.
20 Hudson, *Hill Top Town,* 17.

Abbey House from the north-west in 1809

17th-century staircase rising through three storeys. Houses in Abbey
Row were said to have been destroyed in the Civil War, perhaps during
Sir William Waller's capture of the town in 1643, and there may have
been other destruction arising from the military occupation of
Malmesbury,[21] but it is not possible to identify areas of post-war
reconstruction. The main range of the King's Arms is probably late 17th-
century, as is the substantial building later subdivided into nos. 5 and 7
High Street. The Old Brewery, north-east of the market cross, bears the
date 1672 on a gable, and the much restored frontage of no. 46 High
Street has a date stone for 1671. Stone was the normal building material
by that time, but the chimneys of nos. 5 and 7 High Street are of red
brick and have diagonally set shafts. Away from the centre of the town a
number of smaller houses are of one storey and attics with large gables
rising from the main elevation; examples are no. 3 Back Hill south of
Silver Street, no. 66 High Street, and no. 10 St. John's Street.

The eastern block of King's Wall House, west of King's Wall and
in Westport parish, was built, probably soon after 1700, with an ashlared

21 Moffatt, *Hist. Malm.* 30 n.; below.

front of three bays and three storeys and a shell hood over the entrance. It was extended westwards and northwards shortly afterwards and the new sections were given old-fashioned mullion and transom windows. Other substantial houses of the early and mid 18th century include Cross Hayes House, which is dated 1728 and has an ashlar front of three bays with rusticated end pilasters and a moulded cornice, and no. 32 Cross Hayes, which has a front of five bays surmounted by a small central pediment. Smaller 18th-century houses are behind modern shop fronts, and no. 36 High Street has a date stone for 1763. Unusually for Malmesbury no. 10 High Street has a brick façade, apparently 18th-century, but its elaborate stone architraves and parapet were added or renewed in the later 19th century and its original form is uncertain. In the last quarter of the 18th century and the early years of the 19th much new building took place in the town. The mill by St. John's bridge was replaced by a cloth factory *c.* 1790.[22] No. 25 Abbey Row, dated 1798, has a front of three bays and three storeys with a projecting architrave, a pilastered doorcase with broken pediment, rusticated quoins, and a moulded cornice below a narrow parapet. St. Michael's House, near the market cross, has a plainer elevation of similar proportions and bears the date 1790. No. 63 High Street is of two storeys with attic dormers and

The south part of High Street

22 Below, trade and ind.

a Doric doorcase. It has a front of mixed rubble and brick, perhaps the result of alterations to an earlier building, and was probably rendered. Roughcast elevations are still common on buildings of the later 18th century and early 19th, among them no. 27 Abbey Row, dated 1811, and buildings along the east side of Cross Hayes Lane. Many more buildings, which in the late 20th century had exposed rubble walls, were probably once so treated. At the southern end of High Street[23] and in St. John's Street and Silver Street are cottages, usually of two storeys with stone-slated roofs and brick stacks, which were probably built or altered in the early 19th century.

New building in the town centre after *c.* 1825 was chiefly commercial or institutional. The northern part of Cross Hayes was the site of a town hall and a nonconformist chapel, and another nonconformist chapel stood nearby in Oxford Street. Two schools and a Roman Catholic church were built on the east side of Cross Hayes; the former teacher's house on the same side of Cross Hayes bears the dates 1851 and 1857 and is in baroque style. A hospital was built north of the market cross,[24] and houses in High Street were refronted or rebuilt as shops and banks. No. 44 High Street has a narrow front of three storeys with a shaped attic gable and is of bright red brick with moulded brick decorations characteristic of *c.* 1900. There was little new building in the part of the town which had been in the old Malmesbury parish in the 20th century. After the closure of the station in 1962 factories, a fire station, and an ambulance station were built on and near its site, and new houses were built north of its site in the 1970s and 1980s. Part of the town was designated a conservation area in 1971; the conservation area was extended in 1987.[25]

Most of the 19th-century population increase was achieved by greater density of occupation in the town where there was little space for building on new sites. On the outskirts the union workhouse was built in Brokenborough parish[26] and cottages were built east of Wyniard Mill beyond the borough boundary in the earlier 19th century, and throughout the 19th century and the early 20th the town continued to expand into Westport.[27] Between the early 1930s and the late 1960s the

23 See illus. on p. 19.
24 Below, local govt. (boro. govt.), public services, Rom. Catholicism, prot. nonconf., educ.
25 Inf. from Chief Assistant (Environment), Dept. of Planning and Highways.
26 Above, Brokenborough, introduction.
27 C. Greenwood, *Map of Wilts.* (1820); O.S. Map 6", Wilts. VIII (1889 edn.).

The town hall, built in 1854, and Cross Hayes *c.* 1900.

built-up area of Malmesbury extended further westwards[28] on land which, until 19th- and 20th-century boundary changes, was principally in Brokenborough parish and partly in Bremilham and Westport. Between 1931, when lands called Pool Gastons and Gastons were bought by Malmesbury borough council, and 1941 *c.* 60 council houses were built in Pool Gastons Road and Athelstan Road. The former workhouse was converted into council houses in 1936 and 1938.[29] Another 125 council houses were built between 1946 and 1956 in Alexander Road, Avon Road, Hobbes Close, and Corn Gastons.[30] A school and a swimming pool were built,[31] and another *c.* 40 council dwellings were later built in Newnton Grove and near the swimming pool. The Parklands estate, built on land transferred from Brokenborough to Malmesbury parish in 1984, included *c.* 55 houses and bungalows in 1958; in the late 1960s *c.* 84 more houses, bungalows, and sheltered homes were built.[32] Also in the 1960s the *c.* 100 private houses in White Lion Park, north of Parklands, were built, and in place of the converted workhouse, Bremilham Rise, a row of 27 council houses, was built. Accommodation for old people was later built in the grounds of Burnham House in Burnham Road. The town was extended northwards in the 1980s when *c.* 250 private houses were built east of Tetbury Hill as Reed's Farm.

28 See illus. on p. x.
29 W.R.O., G 21/132/4; G 21/132/6; G 21/132/21.
30 Ibid. G 21/132/2–5.
31 Below, public services, educ.
32 W.R.O., G 7/360/10; above, Brokenborough, introduction.

In the Middle Ages the knight's fees held of Malmesbury abbey apparently constituted an honor for which courts may have been held, and courts for Startley, possibly Chedglow, and Malmesbury hundreds were held at Malmesbury. Assizes were occasionally held at Malmesbury in the 13th century, as were quarter sessions in the late 14th and the 15th. Private sessions allegedly held improperly in the town in 1614 may have been petty sessions;[33] no later reference to quarter sessions held there has been found. In 1927 and for much of the 20th century a bishop suffragan of Malmesbury was appointed to assist in the diocese of Bristol.[34]

Malmesbury was directly involved in the civil wars of both the 12th century and the 17th. After the arrest of Roger, bishop of Salisbury, in June 1139, the castle was taken by King Stephen, lost on 7 October of that year to Robert FitzHubert, and recaptured a fortnight later; whether Robert held it for himself or for the Empress Maud is not clear. In 1144 Malmesbury was attacked by William of Dover, a supporter of Maud, besieged by Robert, earl of Gloucester, her brother, and relieved by the king. In that year, presumably at a time when she hoped that her supporters would take and hold Malmesbury, Maud granted the borough to Humphrey de Bohun with the provision that no new fortification should be made there.[35] William of Dover renewed his attack in 1145 but, although he captured the castellan, the garrison remained loyal to Stephen. The castle changed hands in 1153 when it was captured by Henry of Anjou after a confrontation, but no battle, with Stephen's army. The presence of a garrison was apparently unwelcome to the monks; in 1151 Pope Eugenius III required the soldiers not to trouble the abbey, and *c.* 1173 Alexander III empowered the abbot to excommunicate any of the garrison who harmed the monks.[36]

At the outbreak of war in 1642 Malmesbury apparently held to the parliamentary side and the committee for Wiltshire met there. The town submitted to the royalists on 3 February 1643, the day following Prince Rupert's capture of Cirencester, but on 23 March it was taken by Sir William Waller for parliament. Sir Edward Hungerford was appointed governor but changed his allegiance and surrendered the town to the

33 *V.C.H. Wilts.* v. 19–20, 35, 63–4, 93; above, Malmesbury hund.
34 *Cat. Rec. Bristol Dioc.* comp. I. M. Kirby, 178.
35 *V.C.H. Wilts.* iii. 216–17; *Anct. Chart.* (Pipe R. Soc. x), 45–6.
36 *V.C.H. Wilts.* iii. 217; R. H. Luce, *Hist. Malm.* 25–7; Wm. of Malmesbury, *Gesta Regum Angl.* (Rolls Ser.), ii. 548, 556

royalists on 5 April. Malmesbury may have changed hands twice more before 24 May 1644 when Col. Edward Massey recaptured it for parliament. From then until the late summer or autumn of 1646 a garrison numbering perhaps 1,000 men was kept in the town. A petition was submitted to the county committee, probably early in 1645, complaining of the cost of the garrison to the locality and of its inadequacy as a defence against royalist raids; the petition may have had its result in the new regulations for the garrison issued in July 1645. The garrison had probably been disbanded by November 1646,[37] but other smaller forces were stationed at Malmesbury in 1649 and 1651, and, when renewed disturbances threatened after the Restoration, in 1661 and 1663.[38] The Restoration itself was celebrated in Malmesbury, according to John Aubrey, with 'so many and so great volleys of shot' that part of the abbey tower fell the following night.[39]

Beside St. John's there may have been two medieval hospitals in the town; their sites are not known. In 1245 protection was granted to the brethren of St. Anthony's hospital,[40] and Hugh Mortimer, perhaps he who died c. 1180, apparently confirmed another hospital in Malmesbury to the monks of St. Victor-en-Caux (Seine Maritime).[41]

In 1540 there were inns in Malmesbury called the Crown, the Lamb, the Griffin, and, perhaps, the Red Cross.[42] The Griffin, in High Street, was still open in 1751,[43] but had closed by 1809;[44] no reference to the other three signs after 1540 has been found. In 1592 seven licences to sell ale in the town were granted[45] and in 1620 there were 12 alehousekeepers in the parish including two in Burton Hill.[46] There were between 17 and 20 inns and alehouses within the borough, including the part of it in Westport parish, in the mid 18th century. The number had fallen to 11 by 1827,[47] but had risen to 17 by 1875 perhaps as a result of the expansion of brewing in the town. The total had fallen

37 Accts. of Parl. Garrisons (W.R.S. ii), 27–36.
38 Cal. S.P. Dom. 1649–50, 353; 1651, 371; 1660–1, 478; 1663–4, 301.
39 Aubrey, Topog. Coll. ed. Jackson, 255.
40 Cal. Pat. 1232–47, 459.
41 Complete Peerage, ix. 268; Eton Coll. Mun. 4/1.
42 L. & P. Hen. VIII, xv, p. 551; P.R.O., SC 6/Hen. VIII/3986, rott. 96–98d.
43 W.R.O. 212B/4000.
44 Ibid. 212B/4274
45 Sess. Mins. (W.R.S. iv), 150.
46 Early-Stuart Tradesmen (W.R.S. xv), pp. 29–30.
47 W.R.O., A 1/326/1–3.

again to 12 by 1927.[48] Among the oldest houses were the White Lion in Gloucester Street, first recorded in 1618,[49] the King's Arms in High Street, open in the late 17th century,[50] the Old Bell, called the Castle in 1703[51] and the Bell in 1798,[52] and the George in High Street, open in 1823.[53] The White Lion and the George closed after 1955;[54] the Bell, then the Old Bell hotel, and the King's Arms remained open in 1988. Other public houses in the town in 1988, apart from those in Westport, were the Borough Arms in Oxford Street and the Old Greyhound and the Rose and Crown in High Street.

The *Wiltshire and Gloucestershire Standard* was published in Malmesbury from 1837 until 1840, when the place of publication was moved to Cirencester.[55] A monthly *Malmesbury Journal* was started in the summer of 1841 but only two editions were published,[56] and seven or more editions of a weekly *Malmesbury Free Press* appeared in 1867.[57]

Malmesbury's Horticultural and Floral Society was founded *c.* 1870[58] and in the earlier 20th century held an annual show near Arches Farm in what had been Westport parish.[59] It was disbanded *c.* 1930.[60] The masonic lodge of St. Aldhelm met in Malmesbury from 1901 and in 1906 the Royal Arch Chapter of St. Aldhelm was formed.[61] There was a town brass band in 1895,[62] but in 1945 its instruments were sold.[63] A new band had been formed by 1988.[64] The Athelstan cinema was built north of the market cross in 1935; it had 333 seats[65] and was closed *c.* 1973.[66] There was a bowling green north of Holloway in 1831.[67] A

48 *Kelly's Dir. Wilts.* (1875, 1927).
49 W.R.O. 177/23, deed, Alright to Thorner, 1618.
50 Aubrey, *Topog. Coll.* ed. Jackson, 262.
51 W.R.O. 212B/3908.
52 Ibid. 212B/4201.
53 Ibid. A 1/326/1.
54 Ibid. G 21/516/4.
55 *W.A.M.* xl. 66–9.
56 *Malm. Jnl.* 30 July 1841; 28 Aug. 1841.
57 *Malm. Free Press,* 18 May 1867.
58 W.R.O. 815/24.
59 Ibid. 815/26.
60 Hudson, *Hill Top Town,* 154.
61 *V.C.H. Wilts.* iv. 389.
62 *Kelly's Dir. Wilts.* (1895).
63 W.R.O., G 21/119/3.
64 Local inf.
65 W.R.O., F 12, corresp. file, Athelstan cinema.
66 Inf. from Curator, Athelstan Mus.
67 Glos. R.O., D 674B/P 73.

bowling club had been started in the town by 1923;[68] from 1948 or earlier it had greens by Goose bridge.[69] There was a cricket club in 1895; clubs for football, hockey, and tennis were founded after the First World War. The hockey club had been disbanded by 1927.[70] In 1988 the football and tennis clubs had grounds west of Tetbury Hill and the cricket club a ground north of the former station.

In 1837 Joseph Poole of Malmesbury owned a travelling show, which was later managed by his sons. As the Poole Brothers they developed the 'myriorama', an arrangement of backcloths and mirrors, which was used to illustrate topical events. In the 1890s they toured widely in England and Wales from a base in Westport where the scenery was painted.[71]

In 1980 the town celebrated the supposed 1100th anniversary of the granting of a charter by King Alfred.[72] The date 880 was given as that of the town's charter in a book published in or after 1951 in which the grant attributed by the burgesses in 1381 to Athelstan was apparently ascribed to Alfred;[73] the date 880 was later repeated in a history of Malmesbury.[74]

St. Aldhelm joined the monastic community at Malmesbury as a young man, became abbot, probably in 675, and was from 705 until 709 bishop of Sherborne (Dors.). He was buried in Malmesbury and miracles were worked at his shrine there. William of Malmesbury (d. *c.* 1143) records the tradition that John Scotus Erigena, the philosopher, lived at the abbey in the late 9th century and was murdered there by his pupils. William himself spent most of his life in the monastery at Malmesbury.[75]

BURTON HILL or Burton was a small suburb of Malmesbury immediately south of the town beside the Chippenham road. In the later 13th century its buildings probably included the hospital of St. Mary Magdalene.[76] Part of the hospital may have survived as a chapel which stood at the junction of the Chippenham and Swindon roads in

68 *Kelly's Dir. Wilts.* (1923).
69 *Town Guide* (1948).
70 *Kelly's Dir. Wilts.* (1895 and later edns.).
71 Hudson, *Hill Top Town,* 112–13; *W.A.M.* xliii. 108–9; *Kelly's Dir. Wilts.* (1885, 1895).
72 *W.A.M.* lxxiv/lxxv. 133.
73 W. B. Faraday, *Eng. and Welsh Boroughs,* 15.
74 B. Hodge, *Hist. Malm.* (1968), 4.
75 *V.C.H. Wilts.* iii. 211–14, 217.
76 Ibid. 341; *Reg. Malm.* i. 119.

Burton Hill chapel in 1809

1540.[77] The chapel, used as a private house in 1768 and apparently in 1809,[78] was demolished in the early 19th century when a new house called Canister Hall was built on its site. The three-storeyed brick house was later called the Priory.[79] Burton Hill House was built south of the junction probably in the early 17th century. It was rebuilt in 1840 or 1842 to a design by C. R. Cockerell, the owner's brother, but part or all of the house was burned down in 1846. It was rebuilt again in the same year in a Tudor Gothic style, probably again designed by Cockerell,[80] and enlarged in the later 19th century and the 20th.[81] In the late 18th century a farmhouse, called Manor House in 1823, stood south-east of the junction; it was rebuilt in the later 19th century in Tudor style and from 1925 was used as a hospital.[82] A house later called the Beeches, another which became the Black Horse inn, open as such in 1822, and a turnpike cottage stood near the junction, and cottages were scattered

77 Leland, *Itin.* ed. Toulmin Smith, i. 133.
78 Buckler, watercolour in W.A.S. Libr., vol. vi. 34; see above, illus. on this page.
79 W.R.O. 1165/1, deeds, Dewell to Robins; photo. in Nat. Bldgs. Rec.
80 *W.N. & Q.* viii. 433 and facing pl.; D. Watkin, *Life of C. R. Cockerell,* 253.
81 See illus. on p. 41.
82 *Andrews and Dury, Map* (W.R.S. viii), pl. 16; *Kelly's Dir. Wilts.* (1927); W.R.O. 212A/38/37/161.

south of Burton Hill House in 1773.[83] Between 1773 and 1828 there was much new building beside the Chippenham road north of the junction, presumably to house workers at the cloth mill built near St. John's bridge, and terraces of early 19th-century cottages survive there. Cottages were also built south of Burton Hill House, where a track ran south-west from the Chippenham road,[84] and a turnpike cottage was built there after 1842. Some cottages beside the Chippenham road had apparently been demolished by 1842.[85] In the mid and later 19th century houses in Burton Hill were built or rebuilt for members of Malmesbury's landed, commercial, and professional families.[86] A police station north of the hospital was built later.[87] The Priory and the Black Horse were demolished, probably in 1973 when a roundabout was built at the southern end of the Malmesbury bypass.[88] West of the roundabout 27 council houses and 12 maisonettes were built shortly afterwards,[89] and in the 1980s an estate of *c.* 50 private houses was built north of Burton Hill House.

COWBRIDGE is a settlement which has spread north-westwards from Cowbridge Mill on the Avon along the Swindon road towards Burton Hill. In 1773 only the mill, on a site used since the 13th century or earlier, and a large house beside it were standing.[90] Cottages were built beside the road west of the mill in the early 19th century.[91] Cowbridge House beside the mill was rebuilt *c.* 1853,[92] a farmhouse north of it was probably built then, and the Knoll, another large house 500 m. west of it, is of similar date. In the 1880s a new vicarage house was built north-west of the Knoll.[93] From 1939 Cowbridge House and mill were incorporated into a factory;[94] the old buildings were extended and new workshops and offices built. In Cowbridge Crescent, west of

83 *Andrews and Dury, Map* (W.R.S. viii), pls. 13, 16; W.R.O., A 1/326/3.
84 *Andrews and Dury, Map* (W.R.S. viii), pl. 13; O.S. Map 1", sheet 34 (1828 edn.).
85 W.R.O., tithe award.
86 *Kelly's Dir. Wilts.* (1848 and later edns.).
87 Below, public services.
88 Inf. from Chief Assistant (Environment), Dept. of Planning and Highways.
89 Inf. from Property Maintenance Manager, Dept. of Housing and Property Services, N. Wilts. District Council, Bewley Ho., Marshfield Rd., Chippenham.
90 *Reg. Malm.* i. 176–7; *Andrews and Dury, Map* (W.R.S. viii), pl. 16.
91 O.S. Map 1", sheet 34 (1828 edn.); W.R.O., tithe award.
92 Below, manors.
93 Below, churches.
94 Ibid. trade and ind.

Cowbridge House, 12 houses and 26 prefabricated bungalows were built by the local authority in, respectively, 1941 and 1948 partly to house workers from the factory.[95] Most of those dwellings were later replaced and more houses built in the 1970s and 1980s.

MILBOURNE was a settlement in the Middle Ages but for that period little documentary and no architectural evidence of it survives. In the later 17th century Milbourne was described as a 'discontinued' village on the Oxford–Bristol road,[96] indicating that its farmsteads were then, as in the later 18th century, scattered along the road which formed the village street.[97] The wide verges of the road were common pastures until the earlier 19th century,[98] and the older houses stand well back from the road. The oldest to survive are at the western end, near the junction of the street with Moochers Lane, later Milbourne Lane, which leads north-west to the Cricklade road. Milbourne House, north of the junction, incorporates an east–west range possibly of the late 16th century.[99] In the earlier 17th century a cross wing at the west end and a rear kitchen wing at the east end were added. Extensive 20th-century alterations included the addition of a bay window on the main south front and the fitting of 18th-century panelling. Milbourne Farm, south of the junction, is of 17th-century origin. East of those houses are cottages and farmsteads built in the 18th century or earlier, and the village's eastern end was marked in 1773, as in the later 20th century, by Manor Farm,[1] an early 18th-century stone house of three bays. There was little new building in the 19th century. A row of four cottages on the north side of the village street bears the date 1901, there was infilling north of the street in the 1930s, and 12 semidetached houses were built at the north end of Milbourne Lane c. 1938.[2] In the later 20th century there was more infilling on the north side of the street, houses were built on the west side of Milbourne Lane, and two private estates of bungalows and houses were built, Monks Park on the common pasture south of the street, and Milbourne Park west of Milbourne Lane. When the bypass

95 W.R.O., G 7/760/149; G 7/760/219.
96 Ogilby, *Brit.* (1675), pl. 79.
97 *Andrews and Dury, Map* (W.R.S. viii), pls. 16–17.
98 W.R.O. 900/12.
99 Cf. Dept. of Environment, list of bldgs. of hist. interest (1987).
 1 *Andrews and Dury, Map* (W.R.S.viii), pl. 17.
 2 W.R.O., G 7/760/101.

was built in 1973 the street was closed west of the village and Milbourne Lane became the principal western approach to the village.

WHITCHURCH. There was a settlement, probably including a chapel, at Whitchurch in the 13th century.[3] Perhaps in the late 17th century and certainly in the late 18th Whitchurch comprised a single farmstead. Before 1670 the chapel was incorporated into Whitchurch Farm; its 'steeple' was demolished c.1675.[4] Parts of a late medieval building survive as the western end of the long 17th-century domestic range. That range was altered in the 18th century when a small central pediment above a pedimented porch was added to the north front and much of the interior was refitted. At the centre of a range of brick buildings north-west of the house is a square tower dated 1797. A garage, a small farmstead, several houses, and a water tower were built north of Whitchurch, later Whychurch, Farm beside the Cirencester road in the late 19th century and the 20th.

OTHER SETTLEMENT. The abbot of Malmesbury had a lodge, which may have been in use in the 13th century[5] and was standing in 1540, in Cowfold park.[6] Its site was presumably that of the mansion called Cole Park built south of the town from the later 16th century.[7] A grange in Cowfold park in the early 16th century[8] is likely to have been on the site of either Lawn Farm or Grange Farm, neighbouring farmsteads north-west of Cole Park. Lawn Farm, perhaps used as one of two lodges for officers of the royal stud farm in Cole park in the earlier 17th century,[9] is an L-shaped 17th-century house within which survive parts of two cruck trusses; it was extended and refronted in the early 19th century. The farmhouse of Grange farm was rebuilt in the 1820s.[10] West of Corston village there was a lodge in West park, presumably on the site of West Park Farm, in 1653.[11]

---

3 *Reg. Malm.* ii. 120–1.
4 Aubrey, *Topog. Coll.* ed. Jackson, 267; *Andrews and Dury, Map* (W.R.S. viii), pl. 16.
5 *Rot. Hund.* (Rec. Com.), ii (1), 230, 272.
6 Leland, *Itin.* ed. Toulmin Smith, i. 133; P.R.O., SC 6/Hen.VIII/3986, rot. 116.
7 Below, manors.
8 P.R.O., SC 6/Hen.VIII/3986, rot. 116.
9 Ibid. LR 2/301, f. 233.
10 W.R.O. 161/52, sale partic. of Grange farm.
11 P.R.O., LR 2/301, f. 256.

A building which stood north of Holloway bridge in 1773[12] may have been the Duke of York inn, open in 1822;[13] the inn was rebuilt in the 1960s. Cottages were built north-east of it in the 18th century and the 19th; with some 20th-century buildings they formed the hamlet known in the later 20th century as Blick's Hill.

Most outlying farmsteads in the old Malmesbury parish occupy sites which were in use in the 18th century and probably earlier. Farmsteads on the sites of those later called Whiteheath, north of Corston village, Rodbourne Rail, south of Cole Park, and Burnt Heath, north-west of Whiteheath, were standing in 1729, 1770, and 1773 respectively.[14] Quobwell Farm and Coldharbour Farm, north of the town, were built in the mid 18th century and Southfield Farm, south of Milbourne village, was built between 1773 and 1802. Lower West Park Farm was built on a new site north of West Park Farm between 1842 and 1885,[16] and the Coopers' Arms, beside the Tetbury road north-west of Quobwell Farm, was open as an inn in 1875[17] and converted to a farmhouse after 1927.[18]

MANORS AND OTHER ESTATES. The *BOROUGH* of Malmesbury belonged to the king in 1086. He then received the third penny; the remaining two thirds were held at farm by Walter Hosed. Of 73¾ *masurae* 52, probably including 10 formerly held by Earl Harold, were held by the king, 4 were held by Malmesbury abbey, and the remainder by 15 different lords.[19]

Hugh, provost of Malmesbury, paid £20 for the farm of the borough in 1130.[20] Between 1136 and 1139 King Stephen granted the lordship of the borough to Roger, bishop of Salisbury, his justiciar, who had taken possession of Malmesbury abbey in 1118. The lordship presumably reverted to the Crown after the bishop's disgrace and death in 1139.[21] In 1144 Maud granted it to Humphrey de Bohun but the

12 *Andrews and Dury, Map* (W.R.S. viii), pl. 16.
13 W.R.O., A 1/326/3.
14 Ibid. 568/30, deed, Scrope to Young, 1729; 161/26/2; *Andrews and Dury, Map* (W.R.S. viii), pl.13.
15 *Andrews and Dury, Map* (W.R.S. viii), pl. 37; W.R.O. 900/12.
16 W.R.O., tithe award; O.S. Map 6", Wilts. XIII (1888 edn.).
17 *Kelly's Dir. Wilts.* (1875).
18 W.R.O., G 7/515/9.
19 *V.C.H. Wilts.* ii, pp. 21–2, 113, 115.
20 *Pipe R.* 1130 (H.M.S.O. facsimile), 16.
21 *Reg. Regum Anglo-Norm.* iii, no. 784; *D.N.B.*

grant may not have taken effect.[22] The borough was apparently part of the dowry of Berengaria, wife of Richard I, which was withheld from her by John presumably from Richard's death in 1199.[23] In 1204 John granted the borough to his queen, Isabel, as dower,[24] and in 1215 he gave it in fee farm to Malmesbury abbey.[25] The abbey held it until the Dissolution for £20 a year.[26] The alderman and burgesses held it at fee farm from 1566 until 1598 or later.[27]

By 1628 lordship of the borough had been granted, under the name of *MALMESBURY* manor, to Henry Danvers, earl of Danby[28] (d. 1644),[29] who devised it to his nephew Henry Danvers. From Henry (d. 1654) the manor passed in moieties to his sisters Elizabeth and Anne.[30] Elizabeth (d. 1709) and her husband Robert Danvers, formerly Villiers (d. 1674), held her moiety in 1673.[31] Anne (d. 1659), wife of Sir Henry Lee, Bt. (d. 1659), was succeeded by her daughters Eleanor, later wife of James Bertie, Baron Norreys (cr. earl of Abingdon 1682), and Anne, later wife of Thomas Wharton (Baron Wharton from 1696, cr. earl of Wharton 1706, cr. marquess of Wharton 1715).[32] The settlement made on the Whartons' marriage in 1673 provided for the division of Anne Lee's estates; the Whartons' portion probably included her moiety of Malmesbury manor. The settlement was later disputed[33] but in 1685 Thomas and Anne Wharton held both Anne Lee's and Elizabeth Danvers's moieties.[34] On Wharton's death in 1715 the manor passed to his son Philip, marquess of Wharton (cr. duke of Wharton 1718, d. 1731), whose estates were confiscated when he was outlawed for treason in 1729. In 1733 the estates were settled on trustees for payment of his debts and afterwards for his sisters and coheirs, Jane, wife of Robert Coke, and

22 *Anct. Chart.* (Pipe R. Soc. x), 45–6; above, introduction.
23 *Cal. Papal Reg.* i. 33.
24 *Rot. Chart.* (Rec. Com.), 128.
25 Ibid. 213.
26 *Valor Eccl.* (Rec. Com.), ii. 119, 122.
27 P.R.O., E 310/26/154, nos. 6, 8.
28 *Wilts. Inq. p.m.* 1625–49 (Index Libr.), 432.
29 *Complete Peerage*, iv. 48–9.
30 P.R.O., C 104/86/1, order, Danvers v. Lee, 1672.
31 Ibid. CP 25(2)/746/25 Chas. II Trin.; *Complete Peerage*, x. 687–8.
32 *Complete Peerage*, ix. 649; xii (2), 606–8; Aubrey, *Topog. Coll.* ed. Jackson, pedigree facing p. 217.
33 P.R.O., C 104/86/1, bill, Wharton v. Rochester.
34 Ibid. CP 25(2)/806/1 Jas. II East.

Lucy (d. *s.p.* 1739), wife of Sir William Morice, Bt.,[35] and in 1743 were sold on Jane's behalf. Malmesbury manor was bought by Sir John Rushout, Bt.[36] Sir John was succeeded in 1775 by his son Sir John (cr. Baron Northwick 1797, d. 1800), whose relict Rebecca[37] retained the manor until her death in 1818.[38] She devised it to her younger son the Revd. George Rushout-Bowles.[39] George was succeeded in 1842 by his son George Rushout (Baron Northwick from 1859, d. 1887), whose relict Elizabeth may have held the manor until her death in 1912;[40] the reversion was sold in lots in 1896. The manor then comprised *c.* 80 a. in the town.[41]

The lands which became Malmesbury parish were probably held by Malmesbury abbey from its foundation, but the copies of charters granting them are suspect. The monks claimed to have received an estate called Malmesbury, the site of the abbey, by a grant of 675 from Bishop Leutherius and Rodbourne and Corston by a grant of 701 from King Ine. The boundaries of an estate of 100 hides called Brokenborough, said to have been confirmed to the abbey by King Edwy in 956, were surveyed in the 11th century or the 12th when they included all of what became Malmesbury parish and other lands.[42] In 1066 Gilbert and Godwin each held an estate of 1 hide said to be in Malmesbury; those estates were held by the bishop of Coutances and by Chetel respectively in 1086.[43] The later history of those estates has not been traced, and from 1086 to 1539 Malmesbury abbey owned virtually the whole parish apart from the borough.

Malmesbury abbey claimed to have been granted the estate later called *COWFOLD* as part of the Brokenborough estate by King Edwy in 956, but is likely to have held it much earlier. Between 1066 and 1086, when it was part of the Brokenborough estate, the abbey apparently granted it for knight service.[44] It later recovered it and by the early 13th

---

35 *Complete Peerage*, xii (2), 607–14.
36 W.R.O. 212B/2207.
37 *Complete Peerage*, ix. 751–2.
38 W.R.O. 212B/4264; 212B/4298.
39 P.R.O., PROB 11/1609, f. 232.
40 *Complete Peerage*, ix. 752; W.R.O. 212B/4318.
41 W.R.O. 622/1.
42 Finberg, *Early Wessex Chart.* pp. 69–70, 91; *Arch. Jnl.* lxxvii. 42–54; above, Brokenborough, introduction, manor.
43 *V.C.H. Wilts.* ii, pp. 122, 162.
44 Finberg, *Early Wessex Chart.* pp. 91, 105–6; *V.C.H. Wilts.* ii, pp. 88, 125–6.

century had imparked part of it. In the late 13th century the Cowfold estate apparently included the abbey's Corston land.[45] Cowfold passed to the Crown at the Dissolution, when Corston was a separate estate, and in 1548 as Cowfold manor was granted to Edward Seymour, duke of Somerset.[46] The manor presumably escheated on his attainder in 1552.[47] In 1556 lands at Cowfold, probably part of the manor, were granted to the hospital of the Savoy, London, on its refoundation;[48] they were restored to the Crown by exchange in 1558.[49] In 1560 or earlier Cowfold grange and *c.* 80 a. were granted to Edward Welsh;[50] the greater part of the estate, *c.* 650 a., was retained by the Crown.[51]

Between 1653 and 1656 the Crown's Cowfold estate was sold as COLE PARK to Hugh Audley[52] (d. 1662),[53] who was succeeded by his nephew Robert Harvey.[54] In 1694 the estate, 520 a., was settled on Robert's grandson John Harvey (d. 1712),[55] who was succeeded by his son Audley.[56] In 1725 Cole park was held by another John Harvey[57] (fl. 1767),[58] in 1770 by another Audley Harvey.[59] Audley (d. 1774)[60] devised it for life to his daughter Sarah (fl. 1783), wife of John Lovell, with remainder to her son Peter Lovell.[61] From Peter (d. 1841) it passed in turn to his son Peter (d. 1869) and the younger Peter's son Peter (d. 1909), whose relict Rosalind[62] (d. 1945) devised it to her grandnephew Capt. A. D. C. Francis. In 1945 Capt. Francis sold the house called Cole Park, the parkland, and Rodbourne Rail farm, a total of 120 a., to J. F. Fry.[63] The house and parkland were sold by Fry in 1954 to Frank and

45 *Close R.* 1234–7, 126; *Reg. Malm.* i. 176–7, 203.
46 *Cal. Pat.* 1548–9, 27–8; below, Corston, manor.
47 *Complete Peerage,* xii (1), 63
48 *Cal. Pat.* 1555–7, 544, 546.
49 Ibid. 1557–8, 361.
50 *W.N. & Q.* iv. 456; below.
51 P.R.O., LR 2/301, f. 236.
52 Ibid.; W.R.O. 161/49, settlement, 1656.
53 *D.N.B.*
54 W.R.O. 161/49, settlement, 1656.
55 Ibid. 161/34, settlement, 1694; ibid. tithe award; Burke, *Land. Gent.* (1937), 1412.
56 W.R.O. 161/34, will of John Harvey.
57 Ibid. 161/28/2.
58 Ibid. 161/53, lease, Harvey to Keynes, 1767.
59 Ibid. 161/26/3.
60 *W.N. & Q.* viii. 442.
61 M. Masson, *Cole Park* (priv. print. 1985), 45; W.R.O. 161/34, will of Audley Harvey.
62 Burke, *Land. Gent.* (1937), 1412.
63 Masson, *Cole Park,* 70; inf. from Capt. A. D. C. Francis, the Grange, Corston.

Avril Darling, by the Darlings in 1955 to Mr. E. J. M. Buxton. In 1978 Mr. Buxton sold Cole Park and 8 a. to C. L. McMiram, from whom they were bought in 1980 by Sir Mark Weinberg, the owner in 1987.[64] Mr. P. Roberts bought Lawn farm, c. 270 a., from Capt. Francis c. 1977 and remained the owner in 1987.[65]

The moated site of Cole Park may be that of the abbot of Malmesbury's lodge.[66] A lodge for the royal stud in the park stood there in the late 16th century and the early 17th.[67] A tall red-brick range of the mid or later 16th century,[68] which formed most of the north-east part of the house in the later 20th century, was probably a wing of a house whose main range lay to the north-west. A plan to rebuild the house c. 1625, when Sir George Marshall, lessee of the stud, received £100 of £500 promised for the construction of a new lodge,[69] may have had little effect. The house was described c. 1650 as 'a very fair brick building' of two storeys with a large courtyard and a moat.[70] In the late 17th century a large staircase was built at the south-western corner of the wing, and the hall, immediately north-west of the staircase, was altered or rebuilt. Additions were made, probably then, north-east and south-west of the hall to create a new north-western entrance front. That front and the south-west front were refaced in the later 18th century, perhaps in 1775–6 when building work at the house was recorded[71] and minor additions, apparent from dark headers in the brickwork, were being made to the 16th-century part of the house. The north-west side of that part was refaced in the later 19th century and its north-east end was rebuilt with an oriel overlooking the moat in 1981. About then ground-floor additions were made south-east of the wing and much of the inside of the house was altered and redecorated. The moat, surviving in 1987, is almost square and has walled sides and a paved floor. New buildings of the 18th century include a stable and a coach house flanking an entrance court north-west of the house.

---

64 Inf. from Messrs. Nabarro Nathanson, 50 Stratton Street, Lond.
65 Inf. from Capt. Francis.
66 Above, introduction.
67 P.R.O., LR 2/191, f. 132; LR 2/301, f. 232; below, agric.
68 See illus. on facing page.
69 Hist. MSS. Com. 23, *12th Rep., Coke,* i, p. 184.
70 P.R.O., LR 2/301, f. 232.
71 Masson, *Cole Park,* 40–1.

Cole Park from the north-east

The estate granted to Edmund Welsh in 1560 was later called *GRANGE* farm. Sir James Stumpe held it at his death in 1563;[72] thereafter it passed with Rodbourne manor to Walter Hungerford (d. 1754).[73] By 1752 Hungerford had sold Grange farm to Edmund Estcourt[74] (d. 1758).[75] It passed to Estcourt's relict Anna Maria (d. *c.* 1783) and daughter Anne, who apparently held jointly, and in 1766 was settled on the daughter's marriage to William Earle (d. 1774). Anne Earle (d. 1776) devised the farm to William Edwards her son perhaps by Earle. In 1787 Edwards sold it to Edmund Wilkins (d. 1804), who devised it to his nephew Edmund Gale (d. 1819). Gale's heirs sold the farm in 1829 to Peter Lovell[76] (d. 1841), and Lovell's relict Charlotte (d. 1854)[77] devised it to

72 P.R.O., C 142/135, no. 1.
73 Below, Rodbourne, manor.
74 W.R.O. 161/48, deed, Ratcliffe and Knipe to Wilkins, 1787.
75 *W.N. & Q.* viii. 436.
76 J. Badeni, *Wilts. Forefathers,* 109; W.R.O. 161/52, abstr. of title; below, Little Somerford, manor.
77 Burke, *Land. Gent.* (1937), 1412.

their sons Peter, Frank, and Willes. Peter Lovell apparently bought his brothers' shares of the farm c. 1855;[78] thereafter it passed with Cole Park to Capt. A. D. C. Francis, who held the farm, c. 200 a., in 1987.[79]

WEST PARK, c. 150 a., was held with Cole Park until 1653[80] but by 1694 had been sold separately.[81] Its owners in the late 17th century and the earlier 18th have not been traced. It was held by Richard Watts c. 1770[82] and by the heirs of John Watts in 1780.[83] In 1789 it was sold,[84] probably to George Garlick, the owner in 1790. Garlick and another George Garlick held West park in 1820; by 1827 it had passed to a Mrs. Garlick and Isaac Berry.[85] In 1839 Mary Berry held West park, 139 a.[86] It was owned by Michael Hulbert in 1865,[87] by Henry Wellesley, Earl Cowley, in 1910,[88] and by W. W. West in 1912.[89] By 1927 the estate had been divided into smaller holdings.[90]

Malmesbury abbey's lands at Burton Hill were a distinct estate in the 13th century and at the Dissolution.[91] As the manor of Burton or BURTON HILL they were granted by the Crown in 1552 to John Dudley, duke of Northumberland, who conveyed the manor in 1553 to Sir James Stumpe[92] (d. 1563). It passed to Stumpe's daughter Elizabeth, wife of Henry Knyvett.[93] In 1570 the Knyvetts conveyed the manor to William and George Wynter,[94] perhaps trustees for Sir Thomas Gresham who sold it to Edward Carey and William Doddington in 1574.[95] Carey and Doddington sold Burton Hill manor in 1577 to Adam Archard and

78 W.R.O. 161/43, abstr. from will of Charlotte Lovell; 161/134, letter, Stone to Lovell, 1855.
79 Inf. from Capt. Francis.
80 P.R.O., LR 2/301, f. 233.
81 W.R.O. 161/34, settlement, 1694.
82 Ibid. 490/1112.
83 Ibid. A 1/345/274.
84 P.R.O., CP 25(2)/1447/29 Geo. III East.
85 W.R.O., A 1/345/274.
86 Ibid. tithe award.
87 Ibid. G 21/510/1.
88 Ibid. Inland Revenue, val. reg. 9.
89 Ibid. G 7/500/1.
90 Ibid. G 7/515/9.
91 Reg. Malm. ii. 221–3; Valor Eccl. (Rec. Com.), ii. 120.
92 Cal. Pat. 1550–3, 258, 369; P.R.O., CP 25(2)/65/533, no. 23.
93 P.R.O., C 142/135, no. 1.
94 Cal. Pat. 1569–72, p. 180.
95 W.R.O. 88/1/76.

Thomas Hall,[96] who in the same year sold several parts of it. The rest, still called Burton Hill manor, passed on Archard's death in 1588 to his son Nicholas.[97] In 1616 Nicholas sold the estate to Anthony Risby[98] (d. 1626), who devised it for sale; it then comprised *c.* 40 a.[99] In 1638 it was held by Zacharias Ward.[1] The estate was probably that described as Burton Hill manor which Thomas Ridler and his wife Anne held in 1724.[2] In 1748 Anne, then a widow, held it, perhaps jointly with her daughters Barbara Ridler and Anne, wife of William Pinn.[3] By 1782 it had passed to Joseph Cullerne,[4] who in 1794 sold it to Thomas Brooke. In 1800 Brooke sold the estate to Edmund Wilkins (d. 1804),[5] who devised it to Elizabeth Dewell and her sister Mary.[6] By will dated 1805 Elizabeth devised her interest in the estate for life to Mary (fl. 1809), with reversion to their nephew the Revd. Charles Dewell.[7] In 1823 the whole estate, then the house called the Manor House and 99 a., was settled on Charles.[8] On his death in 1828 it passed to his wife Sarah, later wife of W. R. Fitzgerald, and on her death in 1863 to Charles's nephew C. G. Dewell. In 1863 Dewell sold the estate to the Revd. Thomas Brindle and the Revd. William Brindle.[9] The lands were thereafter dispersed, the house later became part of the Burton Hill House estate, and the lordship was sold in 1867 to T. D. Hill.[10]

The manor house and *c.* 250 a. of Burton Hill manor were bought from Archard and Hall by Richard Cowche[11] (d. by 1588), who was succeeded in turn by his son Richard[12] (d. 1596) and Richard's son

96   *Cal. Pat.* 1575–8, p. 274.
97   P.R.O., C 142/218, no. 42.
98   Ibid. CP 25(2)/371/14 Jas. I Mich.
99   *Wilts. Inq. p.m.* 1625–49 (Index Libr.), 37–8.
 1   P.R.O., CP 25(2)/511/14 Chas. I Mich.
 2   Ibid. CP 25(2)/1079/10 Geo. I Mich.
 3   Ibid. CP 25(2)/1261/21 Geo. II East.; *V.C.H. Glos.* xi, 42 where a slightly different acct. of the fam. is given.
 4   W.R.O., A 1/345/273.
 5   Ibid. 212A/38/42/22.
 6   Ibid. 1165/1, deed, Dewell to Robins, 1809.
 7   Ibid. 212A/38/42/22.
 8   Ibid. 212A/38/37/16.
 9   Ibid. 212A/38/42/24/1.
10   Ibid. 212A/38/40/5–6; below.
11   *Cal. Pat.* 1575–8, pp. 502–4; P.R.O., C 142/326, no. 53.
12   W.R.O. 568/62.

The south front of Cowbridge House, built *c.* 1853

Richard[13] (d. 1611). The estate passed to the last Richard's nephew Richard Cowche,[14] who held it in 1638.[15] Before 1714 John Scrope bought *c.* 170 a. in Burton Hill from a Richard Cowche. As *WHITEHEATH* farm the lands had by 1720 passed to his son Richard, who was succeeded in turn by his son Richard (d. 1787) and Richard's son William, who sold the farm in 1810 to Giles Canter.[16] It was held in 1839 by Giles's son Joseph (d. 1865).[17] In 1910 and 1912 trustees of the Canter family held it;[18] by 1927 it had passed presumably by sale to M. H. Chubb,[19] who still held it in 1939.[20] In 1985 R. Alvis sold 103 a., comprising most of Whiteheath farm, to Mr. P. J. Pritchard, the owner in 1989.[21]

13 P.R.O., C 142/247, no. 25.
14 Ibid. C 142/326, no. 53.
15 W.R.O. 568/62.
16 Ibid. 212A/36/44, abstr. of title.
17 Ibid. tithe award; below, Norton, manor.
18 Ibid. Inland Revenue, val. reg. 9; ibid. G 7/500/1.
19 Ibid. G 7/515/9.
20 *Kelly's Dir. Wilts.* (1939).
21 Inf. from Mr. P. J. Pritchard, Whiteheath Farm.

In 1577 Adam Archard and Thomas Hall sold lands of Burton Hill manor to Henry Grayle.[22] In 1612 Grayle and his son David bought *COWBRIDGE* Mill and other lands, also part of the manor, from Nicholas Archard.[23] Their holding comprised 20 a. and the mill in 1615.[24] In 1706 that estate was sold by George Forman to George Ayliffe,[25] whose son John sold it in 1715 to Walter Trimnell.[26] By will proved 1832 Daniel Young devised it to his daughter Elizabeth.[27] In 1839 the mill and Cowbridge farm, 38 a., were held by S. B. Brooke[28] (d. 1869) whose nephew, the Revd. Charles Kemble (d. 1874), devised it to his wife Charlotte (d. 1890) for life. In 1882 Charlotte settled the reversion of Cowbridge House and *c.* 50 a. on her son Stephen Kemble.[29] The estate was offered for sale in 1893[30] and 1894,[31] and was bought in 1899 by Baldomero de Bertodano[32] (d. 1921).[33] It was sold in 1923,[34] probably to Sir Philip Hunloke, the owner in 1927,[35] who sold it in 1938 to E. K. Cole Ltd.[36] In 1989 Cowbridge House belonged to AT & T Telecommunications UK Ltd.,[37] the farmland to Mr. K. F. Edwards.[38] The house was designed in 1853 by John Shaw with an Italianate south garden front. It had terraced gardens adjacent to it, and stood in a larger garden or small park with lawns and walks.[39]

Lands of Burton Hill manor bought from Archard and Hall in 1577 by Ralph Slifield[40] probably passed to Francis Slifield (d. 1620),

22 *Cal. Pat.* 1575–8, p. 504.
23 W.R.O. 212A/36/34, deed, Grayle to Gymer, 1613.
24 Ibid. 212A/13, lease, Grayle to Forman, 1615.
25 P.R.O., CP 25(2)/979/5 Anne Mich.
26 W.R.O. 212A/36/34, deed, Ayliffe to Trimnell, 1715.
27 Ibid. 803/19.
28 Ibid. tithe award.
29 Ibid. 663/8; 856/3; Wilts. Cuttings, xvii. 13.
30 W.A.S. Libr., sale cat. i, no. 21.
31 W.R.O. 130/78, sale cat.
32 Wilts. Cuttings, xii. 201.
33 *W.A.M.* xli. 307–8.
34 *Country Life*, 9 June 1923.
35 W.R.O., G 7/515/9.
36 Ibid. F 12, corresp. file, E. K. Cole Ltd.
37 Inf. from Mr. G. Halton, AT & T Telecommunications UK Ltd., Cowbridge Ho.
38 Inf. from Mr. K. F. Edwards, Cowbridge Farm.
39 Print in possession of AT & T Telecommunications UK Ltd.; see illus on facing page.
40 *Cal. Pat.* 1575–8, p. 274.

who was succeeded by his brother Matthew.[41] By 1627 the lands had passed to Adam Peddington or Tuck (d. 1628), whose estate of 24 a. and 4 yardlands in Burton Hill, including lands formerly belonging to a Slifield, was divided between his nephews Adam Peddington and John Peddington.[42] The estate may have been that bought from Robert and Margaret Tuck by Edmund Estcourt (d. 1758), who held other lands in Burton Hill.[43]

An estate of *c.* 50 a. in Burton Hill held by Anthony Clase in 1623[44] may have derived from that bought from Archard and Hall by John Young in 1577.[45] Clase (d. 1626) devised the estate to Christopher and Thomas Meade.[46] By 1678 it had passed to Anne, relict of the Revd. Nathaniel Ashe, in 1680 wife of Thomas Petty.[47] It was sold by Anne's daughter Anne Ashe to Matthew Smith in 1693.[48] Smith sold part of it to Edmund Estcourt[49] (d. 1717) and part in 1742 to Estcourt's cousin and heir Edmund Estcourt (d. 1758),[50] who held *c.* 100 a. in Burton Hill. Those lands passed with Grange farm to William Edwards who sold his Burton Hill estate in 1787 to Timothy Dewell (d. 1792). Dewell devised the estate, including *BURTON HILL HOUSE,* to his wife Elizabeth and his sister Mary Dewell. It was sold in 1792 to Francis Hill (d. 1828) and, after litigation over Hill's will, in 1833 to Simon and Isaac Salter. The Salters apparently sold the estate in parcels; the house and 35 a. had been bought by John Cockerell by 1839.[51] Between 1846 and 1849 Cockerell sold his estate to C. W. Miles[52] (d. 1892).[53] It passed in turn to Miles's sons C. N. Miles (d. 1918) and A. C. Miles (d. 1919),[54] after whose death the Burton Hill House estate, then *c.* 120 a., was broken up and sold.[55] Burton Hill House and some land in Malmesbury

41 P.R.O., C 142/388, no. 71.
42 *Wilts. Inq. p.m.* 1625–49 (Index Libr.), 70–1.
43 W.R.O. 161/42, lease, Estcourt to Fothergill, 1764; below.
44 *Wilts. Inq. p.m.* 1625–49 (Index Libr.), 46–7.
45 *Cal. Pat.* 1575–8, p. 274.
46 *Wilts. Inq. p.m.* 1625–49 (Index Libr.), 46–7.
47 W.R.O. 118/97, deed, Petty to Tyte, 1680.
48 Ibid. 568/16, deed, Ashe to Smith, 1693.
49 Ibid. 161/48, deed, Ratcliffe to Wilkins, 1787.
50 *W.N. & Q.* viii. 435–6; Glos. R.O., D 1571/T 108, draft deed, Smith to Estcourt, 1742.
51 *W.N. & Q.* viii. 436–9; W.R.O., tithe award.
52 *W.N. & Q.* viii. 433; W.R.O. 700/137/5.
53 Wilts. Cuttings, xvii. 17.
54 *W.A.M.* xl. 202, 432.
55 W.R.O., G 7/150/2; G 7/500/1; G 7/515/9.

Burton Hill House, built from the 1840s

were probably then bought by H. L. Storey (d. 1933).[56] In 1945 the house and 16 a. were bought for use as a school for handicapped children by the Shaftesbury Society, the owner in 1987.[57]

BURNT HEATH farm, c. 8o a. north of West park, was held by Alexander Staples in 1585 and by George Staples in 1599.[58] Before 1766 the farm was bought from William Robins by William Earle[59] (d. 1774). It presumably passed with Grange farm to William Edwards and was probably sold in or after 1787.[60] In 1839 the farm, c. 60 a., belonged to Richard Perrett[61] and in 1865 to J. G. Lyne.[62] H. C. Lyne was the owner in 1910[63] and 1912.[64] The farm was sold in 1927, after the death of his relict.[65] It was bought in 1957 by Mr. A. R. Highman, the owner in 1989.[66]

56 W.A.M. xlvi. 279–80.
57 Inf. from the head teacher, Burton Hill Ho. Sch.
58 W.R.O. 1269/17, deeds, Staples to Seede, 1585, Staples to Hobbes, 1599.
59 Ibid. 212A/38/52/2A.
60 Above.
61 W.R.O., tithe award.
62 Ibid. G 21/510/1.
63 Ibid. Inland Revenue, val. reg. 9.
64 Ibid. G 7/500/1.
65 W.A.S. Libr., sale cat. xx, no. 41E.
66 Inf. from Mrs. A. R. Highman, Burnt Heath Farm.

Whitchurch was described as a manor in the mid 13th century,[67] and from the mid 16th the manor was usually called *WHITCHURCH* and (or with) *MILBOURNE*.[68] It passed from Malmesbury abbey to the Crown at the Dissolution and in 1545 was granted to Richard Moody[69] (d. 1550). It passed like Garsdon manor to Richard's relict Catherine Basely, to Richard Moody (d. 1612), and to Sir Henry Moody, Bt. (d. 1629).[70] In 1630 Sir Henry's relict Deborah surrendered her life interest to her son Sir Henry Moody,[71] who sold the manor, probably in 1630,[72] to Henry Danvers, earl of Danby, the owner in 1636.[73] From Danby (d. 1644) it passed with Malmesbury manor to Henry Danvers (d. 1654) and, possibly in portions, to Elizabeth, wife of Robert Villiers or Danvers, Anne, wife of Sir Henry Lee, Eleanor, wife of James Bertie, Baron Norreys, and Anne, wife of Thomas Wharton:[74] the whole manor was sold in or after 1681.[75] In 1684 the lordship and some of or all the lands belonged to George Hill who in 1707 sold them, as Whitchurch manor, to Francis Hayes, his mortgagee.[76] Hayes (d. in or before 1724) was succeeded by his son Charles[77] who sold the manor in 1729 to Jonathan Willis[78] (will proved 1732). Willis was succeeded by his daughter Sarah who sold it in 1762 to William Bouverie, Viscount Folkestone[79] (cr. earl of Radnor 1765, d. 1776). William's son Jacob, earl of Radnor,[80] sold it c. 1820 either to John Howard, earl of Suffolk and of Berkshire (d. 1820), or his son Thomas, earl of Suffolk and of Berkshire.[81] In 1839 Lord Suffolk owned c. 950 a., including most of the land around Milbourne and the 360 a. north of the town and almost detached from the rest of Malmesbury parish.[82] With Charlton manor and the titles it

67· *Cal. Chart. R.* 1226–57, 400.
68 e.g. P.R.O., SC 6/Hen. VIII/3986, rot. 129.
69 *L. & P. Hen. VIII,* xx (2), p. 539.
70 *Wilts. Inq. p.m.* 1625–49 (Index Libr.), 152, 155; P.R.O., C 142/92, no. 14; C 142/131, no. 200; above, Garsdon, manor.
71 P.R.O., C 104/91/2, abstr. of title.
72 Ibid. CP 25(2)/509/6 Chas. I Mich.
73 *Wilts. Inq. p.m.* 1625–49 (Index Libr.), 206.
74 Above.
75 P.R.O., CP 25(2)/747/33 & 34 Chas. II Hil.
76 W.R.O. 88/8/15.
77 Ibid. 88/8/16.
78 Ibid. 88/8/19.
79 Ibid. 88/8/35.
80 *Complete Peerage,* v. 542–3; x. 717–18.
81 Ibid. xii (1), 479–80; W.R.O. 88/10/10.
82 W.R.O., tithe award.

descended to Michael Howard, from 1941 earl of Suffolk and of Berkshire.[83] In 1987 Lord Suffolk retained most of the northern part of the estate, then in Quobwell farm, and lands north of Milbourne village. In 1978 Mr. R. A. Clarke bought Manor farm, Milbourne, 200 a., which he owned in 1987.[84]

Lands of Whitchurch and Milbourne manor were apparently sold separately in the late 17th century or the early 18th. They included 30 a. bought from Francis Hayes by Henry Croome (fl.1717). Croome's daughter Rebecca sold the land in 1729 to Humphrey Woodcock (d. 1754), who devised it to his nephew Charles Williamson.[85] In 1756 Williamson bought 179 a., formerly part of the manor, from Frederick St. John, Viscount Bolingbroke.[86] Williamson's estate, including *SOUTHFIELD* farm, passed on his death in 1760 to his niece Sarah Kyffin and her husband Matthew Sloper. In 1770 Sloper sold it to William Bouverie, earl of Radnor,[87] and it again became part of Whitchurch manor. Southfield farm, 175 a. in 1839,[88] was owned by Mr. R. G. Baker in 1987.[89]

In 1717 Henry Croome held a further 26 a. formerly part of Whitchurch and Milbourne manor. The land was sold by another Henry Croome in 1741 to William Earle,[90] who bought 170 a. in Whitchurch and Milbourne from Henry Brooke in 1763.[91] Those lands passed with Grange farm to William Edwards, who in 1787 sold them to Richard Kinneir as *WHITCHURCH* farm.[92] Kinneir or a namesake held the farm in 1839.[93] In 1850 and 1852 it was offered for sale as a farm of 200 a.[94] The farmhouse and 75 a. belonged in 1865 to the Revd. E. E. Elwell.[95] Members of the Elwell family owned it in 1910 and 1927.[96] That farm

83 Above, Charlton, manors.
84 Inf. from Mr. J. H. Guest, Quobwell Farm; Mr. D. W. Clarke, Marsh Farm; Mr. R. A. Clarke, Manor Farm, Milbourne.
85 W.R.O. 88/8/50; 88/10/15; above, Charlton, manors.
86 W.R.O. 88/8/43.
87 Ibid. 88/10/15.
88 Ibid. tithe award.
89 Local inf.
90 W.R.O. 88/10/15.
91 Ibid. 212A/38/52/2A.
92 Ibid. 161/52, abstr. of title.
93 Ibid. tithe award.
94 Ibid. 88/10/10; 137/125/47.
95 Ibid. G 21/510/1.
96 Ibid. Inland Revenue, val. reg. 9; ibid. G 7/515/9.

and other lands, 156 a. in all, were bought in 1941 by John Weaver; 60 a., part of Milbourne farm, were added *c.* 1977, and in 1987 the farm, then called Whychurch, belonged to John's son Mr. Edward Weaver.[97]

Milbourne farm, presumably derived from Whitchurch and Milbourne manor, belonged in 1839 to Isaac Beak.[98] In 1910 Daniel Beak owned 103 a.,[99] and those and other lands, totalling 152 a., were owned in 1927 by William Spong (fl. 1931).[1] Some of the land became part of Whychurch farm;[2] the farmhouse and other land were bought *c.* 1987 by members of the Wickes family.[3]

The lands south-west of the town and mainly in Westport parish, which were held from the 13th century or earlier by the guild merchant and in 1989 by the warden and freemen of Malmesbury, included *c.* 50 a. in Malmesbury parish.[4]

Malmesbury abbey appropriated the parish church of Malmesbury in or after 1191,[5] and owned the *RECTORY* estate until the Dissolution. Thereafter most rectorial tithes passed with the estates from which they derived, but those from the Cowbridge estate were apparently owned separately from the land. In 1735 they were conveyed by Thomas Boucher, perhaps a trustee, to William Carey. In 1789 Carey's son William sold them to Samuel Brooke[6] (d. 1837), whose son S. B. Brooke held both the estate and the tithes in 1839.[7] Rectorial tithes from the lands of Whitchurch and Milbourne manor passed with the manor to Sir Henry Moody, Bt. (d. 1629),[8] but he or a later lord of the manor apparently sold some. Between 1765 and 1774 tithes from part of the manor were bought by William Bouverie, earl of Radnor, lord of Whitchurch and Milbourne manor.[9] In 1839 all rectorial tithes in the parish were merged or held by the owners of the lands from which they arose.[10]

97 Inf. from Mr. E. Weaver, Whychurch Farm.
98 W.R.O., tithe award.
99 Ibid. Inland Revenue, val. reg. 9.
 1 Ibid. G 7/515/9; *Kelly's Dir. Wilts.* (1931).
 2 Above.
 3 Local inf.
 4 Below, Westport, manors, econ. hist.
 5 *Reg. Malm.* i. 374–5.
 6 W.R.O. 212A/36/34, deeds, Boucher to Carey, 1735, Carey to Brooke, 1789.
 7 Ibid. tithe award; above, Charlton, manors.
 8 *Wilts. Inq. p.m.* 1625–49 (Index Libr.), 151–5.
 9 W.R.O. 88/8/40.
10 Ibid. tithe award.

In 1232 Bradenstoke priory owned a house near one of the guildhalls in Malmesbury, and *c.* 1252 William Porter gave the priory a tenement in High Street.[11] In the mid and later 13th century Nicholas of Malmesbury gave a tenement in East Street, William Spicer gave a rent of 1*s.* from a tenement in East Street, and Andrew son of John of Malmesbury gave a rent of 3*s.*[12] The priory retained a small estate in Malmesbury until the Dissolution.[13]

In the Middle Ages small estates in Malmesbury also belonged to two chapels, St. Mary's, possibly the hospital of St. Mary Magdalene, and All Saints'.[14] At their dissolution in 1548 St. Mary's chantry in St. Paul's church had tenements in the town and 17 a. elsewhere in the parish, and St. Mary's chantry in Westport church included *c.* 4 a. and tenements in Malmesbury parish.[15]

St. John's hospital in Nethewall, said in 1389 to have been founded by the burgesses, in the late 13th century occupied a site which comprised lands formerly belonging to William Aldune and Thomas Purs and a parcel called *De Profundis.* In 1247 Walter Bodmin and his wife Emme gave two messuages to the hospital, the property of which was valued at 46*s.* in 1389. It was presumably dissolved and its lands confiscated by the Crown in the mid 16th century. John Stumpe acquired part of the property from John Marsh and William Marsh and part from John Herbert and Andrew Palmer. In 1580 Stumpe conveyed the whole to the alderman and burgesses of Malmesbury,[16] who maintained an almshouse in the former hospital from 1584 or earlier.[17]

AGRICULTURE. On the two small estates called Malmesbury in 1086 there was a total of 1½ ploughteam, 5 bordars, 10 a. of meadow, and 3½ square furlongs of pasture. The bishop of Coutances had demesne of 3 yardlands. A vineyard was planted on a hill north of the abbey in the early 11th century; another, planted in the later 13th century,[18] may have

11 *V.C.H. Wilts.* iii. 281.   12 *Bradenstoke Cart.* (W.R.S. xxxv), pp. 77–8.

13 *Valor Eccl.* (Rec. Com.), ii. 123.

14 *Cal. Pat.* 1572–5, pp. 408–9; 1575–8, pp. 25, 27; below, churches. The hist. of the hosp. of St. Mary Magdalene is related in *V.C.H. Wilts.* iii. 340 (reprinted below, pp. 203–4).

15 P.R.O., E 301/58, nos. 35–6; below, churches; ibid. Westport, church.

16 *W.A.M.* xxix. 124. The hist. of St. John's hosp. is related in *V.C.H. Wilts.* iii. 340 (reprinted below, pp. 201–3).

17 W.R.O., D 1/43/5, f. 21; below, charities.

18 *V.C.H. Wilts.* ii, pp. 122, 162; iii. 214, 221.

given its name to Wyniard Mill on the eastern edge of the town.[19] No later reference to viticulture has been found.

In the Middle Ages and later Malmesbury parish, apart from Corston and Rodbourne, included c. 650 a. to the south in Cole park and West park; c. 600 a. of agricultural land between the parks and the town were worked from farms based in or near Burton Hill, c. 500 a. east of the town were worked from farmsteads in or south of Milbourne, and c. 500 a. north and north-east were worked from Whitchurch or farmsteads north of it.[20]

PARKS. Part of Malmesbury abbey's estate called Cowfold was woodland in the late 12th century[21] and may then or soon afterwards have been imparked. In 1235 the abbot was given two bucks from Braydon forest for his park of Cowfold.[22] In the mid 15th century there was a second park, West park, presumably west of the Malmesbury–Chippenham road.[23] In 1535 the Cowfold estate included a park of 300 a., meadow land of 100 a. in closes, both in hand, and 40 a. of pasture and arable held by a tenant.[24] The tenanted land with other lands and the grange, later called Grange farm, c. 1550 comprised 78 a. including 4 a. in the open fields of Burton Hill.[25]

In the mid 16th century Cowfold, later Cole, park, 300 a., and West park, 200 a., accommodated a royal stud farm,[26] known as the race.[27] The stud was administered by a yeoman or groom of the race. The first may have been Ralph Bolton (fl. 1555–9), who was involved in a dispute when fences around Cowfold park were broken and cattle were driven in.[28] The title yeoman of the race was recorded in 1583, when Ralph Slifield, the yeoman, was commissioned to take for the stud forage of 40 qr. of oats from Wiltshire and another 40 qr. from Gloucestershire.[29] In the early 17th century the yeoman received a fee and a further 26s.

19 P.N. Wilts. (E.P.N.S.), 53.
20 For the areas, W.R.O., tithe award.
21 Reg. Malm. i. 222.
22 Close R. 1234–7, 126.
23 Eton Coll. Mun. 4/105.
24 Valor Eccl. (Rec. Com.), ii. 120.
25 P.R.O., LR 2/191, f. 132.
26 Ibid.
27 B.L. Lansd. Ch. 46.
28 Acts of P.C. 1554–6, 240; Cal. Pat. 1558–60, 172–3; P.R.O., STAC 4/4/56.
29 B.L. Lansd. Ch. 46.

8d. for every colt raised. In 1621 there were also three servants and a farrier at the stud.[30] According to a report made before 1587 the site of the stud was unsuitable; the area was too small, and drainage and soil were poor. It was suggested that fodder should be produced in West park if that from the larger Cole park was insufficient. There were then 34 mares and 31 young horses in Cole park. By the 1590s numbers had fallen to 24 mares and 27 young horses, some of which had been carelessly bred. Walls and fences were in poor repair, and most of the great trees with which the park had been well supplied *c.* 1550 had been felled.[31] Cattle and sheep were kept in the parks; in 1599 there were 85 cows and calves and 80 ewes.[32] Improvements were made in the early 17th century. In 1608–9 a stone wall was built around Cole park,[33] and in 1628 there were 37 mares and 35 young horses.[34] By 1628 the parks had been leased but the stud remained there, on payment of a fee to the lessee,[35] until *c.* 1630.[36]

By 1653 both parks had been disparked. About 500 a. in closes represented the former Cole park; *c.* 70 a. were meadow and some former pasture had been ploughed. Of the former West park, 166 a., some land was arable and 16 a. were wooded.[37] In the 18th and 19th centuries *c.* 200 a. around Cole Park were again parkland. The rest of the former park was in Wood farm, Lawn farm, and Rodbourne Rail farm in the early 18th century.[38] In the 1730s a three-year rotation was practised at Wood farm; clover was grown every third year.[39] In 1767 Lawn farm comprised 145 a. north of Cole Park, including 32 a. of arable.[40] In 1796 Rodbourne Rail farm comprised 119 a. south of Cole Park.[41] South of Lawn farm, Grange farm was 108 a. in 1764 when over half of it was arable.[42] What had been West park was apparently worked as a single

---

30   *Cal. S.P. Dom.* 1611–18, 596; 1619–23, 231.
31   C. M. Prior, *Royal Studs*, 13–23, 64–5; P.R.O., LR 2/191, f. 132.
32   Hist. MSS. Com. 9, *Salisbury*, ix, p. 115.
33   *Cal. S.P. Dom.* 1603–10, 496; P.R.O., E 178/4707.
34   Prior, *Royal Studs*, 70.
35   *Cal. S.P. Dom.* 1628–9, 389.
36   Ibid. 1629–31, 455.
37   P.R.O., LR 2/301, ff. 232–59.
38   W.R.O. 161/27/2; 161/28/1; 161/29/1.
39   Ibid. 161/31/21.
40   Ibid. 161/53, lease, Harvey to Keynes, 1767.
41   Ibid. 161/134, lease, Lovell to Reynolds, 1796.
42   Ibid. 161/42, lease, Estcourt to Fothergill, 1764.

farm until the early 19th century.[43] The lands of the two former parks were mostly pasture in 1839, except for 24 a. of wood east of West Park Farm.[44] In 1927 only *c.* 60 a. around Cole Park remained parkland. Lawn farm was then 229 a., Rodbourne Rail farm 188 a., Grange farm 99 a., and West Park farm 86 a.; there were also three smaller holdings in what had been West park.[45] In the later 20th century all but *c.* 8 a. of the park[46] was agricultural land: Lawn farm and Lower West Park farm were principally dairy farms but there was also some arable.[47]

BURTON HILL. Open arable fields of Burton Hill were the subject of an agreement between Malmesbury abbey and the lord of Bremilham manor in the early 13th century when the abbey proposed to cultivate temporarily inclosed parts of the fallow field. The lord of Bremilham and his tenants apparently held land and pasture in those fields, two of which were called Ham and Kemboro fields.[48] Kemboro field may have lain partly in Westport parish and was still open in the 17th century, when there were also fields called Shelfield and Burton field.[49] From the later 14th century part of the demesne pasture of Burton Hill was shared with one or more tenant.[50] The chief pastures of Burton Hill were presumably Burnt heath and Whiteheath to the south-west. Part of Burnt heath had been ploughed by the early 14th century,[51] and by the late 16th much of it had been inclosed.[52] Much of Whiteheath was a several farm in the early 18th century.[53]

In the late 13th century Malmesbury abbey had 16 tenants, presumably customary, at Burton Hill.[54] In the mid 16th there were 12 customary tenants; 4 held a total of 5 yardlands, the others may have had smaller holdings. Works, including two days cutting and carting hay, had almost certainly been commuted by then. There were five leaseholders,

43 W.R.O., A 1/345/274.
44 Ibid. tithe award.
45 Ibid. G 7/515/9.
46 Above, manors.
47 Inf. from Mr. P. Roberts, Lawn Farm; Mr. G. T. Warr, Lower West Park Farm.
48 *Reg. Malm.* ii. 118, 185–6.
49 *Wilts. Inq. p.m.* 1625–49 (Index Libr.), 46–7; below, Westport, econ. hist.
50 *Feet of F.* 1327–77 (W.R.S. xxix), p. 148.
51 *Reg. Malm.* ii. 151.
52 W.R.O. 1269/17, deed, Staples to Seede, 1585.
53 Ibid. 212A/36/44, abstr. of title.
54 *Reg. Malm.* i. 176–7.

excluding tenants of mills; one, with several pasture and 'lords lands' in Kemboro field, held what may have been the demesne.[55] In 1585 Burnt Heath was a several farm of c. 80 a.[56]

In the 17th and 18th centuries farms derived from Burton Hill manor numbered about five; most were smaller than 100 a., and the largest was Whiteheath farm. There were also holdings of only a few acres. Part of Whiteheath farm was arable but the smaller farms were chiefly pasture and meadow.[57] Part of Kemboro field had been inclosed by 1679[58] and part of Burton field by 1764; apparently the whole of Shelfield remained open.[59] By 1839 all arable had been inclosed and only a few acres of pasture, beside a track between Burnt Heath and Whiteheath farms, remained common. There were then c. 400 a. of pasture and c. 120 a. of arable around Burton Hill. Whiteheath, still the largest farm, was a compact holding of 147 a. west of the Chippenham road. There were seven farms of between 20 a. and 100 a., and c. 130 a. were in holdings smaller than 20 a.[60] In 1866 stock on all those farms included 65 cows, 57 other cattle, 140 sheep, and 70 pigs.[61] Most of the land around Burton Hill was pasture in the 1930s;[62] in the later 20th century farms remained small, dairying continued, but there was also some arable farming.[63] On Whiteheath farm, 103 a. in the 1980s, pedigree cattle were bred and in winter store lambs were kept.[64]

MILBOURNE. South field, south of Milbourne village and recorded in the early 17th century,[65] had probably been an open field, and the men of Milbourne had common grazing for horses and perhaps other beasts on c. 30 a. beside the village street.[66] They also had unrestricted

55 P.R.O., E 318/Box 32/1820; ibid. SC 6/Hen. VIII/3986, rot. 113.
56 W.R.O. 1269/17, deed, Staples to Seede, 1585.
57 Ibid. 212A/13, lease, Grayle to Forman, 1615; 568/30, lease, Scrope to Young, 1729; *Wilts. Inq. p.m.* 1625–49 (Index Libr.), 27–8, 46–7, 70–1.
58 W.R.O. 212A/36/16, deed, Gastrell to Hart, 1679.
59 Ibid. 161/42, lease, Estcourt to Fothergill, 1764.
60 Ibid. tithe award.
61 P.R.O., MAF 68/73, sheet 14.
62 [1st] Land Util. Surv. Map, sheet 103.
63 Inf. from Capt. A. D. C. Francis, the Grange, Corston; Mrs. A. R. Highman, Burnt Heath Farm.
64 Inf. from Mr. P. J. Pritchard, Whiteheath Farm, Corston.
65 *Wilts. Inq. p.m.* 1625–49 (Index Libr.), 152.
66 W.R.O. 88/5/26B.

grazing rights in Braydon forest and its purlieus: the nearest point at which their animals could enter the purlieus was *c.* 4 km. east of the village. Milbourne common, 104 a., allotted to them when the purlieus were inclosed in the early 1630s, remained a common pasture and they could feed *c.* 68 cattle on it. They may also have shared Lot meadow, which in 1792 comprised 15 a. south of the village.[67]

In 1630 the Milbourne portion of Whitchurch and Milbourne manor included a leasehold of 133 a., most of which was a pasture close called Southfield and which may have been largely demesne. The manor also included 920 a. apparently held by copy; there were 4 holdings of over 50 a. each, 9 of between 20 a. and 50 a., and 18 smaller than 20 a. Most of the land was inclosed but 91 a., of which 28 a. were exclusive to copyholders, were still worked in common; whether the 91 a. were in Milbourne or Whitchurch is not clear.[68]

Lands south of Milbourne village were said in 1756 to have been recently inclosed.[69] Lot meadow and Milbourne common were inclosed in 1792 under an Act of 1790; allotments in Milbourne common were made to 10 landholders.[70] The Home common, beside Milbourne village street, was inclosed by an agreement of 1831.[71]

In 1802 Southfield farm, *c.*170 a., was a compact holding south of the village worked from a farmstead recently built on a new site near the parish boundary. What became Manor farm, *c.* 130 a. east of the village, and what became Milbourne farm, *c.* 110 a. scattered around the village, were worked from farmsteads beside the street. There were over 300 a. of pasture, *c.* 75 a. of arable, and *c.* 50 a. of meadow.[72] On Southfield farm *c.* 1800 were 100 sheep, 40 cows and 18 young cattle, and 10 colts.[73] The former Milbourne common, held in parcels in 1802, was in 1839 all in the lord's hand, but there had been few changes in the size or number of farms.[74] In the early 20th century the lands were in three farms of *c.* 150 a. each;[75] there was arable north of the village but not elsewhere in Milbourne in the 1930s.[76]

67 W.R.O., EA/34; ibid. 88/4/43; 88/10/52; ibid. tithe award; *V.C.H. Wilts.* iv. 406.
68 P.R.O., C 104/85/1, deed, Moody to Cowper, 1630.
69 W.R.O. 88/8/43.
70 Ibid. EA/34.
71 Ibid. 88/5/26B.
72 Ibid. 88/5/47; 900/12.
73 Ibid. 490/1041.
74 Ibid. 88/5/47; 900/12; ibid. tithe award.
75 Ibid. G 7/500/1; G 7/515/9.   76 [1st] Land Util. Surv. Map, sheet 103.

WHITCHURCH. In the 17th century and probably earlier Whitchurch had fields called North and Coldharbour.[77] There was common pasture for beasts and sheep on Whitchurch marsh and Wallow marsh, north and north-west of Whychurch Farm, a total of 46 a. in 1792;[78] in the earlier 18th century haywards for the pastures were appointed at Whitchurch and Milbourne manor courts.[79]

Whitchurch farm, possibly demesne land, was held by lease in the early 17th century; it then comprised 174 a., perhaps including land outside the parish, and pasture rights in Whitchurch and Wallow marshes. Other leaseholds in the Whitchurch portion of Whitchurch and Milbourne manor were of no more than 30 a. each. All or part of Coldharbour field may have been open in 1695,[80] but open-field cultivation had probably ceased by the late 18th century. In 1792, under the Act of 1790, Whitchurch and Wallow marshes were inclosed and allotments in them were made to eight landholders.[81] In 1802 most of the Whitchurch portion of the manor lay in three compact farms. The most southerly, Whitchurch, 316 a. including 116 a. in Westport parish, was worked from buildings on a site north-east of Malmesbury which had long been in use; Quobwell, *c.* 290 a. north of Whitchurch, and Coldharbour, *c.* 65 a. further north, were worked from farmsteads probably built on new sites in the 18th century. Over 400 a. were pasture, less than 100 a. arable;[82] the extent and number of the farms had changed little by 1839.[83]

In the earlier 20th century Quobwell farm comprised *c.* 200 a., Coldharbour farm *c.* 100 a., and Whitchurch farm *c.* 75 a.; 50 a. were worked as part of Griffin's Barn farm based in Charlton parish.[84] North of Quobwell Farm was arable in the 1930s; most of the remaining land was then pasture.[85] In 1987 most of what had been Coldharbour farm was part of Quobwell, 311 a., and Griffin's Barn farms; Whitchurch was then *c.* 130 a. All were dairy and arable farms.[86]

77 W.R.O. 149/104/3.
78 Ibid. EA/34.
79 Ibid. 88/5/47.
80 Ibid. 149/104/3.
81 Ibid. EA/34.
82 Ibid. 88/5/47; 900/12.
83 Ibid. tithe award.
84 Ibid. G 7/500/1; G 7/515/9.
85 [1st] Land Util. Surv. Map, sheet 103.
86 Inf. from Mr. J. H. Guest, Quobwell Farm; Mr. E. Weaver, Whychurch Farm.

TRADE AND INDUSTRY. The range of trades in Malmesbury in the mid 13th century is illustrated by the claim of the guild merchant to rights allegedly denied by the abbot of Malmesbury: that only its members might sell cloth, leather goods, fish, sheepskins, or hides within the borough, that no glover from outside Malmesbury might sell gloves made of horse skin, and that no wool merchant might trade with his own weights.[87] The outcome of the dispute is not known. Late 13th-century surnames also suggest that the leather and cloth trades were prominent[88] and there may have been a tannery near Postern Mill.[89] A fulling mill was recorded in the late 12th century[90] and the production of woollen cloth apparently remained Malmesbury's chief industry throughout the later Middle Ages.

In 1542 John Leland reported that 3,000 cloths were produced at Malmesbury yearly.[91] Wool was presumably bought at markets in north Wiltshire and Gloucestershire; a Malmesbury clothier bought yarn at Cirencester from a Northampton supplier.[92] Broadcloths from Malmesbury were sold in London in the early 16th century and the early 17th.[93] The most notable clothier in the town in the earlier 16th century was William Stumpe, who used the buildings of the dissolved monastery to house perhaps as many as 20 looms.[94] The names of nine Malmesbury clothiers of the later 16th century and the earlier 17th are known. Between them they apparently occupied most of the mills on the outskirts of the town. Wyniard Mill, Postern Mill, and Cowbridge Mill were all held by clothiers during that period. A new fulling mill beside St. John's bridge was built c. 1600 by Nicholas Archard, and William Hobbes, who then held Postern Mill, complained that the course of the Sherston branch of the Avon had been altered to his detriment.[95] Archard's business failed and he sold the fulling mill, Cannop's Mill, in 1622.[96]

87 *Reg. Malm.* ii. 393–4.
88 Ibid. i. 118–33.
89 *Medieval Arch.* xxxi, p. 167.
90 *Reg. Malm.* ii. 435.
91 Leland; *Itin.* ed. Toulmin Smith, i. 132.
92 *V.C.H. Wilts.* iv. 144.
93 Ibid. 139–40; *Early-Stuart Tradesmen* (W.R.S. xv), p. 61.
94 *V.C.H. Wilts.* iv. 146–7; G. D. Ramsay, *Wilts. Woollen Ind.* 17, 32–4.
95 *Cal. Pat.* 1550–3, 259; 1575–8, p. 247; *Early-Stuart Tradesmen* (W.R.S. xv), p. 61; *Wilts. Inq. p.m.* 1625–49 (Index Libr.), 70, 431–2; Hist. MSS. Com. 55, *Var. Coll.* i, p. 98; P.R.O., E 134/3 Jas. I East./12.
96 *Wilts. Inq. p.m.* 1625–49 (Index Libr.), 320.

Burton Hill Mill *c.* 1965

Malmesbury was still said to have 'a great name for clothing' *c.* 1650[97] but thereafter references to the industry are less frequent. There was still a dye house at Wyniard Mill in 1653,[98] a clothier and a silk weaver were in the town in 1687,[99] and some woollen manufacture was said to have continued until *c.*1750.[1]

The woollen industry was revived *c.* 1790 when Francis Hill bought Cannop's Mill and built a new cloth mill, Burton Hill Mill, on its site. Hill chose Malmesbury, away from existing areas of cloth production, so that he could install modern machinery without opposition. The mill, which had been enlarged by 1803, used the spring loom or fly shuttle, powered by water, to produce superfine broadcloth. Hill also owned Postern Mill from 1793. Burton Hill Mill was closed *c.*

97 E. Leigh, *Eng. Described,* 208.
98 P.R.O., E 317/Wilts. no. 39.
99 Moffatt, *Hist. Malm.* 161; W.R.O. 212B/3889.
 1 Moffatt, *Hist. Malm.* 162.

1825[2] and in 1831 was used as a corn mill.[3] It was reopened for cloth production by members of the Salter family in 1833[4] and by 1838 steam power had been introduced.[5] Woollen broadcloths were produced throughout the 1840s. Woollen cloth was also dyed and finished at Cowbridge Mill in the 1830s and 1840s.[6] Burton Hill Mill was bought c. 1850 by Thomas Bridget & Co. of Derby and converted to produce silk ribbon. The ownership, but not the use, of the mill changed several times in the later 19th century. In 1862 there were 56 power looms and 281 workers. Numbers employed were said to have risen to 400, perhaps an exaggeration, by 1867. In 1900 there were 150 employees: the mill was closed soon afterwards. It had reopened by 1923[7] and, with an interruption during the Second World War, continued to produce fancy silk and cotton goods until c. 1950.[8] For some years thereafter part of the building was used for dressing furs and skins.[9] The mill was used for the storage and sale of antiques in the 1970s[10] and as workshops for light engineering between 1980 and 1984, and in 1984 it was sold for conversion to flats.[11]

Before Burton Hill Mill was opened lace making was one of the town's chief occupations. Many of the workers were women and were recruited to work in the mill, although they could earn more by making lace. In the 19th century the industry declined in the face of competition from machine-made lace,[12] but women and children continued to make pillow lace throughout the century.[13] In the 1830s and 1850s lace was sent from Malmesbury to Wales and Lancashire.[14] After 1900 there was a revival under the patronage of Mary Howard, countess of Suffolk and of Berkshire, and a Mrs. Jones one or both of whom opened a school in

2   Moffatt, *Hist. Malm.* 159–60; *V.C.H. Wilts.* iv. 167, 172; K. H. Rogers, *Warp and Weft,* 89; W.R.O. 1301/9, deed, Wilkins to Hill, 1793; see above, illus. on p. 53.
3   Soc. Antiq. MS. 817, ix, f. 1v.
4   *V.C.H. Wilts.* iv. 172 n.; J. Bird, *Hist. Malm.* 204.
5   *W.A.M.* liv. 98.
6   Pigot, *Nat. Com. Dir.* (1830), 805; (1842), 21–2; *Kelly's Dir. Wilts.* (1848); Hudson, *Hill Top Town,* 11.
7   *V.C.H. Wilts.* iv. 177; *Kelly's Dir. Wilts.* (1859 and later edns.).
8   W.R.O., F 12, corresp. file, Avon Silk Mills.
9   Local inf.
10 Hudson, *Hill Top Town,* 12.
11 W.A.S. Libr., sale cat. xxix, no. 382; xxxii, no. 5.
12 *V.C.H. Wilts.* iv. 180–1; *W.A.M.* liv. 100.
13 *Kelly's Dir. Wilts.* (1848 and later edns.).
14 W.R.O. 988/2.

Malmesbury to teach lace making,[15] but little or no lace was made in the town after 1914.[16]

Gloves were still made at Malmesbury in the mid 17th century.[17] In the 18th century most of the trades practised there and not connected with textile production were those usual in a market town, and only a few may have been of more than local importance.[18] A firm of parchment makers, William Browning & Co., was recorded in the town in 1750, there was a glover in Westport in 1751, and parchment, gloves, and glue were all made *c.* 1800.[19]

There were two brewers and four maltsters in Malmesbury and Westport parishes in 1830.[20] In 1848 there were breweries in High Street and Cross Hayes; a third, later called Abbey brewery, was south of Abbey House. That in High Street was owned by Thomas Luce who in 1859, with a partner, had breweries in Cross Hayes and Westport; the latter was probably that later called Mill brewery, on the site of and incorporating Postern Mill. By 1867 he had been succeeded by C. R. Luce, who from *c.* 1875 owned both Abbey and Mill breweries.[21] In 1912, when there were 42 public houses tied to his breweries, he sold them to the Stroud Brewery Co.[22] Mill brewery was still in use in 1935–6,[23] but from 1941 was no longer used for brewing.[24] Abbey brewery may also have been closed *c.* 1940.[25] Esau Duck owned Cross Hayes brewery in 1875 and 1885. In 1895 and 1910 the brewery traded as Duck & Reed, in 1915 as Duck & Co.[26] In 1920, when it had 20 tied houses, it was taken over by the Stroud Brewery Co.; it may have been closed with Abbey brewery *c.* 1940.[27]

Edwin Ratcliffe opened a foundry, later known as Westport Ironworks, in the north-western part of the town *c.* 1870. Up to 12

15 Wilts. Cuttings, xvii. 17.
16 *Kelly's Dir. Wilts.* (1915 and later edns.).
17 Aubrey, *Nat. Hist. Wilts.* ed. Britton, 78–9.
18 *Wilts. Apprentices* (W.R.S. xvii), *passim.*
19 Ibid. pp. 35, 60; Moffatt, *Hist. Malm.* 162.
20 Pigot, *Nat. Com. Dir.* (1830), 804–5.
21 *Kelly's Dir. Wilts.* (1848 and later edns.).
22 Wilts. Cuttings, xvii. 17; inf. from Mr. N. Redman, Whitbread & Co. plc, Chiswell Street, Lond. E.C. 1.
23 W.R.O., G 21/516/2.
24 Below.
25 Inf. from Mr. Redman.
26 *Kelly's Dir. Wilts.* (1875 and later edns.); W.R.O., Inland Revenue, val. reg. 9.
27 Inf. from Mr. Redman.

men were employed in the late 19th century and the early 20th in making and repairing agricultural and other machinery.[28] There was an engineering workshop in the foundry buildings in 1988.

From 1877 or earlier bacon was cured in a factory belonging to Adye & Hinwood Ltd. in Park Road. In the 1930s much of the bacon was exported but later most was for home consumption. Some 500 pigs were killed weekly c. 1950, but the number had fallen to 200 by 1956.[29] The factory was closed c. 1965[30] and was demolished. West of it in Park Road from the mid 20th century was a slaughterhouse, used in 1987 by V. & G. Newman, and in 1987 the premises of Ready Animal Foods, pet food wholesalers, were nearby.

In 1923 Wilts. & Somerset Farmers Ltd. had a milk depot in Park Road.[31] The depot belonged c. 1950 to Wiltshire Creameries Ltd.; milk was treated there and up to 60 lb. of cheese produced daily.[32] The depot had been closed by 1974 and in 1986 its site was converted into small industrial units.[33]

The town was a local commercial centre in the 19th century. A bank was opened in St. Dennis's Lane after 1800, and in 1813 Thomas Luce became a partner in it. Luce was later the bank's sole proprietor and sold it in or after 1836 to the Wilts. and Dorset Banking Co. Ltd. The bank became part of Lloyds Bank Ltd. between 1911 and 1915. The North Wilts. Banking Co. took over the business of a smaller Malmesbury bank c. 1836, and its successor, the Capital and Counties Bank Ltd., had a branch in the town until 1915 or later.[34]

Two companies which were moved to Malmesbury shortly before and during the Second World War remained in the town after 1945. E. K. Cole Ltd., manufacturers of 'Ekco' radio, electrical, and electronic equipment, bought Cowbridge House in 1939 and built a factory adjacent to it.[35] In the 1940s and early 1950s radar equipment was produced and there were c. 1,000 employees. Domestic electrical goods were produced after 1958 and continued to be made after 1963 when E. K. Cole Ltd.

---

28 V.C.H. Wilts. iv. 196.
29 Ibid. 222; Town Guide [c. 1950].
30 Inf. from Curator, Athelstan Mus.
31 Kelly's Dir. Wilts. (1923).
32 Town Guide [c. 1950].
33 Inf. from Direct Labour Organisation Manager, N. Wilts. district council, Parsonage Way, Chippenham.
34 Hudson, Hill Top Town, 111; Kelly's Dir. Wilts. (1848 and later edns.).
35 V.C.H. Wilts. iv. 204.

was absorbed into the Pye group of companies. From 1968 Pye–TMC Ltd. and from 1971 TMC Ltd. developed and produced telephone equipment on the site. New buildings were erected in 1975 and 1982. In 1987 AT & T and Philips Telecommunications UK Ltd. acquired the site jointly and in 1988 employed 400 people in research into and the development and manufacture of telephone transmission and switching systems.[36] In 1941 Linolite Ltd., originally makers of lighting fittings but then producing hose clips for use in aeroplanes and tanks, was moved from London to the former Mill brewery in Malmesbury. After 1945 the firm again produced lights, especially gas-filled tubes, and in 1952 employed *c.* 50 people. A new factory was built north of the town in 1985. In 1988 Linolite Ltd., then a subsidiary of the General Telephone and Electronics Corporation, employed 290 people.[37]

After the closure of the railway in 1962[38] several small factories were built on and near the site of the station. In 1988 sheet metal and traffic lights were among the goods produced.

MILLS. In 1066 Earl Harold held a mill at Malmesbury.[39] It may have stood, as did most of the mills recorded later, beside one or other branch of the Avon on or a little outside the borough boundary. Another, whose location is not known, was recorded in the 13th century, and in the late 13th century Malmesbury abbey had a mill on its Cowfold estate;[40] that mill was not afterwards mentioned.

A mill held in the 13th century by William of Westmill[41] may have been in Westport parish, perhaps below the postern gate where a mill stood apparently from the 12th century or the 13th.[42] Postern Mill, which belonged to Malmesbury abbey at the Dissolution, in 1539 incorporated a corn mill and a fulling mill;[43] the fulling mill may have been standing in 1605.[44] In 1610 Postern Mill and a possibly adjacent

---

36 Mass-Observation, *War Factory,* 6; inf. from Mr. G. Halton, AT & T Telecommunications UK Ltd., Cowbridge Ho.
37 *V.C.H. Wilts.* iv. 204; inf. from Mr. P. J. Sear, Managing Director, Linolite Ltd., Malmesbury.
38 Above, introduction.
39 *V.C.H. Wilts.* ii, p. 115.
40 *Reg. Malm.* i. 131, 174–5.
41 P.R.O., CP 25(1)/250/9, no. 48.
42 Inf. from Mr. C. K. Currie, 15 Claudeen Close, Swaythling, Southampton.
43 P.R.O., SC 6/Hen. VIII/3986, rott. 96–98d.
44 Ibid. E 134/3 Jas. I East./12.

corn mill were sold with Wyniard Mill to Sir Peter Vanlore;[45] they may have been the two mills held by John Waite in 1702.[46] Waite and a namesake held one of the mills in 1725.[47] Postern Mill was in use, presumably as a corn mill, in 1830; it was bought by Thomas Luce in 1834 and converted to a brewery soon afterwards.[48]

'Schotesbure' Mill, which stood beside a road leading southwards from the town in the late 13th century or the earlier 14th,[49] was probably that east of St. John's bridge later held of Burton Hill manor and called Cannop's Mill.[50] In the late 13th century, as in the 16th, the bridge was called Mill bridge,[51] and the mill was standing near it in 1480.[52] Between 1535 and 1564 the millers were members of the Cannop family. In 1564 John Cannop was fined for overcharging.[53] From the early 17th century buildings on the site of the mill were used chiefly in the production of cloth.[54]

Cowbridge Mill, standing in the late 13th century,[55] also became part of Burton Hill manor.[56] Although it seems to have been principally a grist mill, it was held by clothiers in the early 17th century and the early 19th.[57] The mill and mill house were rebuilt c. 1850. In 1875 and 1882 the mill was leased to a Malmesbury brewer.[58] Water power was still used in 1894;[59] by 1910 the mill had apparently been converted to generate electricity for Cowbridge House.[60]

A mill beside the abbey garden in 1535[61] was presumably Abbey Mill, north of the abbey church. It was part of Malmesbury manor in

45 P.R.O., E 317/Wilts. no. 39.
46 Ibid. CP 25(2)/979/1 Anne Mich.
47 Ibid. CP 25(2)/1079/11 Geo. I Hil.
48 Pigot, *Nat. Com. Dir.* (1830), 805; (1842), 21; W.R.O. 1301/9, deed, Thomas to Luce, 1834.
49 *Reg. Malm.* ii. 230.
50 P.R.O., C 142/495, no. 60; ibid. E 318/Box 32/1820.
51 Ibid. SC 6/Hen. VIII/3986, rot. 112; *Reg. Malm.* ii, p. xxxiii.
52 W. Worcestre, *Itin.* ed. J. H. Harvey, 283.
53 *Valor Eccl.* (Rec. Com.), ii. 120; W.R.O. 88/2/13.
54 Above.
55 *Reg. Malm.* i. 176–7.
56 P.R.O., E 318/Box 32/1820.
57 *Wilts. Inq. p.m.* 1625–49 (Index Libr.), 93; Pigot, *Nat. Com. Dir.* (1830), 805.
58 *Kelly's Dir. Wilts.* (1875); W.R.O. 856/3.
59 W.R.O. 130/78, sale cat.
60 Ibid. Inland Revenue, val. reg. 9.
61 *Valor Eccl.* (Rec. Com.), ii. 119.

the 18th century and the early 19th, and was leased with Abbey House;[62] in 1808 the tenant was a brewer.[63] The mill was probably in use in 1910 but closed soon afterwards.[64]

Wyniard Mill north of St. John's bridge was also standing in 1535.[65] It passed from Malmesbury abbey to the Crown at the Dissolution and was sold in 1610 to Sir Peter Vanlore, whose relict Catherine, then wife of Peregrine Pelham, held it in 1653.[66] It was bought by John Estcourt *c.* 1662,[67] and passed in the Estcourt and Dewell families, from 1717 with land in Burton Hill and Burton Hill House,[68] until it was sold in 1865.[69] In 1535 and 1585 the mill was leased to members of the Stumpe family and may have been used for cloth production. In 1585 it was said to require extensive repairs.[70] On its site in 1653 were two corn mills and a dye house;[71] repairs costing £100 were made to either one of or both the mills *c.* 1662.[72] In the 19th century millers at Wyniard Mill usually followed an additional trade, in 1839, 1848, and 1867 that of brewer or maltster, in 1859 that of millwright, and in 1885 those of timber merchant and builder. Water and steam powered the mill in 1895; it probably passed out of use shortly afterwards.[73]

A water mill, part of Whitchurch and Milbourne manor in 1539,[74] perhaps stood by the Tetbury Avon north-east of the town. It passed by exchange from Sir Henry Moody, lord of the manor, to Thomas Howard, earl of Suffolk, in 1614.[75] It may have been standing in 1720[76] but was not in use in 1802.[77]

62 W.R.O. 212B/3970; 212B/4157.
63 Ibid. 212B/4264.
64 Ibid. Inland Revenue, val. reg. 9; *Kelly's Dir. Wilts.* (1907 and later edns.).
65 *Valor Eccl.* (Rec. Com.), ii. 121.
66 P.R.O., E 317/Wilts. no. 39.
67 Ibid. E 134/25 Chas. II Trin./4.
68 Above, manors.
69 W.R.O. 212A/38/29.
70 *Valor Eccl.* (Rec. Com.), ii. 121; P.R.O., E 310/26/154, no. 30.
71 P.R.O., LR 2/301, ff. 261–3.
72 Ibid. E 134/25 Chas. II Trin./4.
73 *Kelly's Dir. Wilts.* (1848 and later edns.); W.R.O., tithe award.
74 P.R.O., SC 6/Hen. VIII/3986, rot. 129.
75 W.R.O. 130/1B, deed, Millard to Clerke, 1671.
76 P.R.O., CP 25(2)/1078/7 Geo. I Mich.
77 W.R.O. 88/5/74.

MARKETS AND FAIRS. Malmesbury was a market town until the mid 20th century but as such never seems to have been as popular as Chippenham, Tetbury, or Cirencester, all within 17 km. of it. In the Middle Ages market and fair tolls were taken by Malmesbury abbey[78] and later passed as part of Malmesbury manor to George Rushout, Baron Northwick (d. 1887), whose trustees sold them in 1896 to the borough council.[79] Probably from then until 1941 the markets were administered by a committee of the council.[80]

The 15th-century market cross in 1815, with St. Paul's church behind it

Until 1223 a Saturday market was held partly within and partly outside a graveyard, presumably that of St. Paul's church. Thereafter it was to be held in the New Market,[81] perhaps the area within the abbey precinct where the market cross was built in the 15th century. The market was confirmed by the borough charter of 1635.[82] For much of the 19th century, when it was held in Abbey Row, the area either around

78 *Reg. Malm.* i. 134.
79 W.R.O., G 21/150/10.
80 Ibid. G 21/113/1–5.
81 *Rot. Litt. Claus.* (Rec. Com.), i. 537.
82 Luce, *Hist. Malm.* 102.

the market cross or west of the abbey church, meat and other provisions were sold at it. It ceased *c.* 1890.[83]

A cattle market, held at first on the last Tuesday and later on the last Wednesday of each month, was started *c.* 1790. Like the Saturday market it was held in Abbey Row in the 19th century. In the 1840s and 1850s the market was not held between March and May.[84] It had become a general market by 1950,[85] but a monthly cattle market was again held, on land near the railway station, between 1956 and 1966.[86]

In 1252 Malmesbury abbey was granted a Thursday market to be held in Westport,[87] but no such market is known to have been held. Between 1900 and 1945 a general market was held on Wednesdays in Cross Hayes.[88] References to a pig market in the 1760s and 1770s,[89] and to a corn market in High Street, perhaps at the north end near the market cross, in 1809,[90] imply that those markets were sometimes held in the town.

William I granted to Malmesbury abbey a fair on three or five days including St. Aldhelm's day, 25 May. A five-day fair was granted or confirmed by William II, and extended by Maud to eight days, including the three days before the feast and the four days after it.[91] In 1252 the abbey was also granted a yearly fair on its manor of Whitchurch for three days at the feast of St. James, 25 July.[92] St. Aldhelm's fair was held on St. Aldhelm's mead south-west of the town,[93] and in the 16th century was said to have been so large that a company of soldiers was present to keep order.[94] It and St. James's fair were reduced to one day each and three other fairs, on 17 March, 17 April, and 17 October, were added by the borough charter of 1635.[95] One or more of the fairs may have been held in Horsefair, in Westport, first mentioned by name in the late 17th

83 J. Britton, *Beauties of Wilts.* iii. 89; *Kelly's Dir. Wilts.* (1848 and later edns.).
84 Moffatt, *Hist. Malm.* 163; Pigot, *Nat. Com. Dir.* (1842), 20; *Kelly's Dir. Wilts.* (1859 and later edns.); Britton, *Beauties of Wilts.* iii. 89.
85 *Town Guide* [*c.* 1950].
86 Inf. from the town clerk, Malmesbury.
87 *Cal. Chart. R.* 1226–57, 400.
88 Inf. from the town clerk; see illus. on p. 21.
89 W.R.O. 212B/4045; 212B/4129.
90 Ibid. 212B/4274.
91 *Reg. Malm.* i. 329; *Reg. Regum Anglo-Norm.* ii, nos. 494, 971.
92 *Cal. Chart. R.* 1226–57, 400.
93 Britton, *Beauties of Wilts.* iii. 89.
94 Camden, *Brit.* (1806), i. 130.
95 Luce, *Hist. Malm.* 102.

century;[96] in the 19th century the Triangle in Westport was also called Sheep Fair.[97] In the late 18th century and the early 19th there were three fairs,[98] and between 1842 and 1867 yearly fairs, at which horses, cattle, and sheep were sold, were held on 28 March, 28 April, 5 June, and 15 December. By 1875 the fairs had ceased.[99]

LOCAL GOVERNMENT. The borough of Malmesbury may have had powers of self government from the early Middle Ages.[1] Outside the borough, Malmesbury parish seems likely to have contained several tithings, Burton Hill, Milbourne, Rodbourne, and Corston.[2]

BOROUGH GOVERNMENT. Malmesbury was probably already a privileged borough in 1086.[3] There was a guild merchant in the early 13th century: presumably in 1215 when it became fee-farmer of the borough,[4] and certainly before 1222, Malmesbury abbey excused members of the guild and other inhabitants of the borough from payment of certain scotales in return for a fine and an annual rent to be paid by the hand of the guild steward.[5] In the mid 13th century the guild comprised an alderman, 2 stewards, and 16 or more other members; the 19 apparently formed a body governing the borough and guild. In an exchange with the abbey in the mid 13th century the guildsmen surrendered part of Portmans heath and received Cooks heath, Broad croft and the assart which separated it from Cooks heath, and another assart on Burnt heath.[6] The lands presumably lay south-west of the town mainly in Westport parish, among those which belonged to the borough in the 16th century and were known from the early 17th as King's Heath.[7] The holding was of 700 a. in the early 19th century.[8] In the later 14th century there were in the borough, in addition to the guild, groups

96 Aubrey, *Topog. Coll.* ed. Jackson, 264.
97 Glos. R.O., D 674B/P 73.
98 *Univ. Brit. Dir.* v (1798), 115; Britton, *Beauties of Wilts.* iii. 89.
99 Pigot, *Nat. Com. Dir.* (1842), 20; *Kelly's Dir. Wilts.* (1848 and later edns.).
 1 Above, introduction.
 2 *Taxation Lists* (W.R.S. x), pp. 48–50; W.R.O. 88/2/13; 88/2/40.
 3 Above, introduction.
 4 Ibid. manors.
 5 *Reg. Malm.* i. 446.
 6 Ibid. 150–65.
 7 P.R.O., E 178/5701.
 8 W.R.O., Westport tithe award.

of men called half-hundreds and hundreds. In 1370 the half-hundreds were called Bynport and Westport; the hundreds were called Coxfort, Thornhill, Davids, Fishers, Glovers, and Taylors, names which suggest that the grouping was partly by trade. An agreement of that year, intended to make the assessment of the scotale fairer, required payment only from members of the guild, half-hundreds, and hundreds, and implied that those were the wealthier inhabitants. The half-hundreds and hundreds included members of the guild,[9] and it seems likely that each group had specified rights over the borough's lands.

The borough ascribed an early origin to its privileges. A charter of 1381 confirming them related that King Athelstan confirmed privileges held in the time of his father, that he granted freedom from burghbote, brugbote, wardwyte, horngeld, and scot, and that he gave 5 hides of heath near Norton; the gift was described as a reward to the men of the town for their help in campaigns against the Danes.[10] The attribution of those actions to Athelstan may represent a tradition surviving in 1381 or an attempt to provide a title to rights and privileges long held. The 1381 charter was confirmed at various dates, lastly in 1604.[11]

Many of the functions of government normally performed by the corporation of a borough were retained in Malmesbury by the manor court,[12] and there is little evidence of the corporation's responsibility for the regulation of trade or the administration of justice before the 17th century. In the 16th century the corporation consisted of a company of 13 burgesses including an alderman and two stewards,[13] and three other companies, the twenty-four, the landholders, and the commoners. Every man who was born in the town, married to a woman born there, or resident for three or more years in what was described as an ancient tenement was eligible to become a commoner. He did so by entering one of the six hundreds; by 1600 the half-hundreds of Bynport and Westport had disappeared and Davids had become Davids Loynes hundred. Men apparently entered a hundred primarily to acquire rights to the common land. The companies were distinguished by the extent of their rights in King's Heath. The commoners had only grazing rights but the twenty-four, the landholders, and the burgesses, including the

9 B.L. Add. Ch. 18182.
10 *Cal. Pat.* 1381–5, 54; *W.A.M.* lxxiv/lxxv, 135–6.
11 Luce, *Hist. Malm.* 95.
12 Below, manorial govt.
13 P.R.O., STAC 8/130/3.

alderman, had in addition small several holdings.[14] In the mid 16th century some burgesses' places were vacant, apparently because their portions of King's Heath were poor. At the instigation of John Jewell, bishop of Salisbury, Cooks heath was inclosed and divided between four burgesses c. 1570; the full number of burgesses was thereupon restored.[15]

In the early 17th century the rights of the alderman and burgesses to inclosed lands, then totalling 100 a., were challenged by members of the other companies who claimed that the land should be common. In 1609 it was agreed that a representative of each of the four companies should be appointed to resolve the dispute. The four agreed that the alderman and burgesses should retain their closes on payment to the steward of £20 a year for the general benefit, that closes held by the twenty-four and the landholders should be retained by them, and that the remainder of the land, the greater part, should remain common under new regulations. The settlement was defined in ordinances published by a Chancery decree in 1610. An attempt was made in the same year, presumably by those who had earlier challenged the burgesses' rights, to have the decree dismissed, and in 1611 the burgesses' inclosures were broken. At the annual meeting of the alderman and burgesses in the town hall in 1612 their opponents occupied the burgesses' benches and may have attempted to set up a rival form of government by 12 overseers selected from all members of the corporation, then called the free burgesses. During subsequent litigation it was claimed that government by the alderman and burgesses was an innovation of the 1560s, that previously government of the town was by a head bailiff, two constables, and wardsmen or assistants, elected annually at the court leet of Malmesbury manor, and that the ordinances of 1610 were drawn up without the knowledge of those who later opposed them.[16] The decree, however, seems to have remained in force from 1612, with the slight variation that there were four stewards, one from each company.[17]

A commission issued in 1631 to inquire whether King's Heath was Crown land which had been concealed may have been the product of further disputes within the borough or an attempt by the Crown to reclaim the freehold of the land. Perhaps to settle a dispute or remove

14 P.R.O., STAC 8/290/22.
15 Ibid. C 33/115, f. 36; ibid. E 134/9 Chas. I Mich./75.
16 Ibid. STAC 8/93/2; STAC 8/130/3; STAC 8/138/8; STAC 8/290/22; Luce, *Hist. Malm.* 98.
17 *WAM.* xlvii. 323; Malmesbury boro. rec., ct. bk. 1600–1721.

uncertainty created by the commission, the borough obtained a new charter in 1635. The composition of the corporation was little changed. Thereafter the burgesses were called chief or capital burgesses and the twenty-four were called assistant burgesses, but the landholders and commoners were still so called. Membership of each company was for life; vacancies in each of the senior companies were to be filled by election from the immediately inferior company. The capital burgesses, of whom there were 12 in addition to the alderman, were to elect annually a lawyer as steward, later called the high steward, to advise them. The preamble of the charter referred to a need for better means of keeping the peace within the borough. The alderman, elected annually, was therefore to be a justice of the peace, the coroner, and the clerk of the market. A court was to be held every three weeks for civil cases, and the corporation, meeting in the common hall, was empowered to make regulations for the government and victualling of the borough, enforceable by fines. It was also allowed to appoint two serjeants-at-mace.[18]

Attempts by Charles II and James II to control parliamentary elections brought changes in the constitution of Malmesbury as of most boroughs. In or before 1668 the corporation defended a *quo warranto,* presumably successfully.[19] Another *quo warranto,* issued in 1684,[20] was not contested[21] and a new charter was granted to the borough in 1685. It provided for the capital burgesses to keep their number at 12 (beside the alderman) by choosing new burgesses to fill vacancies from members of the whole corporation, for the high steward, or in his absence the deputy steward, to act as a justice of the peace in addition to the alderman, and for the officers of the corporation to be removable by the Crown. The precinct of the former abbey was for the first time expressly included within the borough.[22] In 1690 the constitution of 1635 was restored[23] and in 1696 a new charter was issued. It confirmed the liberties and franchises held under the charter of 1635, and the provisions of 1685 for the inclusion of the abbey precinct in the borough and the appointment of the high steward or his deputy as a justice.[24]

18 Luce, *Hist. Malm.* 101–2; P.R.O., E 134/9 Chas. I Mich./75.
19 Malmesbury boro. rec., ct. bk. 1600–1721.
20 B.L. Harl. MS. 6013, p. 38.
21 Luce, *Hist. Malm.* 145.
22 *Cal. S.P. Dom.* 1685, pp. 64–5.
23 Malmesbury boro. rec., ct. bk. 1600–1721.
24 *Cal. S.P. Dom.* 1696, 433.

In the early 19th century the qualifications for becoming a commoner, then also known as a free burgess, were apparently a matter of dispute. An inquiry held in 1821 found that the right belonged to every resident of an entire tenement in the borough who was of age, married, and either the son of a commoner or married to a commoner's daughter.[25] In the 1840s the alderman and burgesses attempted to limit admission as commoners to those who lived in ancient tenements, apparently without success.[26] Complaints were made about the administration of justice in Malmesbury and the character of its alderman and burgesses in the 1830s,[27] but the constitution of the borough remained unchanged until 1886. It was then incorporated as a municipal borough, under the Municipal Corporations Act of 1882, with a mayor, four aldermen, and 12 councillors.[28] In 1974 the borough became part of North Wiltshire district.[29]

The principal borough court recorded from 1600 was held annually, usually on the Tuesday after Trinity Sunday in a room in the former St. John's hospital. In the 17th and 18th centuries it was presumably convened, as later, by the alderman; it is not clear how it proceeded. The principal business was probably the election of aldermen and stewards, but the elections are recorded only from 1613. New commoners were admitted to the hundreds on payment of a fine. Regulations were made for grazing on the part of King's Heath not inclosed, called Malmesbury common from the 18th century; those who broke the rules were fined. Until 1614 an account of rents received from those holding closes in King's Heath was presented regularly in the name of the alderman and stewards; thereafter accounts were only occasionally recorded. In the 19th century the alderman and stewards elected at the Trinity court were sworn at a Michaelmas court and other courts were held for the election of capital and assistant burgesses, the nomination of landholders, and the admission of commoners as need arose.[30] No record survives of the three-weekly court provided for by the charter of 1635.

25 *1st Rep. Com. Mun. Corp.* H.C. 116, App. 1, pp. 78–9 (1835), xxii (1).
26 W.R.O. 1305/203.
27 *1st Rep. Com. Mun. Corp.* p. 79; P.R.O., HO 52/27, no. 264; HO 52/31, no. 162.
28 *Kelly's Dir. Wilts.* (1903); W.R.O., F 2/141.
29 *Local Govt. in Eng. and Wales* (H.M.S.O. 1974), 117.
30 Malmesbury boro. rec., ct. bks. 1600–1721, 1722–81, 1793–1868, 1868–1986; inf. from the clerk to the burgesses and freemen, 1 Market Lane; below, Westport, econ. hist.

The borough court meeting at St. John's almshouse in 1924

Courts called borough sessions, at which the alderman and deputy steward presided, are recorded from 1712 to 1741. They were held yearly, usually in April or October, presumably in the same place as the borough court. Orders were made concerning the repair of roads and bridges, apprenticeships, and the setting of poor rates, and weights used in the markets were tested. From 1729 constables were appointed.[31] The borough sought the right to hold separate quarter sessions c. 1750,[32] apparently without success. Borough sessions were still held in 1876,[33] but presumably ceased in 1886.[34] From 1842 or earlier petty sessions for Malmesbury hundred were also held in the town.[35] Petty sessions continued to be held in Malmesbury; from 1973 they were held by Chippenham magistrates sitting in Malmesbury town hall fortnightly.[36]

31 Malmesbury boro. rec., sessions order bk. 1712–41.
32 Ibid. case for separate q. sess. c. 1750.
33 Rep. Com. Mun. Corp. [C. 2490–1], p. 73, H.C. (1880), xxxi.
34 W.R.O., F 2/141.
35 Pigot, Nat. Com. Dir. (1842), 20.
36 Inf. from the town clerk.

Between 1830 and 1854 the alderman exercised the right to act as coroner, granted in the 1635 and 1696 charters.[37] The borough was included in the North Wiltshire coroner's district in 1860.[38]

In the 13th century there were two guildhalls in the borough, one in Malmesbury parish and one in Westport parish.[39] After the Dissolution the corporation bought St. Paul's church and in 1542 used the east end as a town hall.[40] What was called the church house, presumably the east end of St. Paul's, was used for meetings in 1691 and, of the alderman and capital burgesses, in 1709.[41] In 1580 the alderman and burgesses bought the site of St. John's hospital.[42] The building was later used as almshouses, a school, and from 1616 the usual meeting place of the borough court.[43] No. 9 Oxford Street was owned by the corporation and may also have been used for meetings in the 18th century when it was called the Guildhall; such use had ceased by 1794.[44] A town hall was built in Cross Hayes in 1854 and enlarged in 1927.[45] It was used as the offices of the municipal borough council from 1886 and of the town council from 1974.[46]

In 1622 the corporation decided that each burgess should pay 5s. yearly to the alderman towards the cost of a dinner on the day of the borough court. The total allowance to the alderman was increased from £3 to £10 in 1652.[47] An allotment of land on King's Heath, known as the alderman's kitchen, later replaced the payments.[48]

In 1886 the borough lands, including Malmesbury common, were retained by the old corporation under a new name, the warden (later the burgesses) and freemen of Malmesbury. That body also became the trustees of several borough charities. The structure of hundreds and companies was retained and in 1988 three courts were still being held

---

37 Malmesbury boro. rec., coroner's rec. 1830–54.
38 *Lond. Gaz.* 30 Oct. 1860, p. 3898.
39 *Reg. Malm.* i. 121, 123; *Bradenstoke Cart.* (W.R.S. xxxv), p. 76.
40 Leland, *Itin.* ed. Toulmin Smith, i. 131.
41 Malmesbury boro. rec., ct. bk. 1600–1721.
42 *V.C.H. Wilts.* iii. 341.
43 Below, educ., charities; Malmesbury boro. rec., ct. bk. 1600–1721; see above, illus. on p. 67.
44 W.R.O. 177/23, deed, Pinnell to Clarke, 1816.
45 *Kelly's Dir. Wilts.* (1927); see above, illus. on p. 21.
46 *Kelly's Dir. Wilts.* (1895); inf. from the town clerk.
47 Malmesbury boro. rec., ct. bk. 1600–1721.
48 *Endowed Char. Wilts.* (N. Div.), 695.

yearly in the court room of St. John's almshouses to admit commoners, elect officers, and administer property.[49]

In the late 18th century a tradition existed that a common seal had been in use in the 1550s and had born the legend COMMUN[E] SIGILL[UM] BURG[I] DE MALMESBURY.[50] The borough arms, as depicted on a seal matrix cast in the late 16th century or the 17th, were an embattled castle or gateway flanked by two round towers and surmounted by a third from the dome of which flew a pennon; in base the waters of Avon, on each side a teazle or wheat plant; in chief a blazing star and

The borough seal, 1615

crescent, and in the dexter chief three pellets. The matrix, 6.3 cm. in diameter, bears the legend SIGIL[LUM] COM[MUNE] ALD[E]R[MAN]I ET BURGEN[SIUM] BURGI DE MALMESBURY IN COM[ITATU] WILTS. A second matrix, 5.6 cm. in diameter, has the same device, except that the three pellets are in the sinister chief, and a similar legend, with the addition of

49 Malmesbury boro. rec., ct. bk. 1868–1986; *Town Guide* (1986).
50 Moffatt, *Hist. Malm.* 132.

the date 1615. Two smaller matrices, one perhaps of the early 17th century, bear reduced versions of the arms shown on the matrix of 1615 and of the undated legend.[51]

The borough possessed two silver-gilt maces, possibly of the mid 17th century, each 71 cm. long, and two silver maces, hallmarked for 1703, each 82 cm. long. A cross on the head of one of the older pair was renewed in brass. Both the seals and the maces were held by the warden and freemen from 1886 and remained in use in the later 20th century.[52]

In 1950 arms were granted to Malmesbury borough council: parted saltirewise argent and gules, a cross botony in chief a Saxon crown and in base an orb, all gold, on a chief sable a lion passant between a mitre and a crozier erect, all gold.[53]

MANORIAL GOVERNMENT. Malmesbury abbey claimed to be free of shire and hundred courts and to have other liberties in estates including Cowfold by a charter of 1065, but the relevant part of the charter, if not the whole, is almost certainly spurious.[54] The abbey nevertheless held those liberties in the mid 13th century for all its estates in Malmesbury parish.[55]

Records of views of frankpledge and other courts held for Malmesbury manor survive for several periods from the mid 16th century. From the mid 18th century the courts were described as courts leet and courts baron for the manor of Malmesbury and Westport. In the 1560s, in the late 1640s, and between 1750 and 1780 courts were usually held in spring and autumn each year.[56] Military activity prevented courts from being held in the early 1640s.[57] Many functions of town government were apparently performed in Malmesbury by the manor courts rather than or in addition to the borough courts. At the view held in 1561 bakers, butchers, and innkeepers were presented for breaches of the assize, and fines were imposed on those who had neglected to repair King's Wall; whether the street of that name or part of the town wall needed repair is not clear. In the later 18th century the jurors at the court leet

51 *W.A.M.* xxviii. 43–4.
52 Ibid. 42–4; inf. from the town clerk.
53 C. W. Scott-Giles, *Civic Heraldry of Eng.* 386.
54 *Reg. Malm.* i. 323; *V.C.H. Wilts.* ii, p. 88 n. 68.
55 Above, Malmesbury hund.
56 P.R.O., C 116/273, pp. 6–9, 16; ibid. SC 2/209/16; W.R.O. 212B/3977; 1165/3.
57 Hist. MSS. Com. 55, *Var. Coll.* i, p. 110.

presented defaulters from the court, roads in need of repair, and rubbish and pigsties in Cross Hayes and High Street. In 1752 they reported the lack of a ducking stool. Constables were appointed from the 1750s. A court leet was held once a year from the 1780s; none was held after 1806. In 1561 offences by victuallers were also presented at the court baron. Later the court baron, at which the homage presented, dealt mainly with the tenure of copyhold premises in the town. From *c.* 1780 until 1914 courts were held irregularly, apparently at need.[58]

Courts and views held for Burton Hill manor were recorded with those for Rodbourne manor under the rubric of Cowfold manor with Rodbourne and Burton Hill for the years 1559, 1563–4, 1569, and 1571–3. The courts and views were held in spring and autumn yearly, probably at a house in Cole park. Between 1559 and 1564 and in 1573 views were held for Burton Hill at which a tithingman presented and a jury affirmed his presentments. Between 1569 and 1572 views were held jointly for Burton Hill and Rodbourne; there was a single jury but a tithingman from each presented. Burton Hill business included stray animals and overcharging by millers and a butcher. Courts baron for Burton Hill were held separately. The homage presented defaulters from the court, deaths of copyholders, and tenements in need of repair. The use of common pastures was regulated and, at the autumn court, a tithingman and a reeve were appointed.[59]

Courts leet and courts baron for Whitchurch and Milbourne manor are recorded for the years 1763–1816. The courts were usually held annually in autumn; additional courts were held to admit copyholders. At the autumn court two haywards, one each for Milbourne common and Whitchurch marsh, were appointed. Orders were made for footpaths to be repaired and, in 1766, a new pound to be built; encroachments on waste ground were presented.[60]

PARISH GOVERNMENT. In 1632 those who lived in Cole park and West park were ordered to contribute to poor relief in the parish,[61] which was presumably administered without differentiating the town and the outlying parts. In 1636 it was reported that 60 houses within the

58 *Wilts. Q. Sess. Rec.* ed. Cunnington, 159; P.R.O., C 116/273, pp. 6–9, 16; ibid. SC 2/209/16; W.R.O. 212B/3977; 1165/3–6.
59 W.R.O. 88/2/7; 88/2/13; 88/2/21; 88/2/29.
60 Ibid. 88/5/47.
61 P.R.O., ASSI 24/20, f. 55v.

precinct of the former abbey contained 47 persons needing relief; the implication was that the precinct was being treated as extraparochial but the parish should provide relief. Seven houses within the precinct were then in Westport parish.[62] Probably by 1760, however, and certainly by 1776 the Abbey had become a separate parish relieving its own poor.[63]

In 1642 £30 a week for six weeks was ordered to be collected from Malmesbury and parishes within 5 miles of it to relieve its poor, then affected by plague. Only £68 was collected and in 1646 the constables, churchwardens, and overseers were still seeking compensation for money spent during the epidemic.[64]

In the later 18th century the Malmesbury vestry set a rate and delegated its collection and the distribution of relief to 6 overseers, 2 for the town and 1 each for Burton Hill, Corston, Rodbourne, and Milbourne (presumably with Whitchurch). In 1779 John Chamberlain was appointed by the vestry to administer poor relief throughout the parish. From 1780, however, the six overseers again received and made payments. Relief in the parish, excluding Corston and Rodbourne, cost c. £150 in 1760–1. It was given regularly at a cost of £82 to 26 people; 22 apparently lived in the borough and 2 each in Milbourne and Burton Hill tithings. Occasional relief and other expenses cost £70; payments were made for clothing, bedding, rents, and funerals. In 1770–1 regular relief was given to 28 in the borough, 1 in Milbourne, and 3 in Burton Hill; in 1779–80 it was given to c. 40 in the borough, 6 in Milbourne, and 1 in Burton Hill.[65] In 1802–3 in Malmesbury parish, including Corston and Rodbourne, regular relief was given to 129 adults, some of whom were in the workhouse, and 168 children; 52 inhabitants and 107 people from outside the parish received occasional payments. The total cost was £972. During the next decade fewer people were relieved. In 1815 regular relief was given to 111 and occasional relief to 59. Costs, however, rose; £1,102 was spent on the poor in 1815.[66] A peak was reached in 1818 when £1,928 was spent. Thereafter expenditure fell until 1824, when £1,086 was spent, and usually remained between

62 *Wilts. Q. Sess. Rec.* ed. Cunnington, 117–19.
63 *Poor Law Abstract, 1804,* 566–7; W.R.O. 1589/33.
64 Hist. MSS. Com. 55, *Var. Coll.* i, pp. 108, 110.
65 W.R.O. 1589/33.
66 *Poor Law Abstract, 1804,* 566–7; *1818,* 498–9.

£1,000 and £1,200 until 1835[67] when Malmesbury poor-law union was formed.[68]

In the later 18th century the east end of St. Paul's church housed some of the poor.[69] There was a workhouse in 1781,[70] which in 1803 had 46 inmates.[71] It was probably the building in Holloway held in 1805 by the churchwardens and overseers on a 21-year lease,[72] and may previously have been part of Jenner's almshouses.[73] In 1814 there were 23 inmates.[74] In 1825 a new poorhouse for the parish was built on the site of part of Jenner's almshouses at the junction of Oxford Street and Holloway; in 1834 the remaining almshouses also housed poor families placed there by the parish.[75] Such use presumably ceased when the union workhouse on the outskirts of the town in Brokenborough parish was opened in 1838.[76]

Poor relief in the Abbey parish cost £15 in 1775–6 and £30 in 1802–3, when four adults and four children were regularly relieved. Expenditure had risen to £50 by 1814, when seven people received regular relief. There is no record of occasional relief being given in the parish.[77] Between 1815 and 1835 the cost of poor relief was usually £35–£45; it was a little higher in 1816, 1820, and 1827–8, and lower in 1822–4.[78] The Abbey parish became part of Malmesbury poor-law union in 1835.[79]

PUBLIC SERVICES. Constables of Malmesbury were first recorded in the 1640s; it is not clear by whom they were appointed. In 1642 two constables complained to the justices at quarter sessions of the additional expense that they had incurred during the plague of that year and in watching and warding, providing and mending arms, and attending and

67 *Poor Rate Returns, 1816–21,* 188–9; *1822–4,* 228; *1825–9,* 219; *1830–4,* 212–13.
68 *Poor Law Com. 2nd Rep.* App. D, 559.
69 Camden, *Brit.* (1806), i. 142.
70 W.R.O. 1589/34.
71 *Poor Law Abstract, 1804,* 566–7.
72 Moffatt, *Hist. Malm.* 99; W.R.O. 1589/46B.
73 *Endowed Char. Wilts.* (N. Div.), 677; below, charities.
74 W.R.O. 1589/35.
75 *Endowed Char. Wilts.* (N. Div.), 677.
76 *W.A.M.* xlvii. 565.
77 *Poor Law Abstract, 1804,* 566–7; *1818,* 498–9.
78 *Poor Rate Returns, 1816–21,* 188–9; *1822–4,* 228; *1828–9,* 219; *1830–4,* 212–13.
79 *Poor Law Com. 2nd Rep.* App. D, 559.

transporting prisoners. In 1644 a constable sought release from the office, in which he had served for three years apparently because manor courts had not been held. In 1646 a similar request was made by both constables, who claimed to have suffered great loss, particularly through plunder and imprisonment by royalist troops.[80] Between 1729 and 1741 two constables each for Malmesbury and Westport were appointed at the borough sessions, and from 1753 two constables for Malmesbury, two for Westport, and one for the Abbey parish at the manor court. Two sidesmen for Malmesbury and two for Westport were also sworn at the manor courts from 1753.[81]

From 1840 Malmesbury parish outside the borough was policed by the county constabulary.[82] The borough force was separate, presumably from *c.* 1840, until in 1887 it became part of the county constabulary.[83] A police station in the town belonging to the county police in 1844[84] was replaced in 1854 by a new building in Burnham Road.[85] A new station in Burton Hill was built *c.* 1955.[86]

The abbot of Malmesbury had a prison in the 12th and 13th centuries.[87] Prisoners were sent from the hundred courts to a gaol in Malmesbury in 1613,[88] and in 1682 the justices at quarter sessions ordered that a gaol be built there.[89] In 1831 a building east of the abbey gateway was used as the town prison.[90]

A fire brigade, formed in 1851, had a station in 1866, perhaps that in Ingram Street in use *c.* 1894. From 1907 to *c.* 1948 the brigade was based at the town hall. It was moved to a station in Gloucester Road *c.* 1948 and a new station was opened there in 1969.[91]

In 1798 an Act for paving the footways and for cleaning and lighting the streets of the borough[92] established a body of improvement

80 *Wilts. Q. Sess. Rec.* ed. Cunnington, 159; Hist. MSS. Com. 55, *Var. Coll.* i, p. 110.
81 Malmesbury boro. rec., sessions order bk. 1712–41; W.R.O. 212B/3977; 1165/3.
82 W.R.O., F 5/100/1.
83 Ibid. A 1/150/28, p. 628.
84 W.R.O., F 5/100/1.
85 Ibid. A 1/592, plan of police station, deed, Lloyd to Jacob, 1853.
86 Inf. from Chief Constable, Police Headquarters, Devizes.
87 *Reg. Malm.* ii. 318, 364.
88 *Acts of P.C.* 1613–14, 92–3.
89 *W.A.M.* xliv. 387.
90 Glos. R.O., D 674B/P 73.
91 *Kelly's Dir. Wilts.* (1903, 1907); TS. notes on fire brigade in Athelstan Mus.; inf. from the town clerk.
92 *L.J.* xli. 655.

commissioners, and in 1872 the town became an urban sanitary district under the authority of the same body.[93] Its duties apparently passed to the borough council in 1886.[94]

In 1835 it was proposed to supply gas to the town; a gasworks north of St. John's bridge may have been built then[95] and was standing in 1848.[96] The Malmesbury Gas & Coke Co. was vested in the South Western Gas Board in 1949.[97] Electricity was supplied to the town by the Western Electricity Distributing Corporation in 1923.[98] The Malmesbury Water Works Co. Ltd. built a pumping house in Holloway in or soon after 1864 and a water tower south-east of Abbey House probably at the same date. The waterworks was transferred to the borough in 1900.[99] Another water tower, to serve Malmesbury rural district and the borough, was built north of Whychurch Farm between 1947 and 1953[1] and was replaced by a new tower and pumping station in 1985.[2] In 1904 and 1920 proceedings were instituted by Wiltshire county council against the borough council to prevent the discharge of sewage into the Avon.[3] A sewage works was built north of Cowbridge Farm c. 1962.[4]

A cemetery and a mortuary chapel for Malmesbury and Westport parishes were opened on 1 ha. west of the Tetbury road in Westport in 1884.[5] A cottage hospital north of the market cross was opened in 1889 and rebuilt in 1897. It was transferred to the Manor House, Burton Hill, in 1925;[6] that house, much extended, was still used as a hospital in 1988. An isolation hospital was opened on a site then in Brokenborough parish c. 1890. It was a wooden building with 6 beds in 2 wards, but without cooking apparatus, bath-house, or bath. The hospital was closed in 1933.[7]

93   V.C.H. Wilts. v. 258; W.R.O. 1269/16.
94   Above, introduction.
95   Inf. from Dr. H. Nabb, British Gas plc (South Western), Bristol; W.R.O. 1269/16.
96   Kelly's Dir. Wilts. (1848); O.S. Map 6", Wilts. VIII (1889 edn.).
97   Inf. from Dr. Nabb.
98   'Malm. Electricity Special Order, 1923', Electricity (Supply) Acts, Special Orders (Min. of Transport).
99   W.R.O., G 21/150/1.
 1   Ibid. G 21/127/1, p. 3; Hudson, Hill Top Town, 145.
 2   Inf. from Supply Controller, Wessex Water, Quay Ho., the Ambury, Bath.
 3   V.C.H. Wilts. v. 277, 327.
 4   Hudson, Hill Top Town, 151.
 5   Kelly's Dir. Wilts. (1939).
 6   Ibid. (1907, 1939); V.C.H. Wilts. v. 343.
 7   V.C.H. Wilts. v. 345; above, Brokenborough, introduction.

In 1851 a mechanics' institute in Malmesbury had 92 members and a library of 900 books.[8] A library in the town was open on two evenings a week in 1926, and in 1935 was in the town hall. Thereafter it was moved several times; from 1972 it occupied part of the former Malmesbury Church of England school in Cross Hayes.[9] In 1931 the Athelstan Museum was opened in the town hall.[10] It was moved to a building in Gloucester Road c. 1970[11] but from 1979 was again in the town hall.[12]

Between 1931 and 1956 Malmesbury borough council built most of the new houses west of the town and the houses and prefabricated bungalows in Cowbridge Crescent. The council also built the swimming pool in Old Alexander Road opened in 1961. The Parklands estate was built for Malmesbury rural district council,[13] and North Wiltshire district council built the houses and maisonettes at Burton Hill.[14] In 1971 Wiltshire county council bought Burnham House as a residential home for the elderly, and later built the additional accommodation in its grounds.[15]

PARLIAMENTARY REPRESENTATION. Malmesbury returned burgesses to the parliament of 1275 and to a total of 74 parliaments before 1449; only New Salisbury, Wilton, and Marlborough of the boroughs in Wiltshire were more frequently represented. Until 1832 the borough usually had two M.P.s. The earliest surviving indentures are between the sheriff and the alderman and burgesses; in 1455 the borough's representatives were selected by the alderman and at least 13 burgesses.[16] The franchise had probably been restricted to the alderman and 12 other burgesses, later called the capital burgesses, by the late 16th century. The first record of an election by those 13 dates from 1640.[17] Conflicts over King's Heath and borough government in the early 17th

8 J. W. Hudson, *Hist. Adult Educ.* 231.
9 Inf. from Director, Libr. and Mus. Service, Co. Hall, Trowbridge.
10 Wilts. Cuttings, xvii. 10.
11 Hudson, *Hill Top Town*, 22.
12 Inf. from the Curator, Athelstan Mus.
13 Above, introduction; W.R.O., G 21/100/12.
14 Inf. from the Property Maintenance Manager, N. Wilts. District Council, Bewley Ho., Marshfield Rd., Chippenham.
15 Inf. from Property Services Dept., Co. Hall, Trowbridge.
16 *V.C.H. Wilts.* v. 73, 75; *W.A.M.* xlvii. 177–258.
17 *Hist. Parl., Commons,* 1660–90, i. 452.

century may have derived in part from attempts to extend the franchise,[18] but no complaint about electoral rights was recorded.

In the 15th century over half the borough's M.P.s whose names are known were residents of Malmesbury. In the mid 16th century leading clothiers were among the M.P.s. William Stumpe (d. 1552) sat in the parliaments of 1529 and 1547–52, and Matthew King in those of 1553–5 and 1558.[19] Sir James Stumpe was returned in 1555. A controlling interest in the borough's parliamentary elections apparently passed to Sir James's son-in-law Sir Henry Knyvett, who himself represented Malmesbury four times in the later 16th century, and later to Knyvett's son-in-law Thomas Howard, earl of Suffolk.[20]

For much of the 17th century at least one and sometimes both of Malmesbury's M.P.s were drawn from families with local interests: members of the Moody, Poole, Hungerford, Lee, Washington, and Estcourt families represented the borough.[21] Sir John Danvers, elected in place of Anthony Hungerford in 1645, was a signatory to Charles I's death warrant.[22] Elections were occasionally influenced by the earls of Berkshire, resident at Charlton Park, but more usually by members of the Danvers family and their heirs as lords of Malmesbury manor or by the holders of the post of high steward created by the borough charter of 1635. The high steward's influence presumably derived from his duty under the charter to advise the alderman and burgesses on all business concerning the borough. The post was held by members of the Estcourt family of Sherston Pinkney, in Sherston, between 1641 and 1659 and between 1671 and 1677.[23] Later high stewards were usually men of wider influence, often peers.[24]

A letter of 1684 refers to recent elections in Malmesbury as popular, but returns of that year do not indicate any increase in the number of electors. In 1689 Thomas Wharton, later marquess of Wharton and then lord of Malmesbury manor, took advantage of uncertainty over the borough charter to extend the franchise to assistant burgesses, landholders,

18 Above, local govt. (boro. govt.).
19 *Hist. Parl., Commons,* 1439–1509, i. 711; 1509–58, i. 227; ii. 467–8; iii. 403–5; above, trade and ind.
20 *Hist. Parl., Commons,* 1558–1603, i. 274–5.
21 Ibid. 1660–90, i. 453; *W.A.M.* xlvii. 216–19.
22 *D.N.B.*
23 *Hist. Parl., Commons,* 1660–90, i. 453; Luce, *Hist. Malm.* 101.
24 *V.C.H. Wilts.* v. 218.

and commoners; a total of 172 voted in the election of that year.[25] The old franchise was presumably restored in 1690 with the 1635 constitution of the corporation, and the franchise was not defined in the new charter of 1696. In the 1720s and 1730s a standard tariff, by which each of the 13 voters received £100 for a general election and £20 for the re-election of a member who had taken office, secured uncontested elections. In the mid 18th century Henry Fox (cr. Baron Holland 1763) and Henry Howard, earl of Suffolk and of Berkshire (d. 1779), competed for control of the borough. Fox, high steward from 1751 to 1760, proposed a compromise by which they shared both the representation and the electoral costs, paying each capital burgess a total of £30 a year and jointly providing for them two feasts each year.[26]

Lord Suffolk and his supporter Edmund Wilkins, a Malmesbury apothecary, were successively high steward 1762–9. Wilkins transferred his support to Fox and from 1769 to 1775 served as deputy high steward to Charles James Fox, who was M.P. for Malmesbury 1774–80. Wilkins was again high steward from 1775 to 1806. He controlled parliamentary elections by refining the system of annual pensions and reinforcing it by a bond of £500 entered by each capital burgess. Until 1789 he sold the borough at each election to the highest bidder; later he consistently supported government candidates. He was succeeded in control of the borough by Edmund Estcourt, who raised the pension to £50 yearly. Control of the borough's two seats was sold at least twice before 1832. The narrow franchise and the corruption and illiteracy of the burgesses were frequently attacked in the late 18th century and early 19th, and in 1796, 1802, 1806, and 1807 provided the grounds for petitions for elections to be overturned. The borough lost one seat in 1832,[27] and the remaining seat in 1884, when it was merged in the Chippenham division of the county.[28]

CHURCHES. In 1191 Malmesbury abbey was granted the right to appropriate the parish church, St. Paul's church 'in atrio monasterii', to endow lights in the abbey church.[29] By the mid 13th century a vicarage

---

25 *Hist. Parl., Commons,* 1660–90, i. 453.
26 Ibid. 1715–45, i. 348–9; 1754–90, i. 417–18.
27 Ibid. 1754–90, i. 417–18; 1790–1820, ii. 422–4; *V.C.H. Wilts.* v. 219; see below, illus. on facing page.
28 *V.C.H. Wilts.* v. 311–12.
29 *Reg. Malm.* i. 374–5.

A parliamentary election, as lampooned in 1792

had been ordained.[30] Between 1650 and 1658 the vicarage was united
with Westport vicarage[31] but the benefices were separated after 1660.[32]
The vicarages and parishes were united under the name Malmesbury
with Westport St. Mary in 1946, and in 1984 the new benefice and
parish of Brokenborough was added.[33] Chapels at Corston and
Rodbourne were dependent on St. Paul's church from the 14th century
or earlier until 1881.[34]

    The abbot of Malmesbury was patron of the vicarage presumably
from its ordination and certainly from 1301. He presented at most
vacancies until the Dissolution. The bishop of Salisbury may have collated
a vicar in 1332, and in 1387 a vicar, who obtained the living by exchange,
was apparently instituted without the abbot's consent. After the

30 Ibid. ii. 75.
31 *W.A.M.* xli. 5; *Cal. S.P. Dom.* 1658–9, 220.
32 Phillipps, *Wilts. Inst.* ii. 27, 29–31.
33 *Lond. Gaz.* 1 Nov. 1946, p. 5361; inf. from Ch. Com.
34 Below, Corston, church; Rodbourne, church.

Dissolution the Crown presented[35] until 1866 when the advowson was sold to S. B. Brooke.[36] It passed with his Cowbridge estate to the Revd. Charles Kemble and to Charlotte Kemble[37] (d. 1890), who devised the advowson to her daughter Charlotte Kemble.[38] By 1907 the advowson had passed to the Church Trust Fund,[39] the patron of Malmesbury with Westport and Brokenborough in 1987.[40]

After a pension of £5 was paid to Malmesbury abbey the vicarage, worth £4 6s. 8d., was one of the poorer livings in Malmesbury deanery in 1291;[41] probably excluding a pension of £4 to the abbey, it was valued at £8 in 1535, close to the average for the deanery.[42] About 1830 the vicar's net annual income was £265, average for a Wiltshire living.[43]

Tithes, apart from those of grain and hay, were due to the vicar from the whole parish except some demesne of Malmesbury abbey. In the mid 13th century offerings and tithes owned by St. John's hospital were replaced by 40d. and ½ lb. wax a year.[44] In 1839 a total of 823 a., mostly what had been Cole park and West park, was tithe free; moduses totalling 12s. were paid in place of vicarial tithes from a further 185 a., said to be former demesne of the abbey. The vicar's tithes were then valued at £430 and commuted.[45]

The vicar had a house, perhaps in King's Wall, c. 1300;[46] it is not known whether it was part of the glebe. In 1412 Edmund Dauntsey and John Thornbury endowed the vicarage with a house and 5 a.[47] In 1671 the glebe comprised 3½ a., a cottage, and a house.[48] The house, of one bay in 1704,[49] stood in Gloucester Street opposite St. Paul's church. In

35 Phillipps, *Wilts. Inst.* (index in *W.A.M.* xxviii. 225); *Clerical Guide* (1829); *Clergy List* (1859).
36 Ch. Com. file 34228.
37 Above, manors.
38 Wilts. Cuttings, xvii. 13.
39 Bristol R.O., EP/A/3/218.
40 Inf. from Gen. Secretary, Church Pastoral Aid Soc., Falcon Ct., 32 Fleet Street, Lond.
41 *Tax. Eccl.* (Rec. Com.), 189.
42 *Valor Eccl.* (Rec. Com.), ii. 137; P.R.O., E 123/7, f. 285v.
43 *Rep. Com. Eccl. Revenues,* 840–1.
44 *Reg. Malm.* ii. 75–8.
45 W.R.O., tithe award.
46 *Reg. Malm.* i. 121.
47 *Cal. Pat.* 1408–13, 417.
48 W.R.O., D 1/24/141/1.
49 Ibid. D 1/24/141/2.

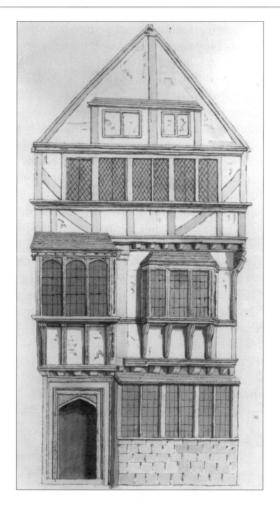

The vicarage house in 1790

the earlier 19th century it was used as a shop and vicars lived in lodgings.[50] From *c.* 1882 incumbents lived in a house, then newly built beside the Swindon road, belonging to Westport vicarage.[51] A new vicarage house was built in Holloway, and that beside the Swindon road was sold, in 1969.[52]

50 Ch. Com. file 34228; ibid. NB 5/116ʙ; Soc. Antiq. MS. 817, ix, f. 9; see above, illus. on this page.
51 Ch. Com. file, NB 5/116ʙ.   52 Ibid. 83703.

Its name suggests that Whitchurch may have been the site of an early chapel. Such a chapel may have invoked St. James in 1252, when Malmesbury abbey was granted a St. James's fair on its land at Whitchurch.[53] In 1535 offerings made from or at Whitchurch to an image of St. James were taken by the abbey.[54] Alms were distributed in a chapel at Whitchurch by the abbey or by the lessee of its Whitchurch estate at mass on the eve and feast of St. James in the early 16th century.[55] After the Dissolution presumably no service was held in the chapel, which from the 1560s or earlier passed with Whitchurch manor.[56] By 1670 it had been incorporated in Whychurch Farm.[57] In 1268 Nicholas of Malmesbury gave land at Fowlswick in Chippenham for a chaplain to say masses for his parents in the chapel of 'la Charnere' in Malmesbury.[58] No other reference to the chapel has been found. All Saints' chapel stood in High Street, perhaps on the eastern side, in the late 13th century and in 1545.[59] In 1544 the Crown granted a house called 'St. White's hermitage' at Burton Hill;[60] what, if any, ecclesiastical purpose the hermitage had before the Dissolution is not clear. In 1268 William Porter gave a rent of 1s. a year for a light in St. Paul's church.[61] A chantry was endowed at the altar of St. Mary in the church probably before 1300;[62] in 1388 the Crown presented a chantrist.[63] At the chantry's dissolution in 1548 its priest had an income of £6 11s. from Malmesbury and Westport and was described as a very honest poor man.[64]

Some parishioners apparently heard mass in the chapel of St. John's hospital until the mid 13th century, when attendance there was forbidden to all but those wearing the habit of the hospital.[65] In 1378 the vicar John Swan travelled to Rome for the sake of his conscience;[66] he resigned

53 *Cal. Chart. R.* 1226–57, 400.
54 *Valor Eccl.* (Rec. Com.), ii. 119.
55 P.R.O., E 315/102, ff. 28–9.
56 Ibid. C 3/109/19.
57 Aubrey, *Topog. Coll.* ed. Jackson, 267.
58 *Reg. Malm.* ii. 125, 127.
59 Ibid. ii. 340–1; P.R.O., E 318/Box 18/874.
60 *L. & P. Hen. VIII,* xix (2), p. 414.
61 *Reg. Malm.* ii. 113.
62 Ibid. i. 119; ii. 192–3.
63 *Cal. Pat.* 1385–9, 511.
64 P.R.O., E 301/58, no. 35.
65 *Reg. Malm.* ii. 75–8.
66 *Cal. Close,* 1377–81, 528.

the living in that or the following year.[67] William Sherwood held the vicarage and a rectory in Oxford, and in 1477 was dispensed to hold a third living.[68] Richard Turner, vicar from 1535, in 1539 condemned the dissolution of the monasteries;[69] he seems to have suffered no penalty but had resigned the living by 1544.[70]

In the early 16th century parishioners may have attended services in the abbey church and St. Paul's fell into disrepair. In 1541 the nave of the church of the dissolved abbey was licensed as the parish church because St. Paul's had 'fallen even unto the ground'.[71] The former abbey church was then in the king's hand and in the keeping of William Stumpe.[72] In 1542 John Leland reported that the townsmen, among whom Stumpe was the chief contributor, had bought the church from the king.[73] Stumpe was probably then only the lessee of the site of the abbey; in 1544 he was granted the site by the Crown[74] and may then have given or sold the church to the parish.

There were said to be 860 communicants in Malmesbury and Westport parishes in 1548, and the Crown was then petitioned for assistant clergy to replace chantry priests who had formerly helped incumbents in both parishes.[75] John ApRice, vicar of Malmesbury from 1544 until c. 1564, had two other benefices and in 1556 no licence for plurality.[76] In 1551 the church had no copy of Erasmus's *Paraphrases* or Book of Homilies.[77] ApRice's successor John Skinner was deprived in 1564 or 1565,[78] for what reason is not known. In 1583 the vicar, James Steele, was alleged to have leased the vicarage and to have left the town.[79] In 1585, when he may still have been absent, the churchwardens complained that services were not held at the proper times and that there was no curate.[80]

67 Phillipps, *Wilts. Inst.* i. 63.
68 *Cal. Papal Reg.* xiii (2), 596.
69 *L. & P. Hen. VIII,* xiv (2), p. 351.
70 Phillipps, *Wilts. Inst.* i. 210.
71 *W.A.M.* i. 249.
72 Ibid. viii. 587.
73 Leland, *Itin.* ed. Toulmin Smith, i. 132.
74 *L. & P. Hen. VIII,* xix (2), p. 414; P.R.O., E 318/Box 20/1074.
75 P.R.O., E 301/58, no. 36.
76 Phillipps, *Wilts. Inst.* i. 210, 221; W.R.O., D 1/43/2, f. 22.
77 W.R.O., D 1/43/1, f. 23v.
78 Phillipps, *Wilts. Inst.* i. 221–2.
79 P.R.O., E 123/7, f. 285v.
80 W.R.O., D 1/43/6, f. 31Av.

The abbey church from the south

In 1651 the alderman and burgesses granted to Robert Harpur, the vicar, rights of pasture on King's Heath as a mark of esteem.[81] In 1661 the bishop of Salisbury mentioned Malmesbury among places, whose incumbents were 'busy, turbulent' men, which he was unable to bring to good order; Simon Gawen was expelled from the vicarage in 1662.[82] Between 1643 and 1686 there were several cases of witchcraft in the town,[83] and Aubrey reported that seven or eight witches from Malmesbury were hanged in the 1670s.[84]

Vicars of Malmesbury received 20s. a year from each of three annual sermon charities, founded by Michael Wickes, Elizabeth Hodges, and Robert Cullerne in 1695, c. 1723, and in 1758 respectively. No payment was received from Hodges's charity in or after the late 19th century,[85] but payments from Wickes's and Cullerne's were still made in the late 20th.[86]

81 Luce, *Hist. Malm.* 99.
82 *Calamy Revised,* ed. Matthews, 218.
83 *W.A.M.* xxiv. 159–64; *Wilts. Q. Sess. Rec.* ed. Cunnington, 225.
84 Aubrey, *Nat. Hist. Wilts.* ed. Britton, 121–2.
85 *Endowed Char. Wilts.* (N. Div.), 672–3, 678–9.
86 Ibid. 685, 688, 690; inf. from the vicar.

John Copson, vicar 1749 to *c.* 1786, was from 1765 also vicar of Kemble (now Glos.).[87] In 1783 he lived at Kemble and a curate, who was also curate of Ashley (now Glos.), served Malmesbury, including Corston and Rodbourne chapels. Services were then held at Malmesbury on Sunday afternoons and additionally at festivals and in Lent. Communion was celebrated four times a year and there were usually *c.* 50 communicants.[88] From 1879 until the benefices were united Malmesbury and Westport vicarages were held in plurality.[89]

ST. PAUL'S church was so called in 1191.[90] In 1542 all that remained of it was the west tower, then used as a house, and part of the east end, used as a town hall.[91] Reports in 1556 and 1585 that a church in Malmesbury needed repair[92] may refer to St. Paul's and, if they did, indicate some hope of its restoration as the parish church. Part of it may have continued in ecclesiastical use until the 1630s; there were said to have been marriages and sermons at St. Paul's until then.[93] The east end was probably used for meetings of the corporation until the 18th century,[94] and in the late 18th century was apparently a poorhouse.[95] When it was demolished in 1852 it was said to have long been used as a timber warehouse.[96] The tower was standing in 1988 and then as earlier housed bells rung for services in the abbey church.[97] It was built in the 14th century, of limestone rubble with ashlar dressings, and has three stages.

Before the Dissolution the abbey church[98] was apparently dedicated to St. Mary and St. Aldhelm.[99] In the early 20th century an additional or alternative dedication was to *ST. PETER AND ST. PAUL.*[1] In 1988 all four saints were invoked.[2] Nothing survives of the churches and other

87 Phillipps, *Wilts. Inst.* ii. 73, 93; *W.N. & Q.* viii. 225.
88 *Vis. Queries, 1783* (W.R.S. xxvii), pp. 150–1.
89 *Clergy List* (1892); *Crockford* (1907 and later edns.).
90 *Reg. Malm.* i. 374–5.
91 Leland, *Itin.* ed. Toulmin Smith, i. 171.
92 W.R.O., D 1/43/2, f. 22v.; D 1/43/6, f. 31Av.
93 Nightingale, *Wilts. Plate,* 203; Soc. Antiq. MS. 817, ix, f. 9.
94 Above, local govt. (boro. govt.).
95 Camden, *Brit.* (1806), i. 142.
96 Soc. Antiq. MS. 817, ix, f. 3v.
97 Below.
98 See illus. on p. 84.
99 *V.C.H. Wilts.* iii. 228.
 1 *Kelly's Dir. Wilts.* (1903, 1911).
 2 Inf. from the vicar.

buildings of the abbey which stood before the 12th century.[3] Parts of
the crossing, transepts, and nave[4] of the 12th-century church survive
and footings found by excavation indicate a semicircular ambulatory at
the east end. The surviving parts suggest that the church had arcades, a
triforium, a clerestory, and a timber roof, and that the whole was built to
one design in the later 12th century. The arcades were of nine bays and
the transepts each of three bays; chapels probably extended eastwards
from the outer bay of each transept.[5] The south doorway and porch

The west tympanum in the porch of the abbey church

were richly decorated with stone sculptures representing the apostles
and scenes from the Old and New Testaments.[6] The cloister was to the
north and was probably surrounded by other buildings although only
one wall, to the east and presumably part of the chapter house, has been
traced. Because the ground falls steeply north of the cloister, the dormitory
and its undercroft seem likely to have run east–west. The vaulted 13th-

3 *V.C.H. Wilts.* iii. 228.
4 See illus. on p. 146.
5 *Archaeologia*, lxiv, pl. lxvi.
6 *Jnl. Brit. Arch. Assoc.* [3rd ser.], xxviii. 40–54; see above, illus. on this page.

century undercroft incorporated in Abbey House[7] may have been at the end of or beside the dormitory range. Another probably 13th-century range, incorporated in the Old Bell hotel west of the church,[8] may have been part of a building which, according to the usual plan of a monastery, consisted of the inner gatehouse and the abbot's lodging. By the 16th century, however, the abbot's lodging was apparently south-east of the church. Late 13th-century improvements and additions included alterations to the chapter house and the building of a new infirmary;[9] neither building survives. In the early 14th century the nave and transepts were vaulted and the clerestories altered and, at the west end, rebuilt. Flying buttresses were added to the nave to support the vault, the parapets of the nave and aisles were reconstructed, and the porch walls were made thicker, perhaps to support a tower. A first-floor room but no tower, was built over the porch. A tower was built over the two western bays of the nave c. 1400. A central tower, perhaps built in the 12th century, was apparently heightened and topped with a tall spire of wood and lead in the later Middle Ages. It fell probably in the early 16th century.[10] The west tower was standing in 1660 but fell soon afterwards, destroying the south-west corner of the nave.[11] When the nave became the parish church a wall was built between it and the crossing. After the west tower fell a wall was built across the nave three bays from the west end. That wall had a window with wooden tracery which in 1823 was replaced by one in stone made to designs by H. E. Goodridge. A plaster vault, presumably imitating the surviving 14th-century vaulting, was then built over the western bays of the nave and a gallery and an organ were built against the west wall.[12] Major alterations since then include the extension of the south aisle and clerestory in 1900,[13] the vaulting of the porch in 1905,[14] and the restoration of the upper room in 1912.[15] Between 1926 and 1928 the plaster part of the nave vault was renewed in stone and the gallery was removed.[16]

7 Above, introduction.
8 Ibid.
9 *Archaeologia,* lxiv. 401–5.
10 Leland, *Itin.* ed. Toulmin Smith, i. 131; *W.A.M.* xxxviii. 473.
11 Aubrey, *Topog. Coll.* ed. Jackson, 255–6.
12 *Gent. Mag.* ii. 170 n.; Wilts. Cuttings, i. 154.
13 Bristol R.O., EP/J/6/2/164, pet. for faculty.
14 *W.A.M.* xxxviii. 479.
15 Bristol R.O., EP/J/6/2/164, faculty papers, 1912.
16 *W.A.M.* xliii. 498–9; Wilts. Cuttings, xi. 196–8.

A chalice valued at 40s. was stolen from St Paul's church in 1383 or 1384;[17] no other record survives of plate used in that church. Chalices of 1575 and 1631, the latter given in 1632, and a paten of 1702 belonged to the parish c. 1890.[18] That plate, a chalice of 1703, and other plate mainly of the late 19th century and the 20th, some from Westport church, belonged to the parish in 1988.[19]

In 1987 eight bells hung in the tower of St. Paul's. The oldest was one cast in Bristol c. 1500; one of 1610 was cast by a member of the Purdue family. A bell of 1640, perhaps cast by A. Hughes, and one of 1703 by William Cor were recast by Mears & Stainbank in 1910, and a bell of 1739 was recast in 1896 by Llewellins & James. Three new bells were cast in 1951 by Gillett & Johnston.[20]

Registers of baptisms, marriages, and burials survive from 1591.[21]

ROMAN CATHOLICISM. In 1865 a site in Cross Hayes was bought for a Roman Catholic church,[22] which was in the charge of Missionaries of St. Francis de Sales from 1867.[23] By 1876 that church had been replaced by a new stone building in a plain 14th-century style.[24] The former church was used as a school from 1876 or earlier until c. 1932.[25] By will proved 1923 C. J. Pollen gave the income from an invested sum, then £22 yearly, for the use of a Roman Catholic priest in Malmesbury.[26]

PROTESTANT NONCONFORMITY. Simon Gawen, ejected from Malmesbury vicarage in 1662, preached in the town until his death in 1672.[27] Other dissenting ministers in the town in the late 17th century included Henry Chandler, a Presbyterian recorded there in 1687,[28] and Samuel Clifford, formerly rector of East Knoyle, who preached in Malmesbury between 1695 and 1699.[29] Until the late 18th century

17 *Proc. before Justices,* ed. B. H. Putnam (Ames Foundation), 387.
18 Nightingale, *Wilts. Plate,* 202.
19 Inf. from the vicar.
20 Walters, *Wilts. Bells,* 128–30; inf. from the vicar.
21 W.R.O. 1589/1–16.
22 Ibid. 212A/38/37/27.
23 *V.C.H. Wilts.* iii. 96.
24 J. Bird, *Hist. Malm.* 202.
25 Below, educ.
26 W.R.O., Char. Com., Malmesbury, 1.
27 *Calamy Revised,* ed. Matthews, 218.
28 Dr. Williams's Libr., Wilson MS. F i, p. 155.
29 *Calamy Revised,* ed. Matthews, 122.

nonconformity in the town was concentrated in the Westport part. In 1676 there were 5 nonconformists in Malmesbury, 18 in Westport;[30] in 1715 a Presbyterian minister in Westport was said to serve a congregation of 160;[31] and in 1783 the curate of Malmesbury reported that there were many dissenters of various denominations in the parish, but that their teachers lived elsewhere,[32] presumably in Westport.

An Anabaptist parishioner of Malmesbury refused to allow his child to be baptized in 1660[33] and in 1672 a house in Malmesbury may have been licensed for Baptist meetings.[34] A chapel was built in Westport parish, in Abbey Row on the boundary with Malmesbury parish, in or before 1695 and another built on the same site for Strict Baptists in 1802 was open in 1987.[35]

Several Quaker families lived in Burton Hill between 1669 and 1750.[36] A house in Malmesbury parish, probably in Burton Hill, was certified in 1695 for Quaker meetings.[37] A Quaker Sunday school was opened in Malmesbury in 1827, and in 1833 had 50 pupils,[38] but there is no record of a meeting in the town.

Between 1739 and 1741 John Wesley preached three or four times in Malmesbury.[39] John Davis (d. 1796), chaplain of Lea and Cleverton and curate of Garsdon, held evangelical services in a cottage in the town[40] and some of his congregation may have become Methodists *c.* 1800.[41] In 1814 and 1825 Primitive Methodists met in the former Ebenezer chapel in Silver Street,[42] but they had no permanent church in the town until 1856 when a chapel was built in Bristol Street in Westport parish.[43] A chapel in the Triangle in Westport was open in 1987. Wesleyan Methodist services were held in the town hall from 1882 to 1886, when

30 *Compton Census,* ed. Whiteman, 128.
31 Dr. Williams's Libr., Wilson MS. F i, p. 155.
32 *Vis. Queries, 1783* (W.R.S. xxvii), p. 150.
33 Soc. Antiq. MS. 817, ix, f. 9.
34 *Meeting Ho. Certs.* (W.R.S. xl), pp. 174–5.
35 Below, Westport, nonconf.
36 *W.N. & Q.* ii. 290, 463, 519; iii. 228–9; iv. 212, 287; v. 224–5, 305, 515, 517, 550; vi. 82, 133–4.
37 *Meeting Ho. Certs.* (W.R.S. xl), p. 5.
38 *Educ. Enq. Abstract,* 1042.
39 J. Wesley, *Works* (1872), i. 253, 259, 273, 299.
40 *V.C.H. Wilts.* iii. 132.
41 Moffatt, *Hist. Malm.* 159.
42 Britton, *Beauties of Wilts.* iii. 90; G. L. Jenkins, *Nonconf. in Malm.* (1895), 26; below.
43 Wilts. Cuttings, xxvii. 311; below, Westport, nonconf.

a chapel was opened in Cross Hayes.[44] The chapel had been closed by 1919.[45]

In 1745 John Cennick, a follower of George Whitefield, invited the Moravian Brethren to take charge of congregations in north Wiltshire founded by his preaching, including one in Malmesbury.[46] A Moravian church may have been in the town since 1742.[47] In 1770 a chapel was built near the junction of Oxford Street and Cross Hayes Lane. On Census Sunday in 1851 morning service was attended by 96 adults and 51 children; 122 adults attended evening service and a school was held in the afternoon.[48] The chapel was open in 1987. Registers of births and baptisms for the years 1827–40 and of burials 1826–40 survive.[49]

A cottage in Malmesbury certified in 1792 for Independent meetings[50] may have been used for John Davis's evangelical services.[51] Before 1800 two cottages in Silver Street were converted for use as the Ebenezer chapel by all or part of his congregation. In 1812 the congregation was united with that of Westport Congregational church, formerly the Presbyterian or Independent chapel, and the Ebenezer chapel was sold soon afterwards. A new meeting house was opened in Silver Street as a branch of the Westport church in 1836, and from 1841 was a separate church. The building was enlarged or rebuilt in 1848. On Census Sunday in 1851 the three services in the chapel, again called the Ebenezer chapel, were each attended by a congregation of between 150 and 200; attendance was said to be lower than usual.[52] In 1914, because there was no settled minister, it was proposed to reunite the chapel with Westport Congregational church; the proposal was resisted by the Silver Street deacons,[53] apparently successfully. The chapel had been closed by 1974.[54]

Other meeting houses in Malmesbury were certified in 1825 and 1827, and in 1842 a hall was certified.[55] From 1948 meetings of an

44 Jenkins, *Nonconf. in Malm.* 49.
45 W.R.O., G 21/160/2.
46 *V.C.H. Wilts.* iii. 130–1.
47 Jenkins, *Nonconf. in Malm.* 49.
48 P.R.O., HO 129/252/2/6/4.
49 Ibid. RG 4/2237.
50 *Meeting Ho. Certs.* (W.R.S. xl), p. 40.
51 Above.
52 Jenkins, *Nonconf. in Malm.* 21–3, 27; P.R.O., HO 129/252/2/1/2.
53 W.R.O. 1418/22.
54 *Wilts. Gaz.* 10 Jan. 1974.
55 *Meeting Ho. Certs.* (W.R.S. xl), pp. 108, 114, 154.

Assemblies of God Pentecostal church were held in the town; the church occupied a building in Silver Street from 1967 and was open in 1987.[56]

EDUCATION. A school may have been opened in the former hospital of St. John after the building was acquired by Malmesbury corporation in 1580.[57] The agreement of 1609 concerning the borough's government required that, of £20 paid annually by the alderman and burgesses for their inclosures on King's Heath, £10 should be paid to a schoolmaster.[58] From 1629 or earlier the payment was in the form of a rent charge on some of the inclosures.[59] The payment was confirmed by the borough charter of 1696. In 1695 Michael Wickes endowed the schoolmaster with an additional £10 a year from land in Great Somerford.[60] The school was apparently held in the part of the former hospital also used as a court room.[61] Instruction was free; in 1714 a master was dismissed for leaving the town and appointing a deputy who demanded fees.[62] There were 25 pupils in 1818,[63] and in 1858, when 50 pupils attended in wet weather and 20 in fine, the school was described by its master as little better than a refuge on a wet day.[64] In the late 19th century the school was attended only by sons of members of the corporation or freemen of Malmesbury. It was closed in 1890 and the warden and freemen of Malmesbury gave the rent charge to the National school provided that it accepted 20 sons of freemen. Payment of the rent charge to the school ceased on introduction of free elementary education in 1891.[65] Under a Scheme of 1910 the rent charge provided exhibitions at secondary schools or technical institutions for boys and girls resident in Malmesbury, preferably the children of freemen.[66] After 1890 occasional payments were made from Wickes's charity to schools in the town.[67]

56 Inf. from Mr. H. Latham, 4 Silver Street.
57 *W.A.M.* liii. 123.
58 P.R.O., STAC 8/290/22; above, local govt. (boro. govt.).
59 *W.A.M.* liii. 123.
60 *Endowed Char. Wilts.* (N. Div.), 672–3; below, charities.
61 *W.A.M.* liii. 123; *Endowed Char. Wilts.* (N. Div.), 683.
62 Malmesbury boro. rec., ct. bk. 1600–1721.
63 *Educ. of Poor Digest,* 1032.
64 *Acct. of Wilts. Schs.* 32.
65 P.R.O., ED 49/8215; below.
66 Char. Com. file.
67 P.R.O., ED 49/8215.

In 1634 Robert Arch gave 11 a., mostly in Lea and Cleverton parish, for the general good of Malmesbury borough.[68] In 1818 the income of £55 was used for a school attended by c. 150 pupils.[69] By 1834 the income had fallen to £33. It then paid for a free school for 45 girls held in a room over the porch of the abbey church; lace making was among the subjects taught.[70] The school was open in 1873[71] but apparently closed soon afterwards. In 1908 the endowment was used for Malmesbury and Westport church schools,[72] and in 1911 provided scholarships for pupils from the town attending secondary schools.[73]

By will dated 1723 Elizabeth Hodges gave £30 yearly to schools in Malmesbury and other bequests to schools in nearby parishes. The provisions of the will were executed in 1730 when a Chancery decree ordered the foundation of a school for 15 boys.[74] The school's income and the number of its pupils were unchanged in 1846.[75] In 1869 the school was amalgamated with Westport Church of England school.[76] A Scheme of 1915 provided that the endowment should promote the education of children in the town by the award of exhibitions or other means. The annual income was between £10 and £15 in the 1960s.[77] In 1987 a share of the £67.50 given by the charity was received by schools in Malmesbury.[78]

A school for Malmesbury and Westport parishes was built in or before 1851 beside Sherston Road on a site then said to be in Westport parish,[79] but probably that in a detached part of Bremilham parish on which additional buildings, including a teacher's house, were erected in 1855–7. In 1857 it was attended by 63 boys and 34 girls.[80] From 1859 Westport Church of England school was a National school for boys

---

68 Endowed Char. Wilts. (N. Div.), 674.
69 Educ. of Poor Digest, 1032.
70 Endowed Char. Wilts. (N. Div.), 674.
71 P.R.O., ED 21/18532.
72 Below.
73 W.R.O., Char. Com., Malmesbury, 1.
74 Educ.of Poor Digest, 1032.
75 Endowed Char. Wilts. (N. Div.), 687–8; Nat. Soc. Inquiry, 1846–7, Wilts. 8–9.
76 Glos. R.O., D 1571/R 44; below.
77 Char. Com. file.
78 Inf. from clerk to Eliz. Hodges Trust, Courtfield, Tetbury, Glos.
79 W.R.O. 782/69; P.R.O., ED 7/131, no. 185.
80 Return of Non-Provided Schs. 25; Endowed Char. Wilts. (N. Div.), 696; Acct. of Wilts. Schs. 48; P.R.O., ED 7/131, no. 185.

only,[81] and in 1872 there were 247 pupils.[82] Another Church of England school for Malmesbury parish, built in 1857 in Cross Hayes, was for girls and infants.[83] In 1858 it had 220 pupils.[84] Average attendance at the two schools totalled 471 in 1909–10, 301 in 1921–2.[85] Both were closed in 1964 when a new primary school was opened in the old grammar school in Tetbury Hill.[86] A new school was built on the Tetbury Hill site in 1983; in 1988 it had 290 pupils on roll.[87]

A secondary school was opened in the town hall in 1896. It moved to new buildings on the west side of Tetbury Hill in 1903.[88] As Malmesbury grammar school it was attended by c. 240 in 1948.[89] A new school was built 750 m. north of it in 1964. A secondary modern school was built north of Sherston Road in Brokenborough parish in 1954;[90] it then had 450 pupils. The buildings of that school, the grammar school, and Westport Church of England school were used by a comprehensive school known as Malmesbury school from 1971; in 1988 it had 809 pupils on roll.[91]

The Roman Catholic school, built in Cross Hayes in 1869,[92] using the former church by 1876,[93] run by Sisters of St. Joseph of Annecy from 1884,[94] was known as St. Joseph's school. In 1892 average attendance was 60;[95] numbers changed little before 1922.[96] A new school was built in Holloway in 1932–3; it had c. 90 pupils in 1935–6.[97] In 1988 there were 98 children on roll from Malmesbury, Brinkworth, Hullavington, Crudwell, and Sherston.[98]

81 *Kelly's Dir. Wilts.* (1859 and later edns.).
82 P.R.O., ED 21/18532.
83 *Endowed Char. Wilts.* (N. Div.), 696–7; date on bldg.
84 *Acct. of Wilts. Schs.* 32.
85 *Bd. of Educ., List 21, 1911* (H.M.S.O.), 550; *1922*, 361.
86 Hudson, *Hill Top Town*, 31–2; below.
87 Inf. from Chief Educ. Officer, Co. Hall, Trowbridge.
88 Inf. from Mr. G. Allnatt, Malmesbury Sch.
89 *Town Guide* (1948).
90 Hudson, *Hill Top Town*, 31–2.
91 Inf. from Mr. Allnatt.
92 P.R.O., ED 7/131, no. 96.
93 Bird, *Hist. Malm.* 202.
94 *V.C.H. Wilts.* iii. 97.
95 P.R.O., ED 7/131, no. 186.
96 *Bd. of Educ., List 21, 1911* (H.M.S.O.), 550; *1914*, 552; *1919*, 362; *1922*, 361.
97 Ibid. *1936*, 425; W.R.O., F 8, corresp. file, primary schs., special ser., Malmesbury R.C. St. Joseph's.
98 Inf. from the head teacher, St. Joseph's Sch.

Other schools in the town included one kept by J. M. Moffatt (d. 1802), minister of Westport Presbyterian chapel,[99] and one held by the three daughters of Thomas Milsome in 1806.[1] In 1830 there were five and in 1842 seven schools in addition to the endowed schools in the town; most were probably in Westport parish. They included two ladies' boarding schools in 1830; in 1842 one was in Burton Hill.[2] Burton Hill House was used as a private school during the Second World War. Since 1945 it has been a residential school for physically handicapped children. In 1987 there were 32 pupils.[3]

CHARITIES FOR THE POOR. From 1584 the alderman and burgesses were using the former hospital of St. John as an almshouse and possibly a school,[4] and from 1609 they gave £10 of the £20 paid for their inclosures on King's Heath to maintain five inmates of it; from 1629 or earlier the £10 was a rent charge on particular inclosures,[5] and in 1696 its payment was confirmed by the borough charter. From 1695 the almshouse also received £10 a year from Michael Wickes's charity. In the early 20th century it comprised three cottages, providing accommodation for six widows of freemen of Malmesbury.[6] Between 1927 and 1967 it was rarely full and was sometimes empty. It was converted to house three people and filled in 1967.[7]

In 1612 Thomas Cox gave the income from 40s. to be distributed to the poor of Malmesbury on Good Friday annually.[8] Nothing more is known of the bequest. In 1641 Robert Jenner built almshouses near the corner of Oxford Street and Holloway for eight people.[9] In 1643 he gave a rent charge of £40 from Widhill manor in Cricklade for their upkeep and by will dated 1651 provided for the payment to continue. In the later 17th century and the early 18th actions were brought against his heirs for failure to pay the rent charge; payment ceased before *c.*

99 *V.C.H. Wilts.* iii. 123 n.; *D.N.B.*
  1 W.R.O. 805/22.
  2 Pigot, *Nat. Com. Dir.* (1830), 805; (1842), 20.
  3 Inf. from the headmaster, Burton Hill Ho. Sch.
  4 W.R.O., D 1/43/5; above, educ.
  5 P.R.O., STAC 8/290/22; above, local govt. (boro. govt.).
  6 *Endowed Char. Wilts.* (N. Div.), 672–3, 684; below.
  7 *Almshos. Gaz.* lxx. 2–3; *Country Life,* 3 Dec. 1959; W.R.O., Char. Com., Malmesbury, 1.
  8 Soc. Antiq. MS. 817, ix, f. 9.
  9 W.R.O. 161/133, Sansum v. Jenner; 1589/28.

1740. Four of the almshouses were demolished in 1825 and the remainder in the later 19th century.[10]

In 1654 Henry Grayle gave a rent charge of £10 yearly from lands in Great Somerford to apprentice poor children of Malmesbury. In the 19th century two children were usually apprenticed each year. Three boys were apprenticed in 1904; beneficiaries were usually from the borough but sometimes from St. Paul Malmesbury Without.[11]

E. Waite (d. 1661) gave by will £3 a year to the poor of the borough and Burton Hill. By a deed of 1774 Anne Rowles gave two thirds of the income from £100 to the poor of Malmesbury parish. In the 1830s the income from the two charities was distributed together; each beneficiary received 6d. In 1904 Waite's charity was distributed separately; adults received 6d. each and children 3d.[12] No record has been found of payments after 1910.[13] By a Scheme of 1907 Rowles's charity was united with that of William Arnold. The combined income, then c. £17, was thereafter used to buy coal for elderly residents or widows in the borough and Burton Hill.[14] In the later 20th century the income was allowed to accumulate and few payments were made.[15]

In 1695 Michael Wickes gave the income from lands in Great Somerford for charitable purposes in Malmesbury, including payments to St. John's almshouse, the free school, and the vicar of Malmesbury. The residue was to be distributed as the trustees thought fit. There was apparently little residue until the school was closed in 1890.[16] Thereafter the money was given to other Malmesbury institutions; in 1914 recipients of a total of £68 included the cottage hospital, the lying-in society, and the mayor's coal fund.[17]

Benefactions under the will of Elizabeth Hodges, dated 1723, included £10 yearly for poor housekeepers of Malmesbury. From 1820 equal payments were made to 20 of the second poor; beneficiaries were nominated for life. Similar payments were made in 1904.[18] The charity's

---

10 *Endowed Char. Wilts.* (N. Div.), 677; above, local govt. (par. govt.).
11 *Endowed Char. Wilts.* (N. Div.), 678, 689.
12 Ibid. 678, 689–90.
13 W.R.O., Char. Com., Malmesbury, 1.
14 Ibid.; Char. Com. file; below.
15 Inf. from Mr. T. Winch, Westport Granary.
16 *Endowed Char. Wilts.* (N. Div.), 672–3, 685.
17 W.R.O., Char. Com., Malmesbury, 1.
18 *Endowed Char. Wilts.* (N. Div.), 675, 679–80, 688.

income remained *c.* £10 in 1960.[19] In 1987 payments totalling £175 were made to poor residents of Malmesbury and of three other parishes named in the founder's will.[20]

By a deed of 1758 Robert Cullerne gave £17 10*s.* of a rent charge of £20 from lands in Lea and Cleverton to be given to the poor of Malmesbury (presumably the borough), of Burton Hill, and of Westport; each family was to receive 5*s.* annually. In 1904 payments were probably to individuals and each received 2*s.* 6*d.*,[21] in 1975–6 payments of 25p each were made to 87 applicants,[22] and similar payments were made in 1987.[23]

By will dated 1778 William Arnold gave the income from £400 to buy bread for the poor of Malmesbury. In 1904 the income, £14 8*s.* 4*d.*, was used to buy bread for the poor of the borough and Burton Hill.[24] By a Scheme of 1907 the charity was united with that of Anne Rowles.[25]

May Moore (d. 1978) gave by will a house in Abbey Row and £10,000 to house and care for the elderly. In 1983 it was declared that the endowment should be used to provide grants, clothing, or travel for elderly residents within the boundaries of the former borough, and that an administrator should occupy the house. The yearly income was then *c.* £1,300.[26]

CORSTON

CORSTON was a village, chapelry, and tithing in the south-western corner of Malmesbury parish. In 1839 its lands measured *c.* 1,140 a. (461 ha.).[27] They may have been those of a 10-hide estate beside the 'Corsaburna', later called Gauze brook,[28] apparently the subject of a grant in 701.[29] In

19 Char. Com. file.
20 Inf. from clerk to Eliz. Hodges Trust, Courtfield, Tetbury, Glos.
21 *Endowed Char. Wilts.* (N. Div.), 678–9, 690.
22 Char. Com. file.
23 Inf. from Mr. J. A. G. Toogood, Forrester & Forrester, 59 High Street.
24 *Endowed Char. Wilts.* (N. Div.), 679, 691.
25 Above.
26 Char. Com. file.
27 W.R.O., tithe award.
28 Finberg, *Early Wessex Chart.* p. 70; *V.C.H. Wilts.* ii, pp. 4, 88–9.
29 Below, manor.

1086 Corston was part of Malmesbury abbey's large estate called Brokenborough. Corston's boundaries had apparently been fixed by *c.* 1100 when all except its northern one were surveyed with others of the Brokenborough estate; they may have been roughly those of *c.* 1840, when the northern boundary was a little north of Gauze brook, but few landmarks on them *c.* 1100 can now be traced.[30] In the later 13th century Corston was apparently part of the abbey's Cowfold estate,[31] but later may again have been a separate estate; possibly in the 12th century, certainly before 1341, a church was built there.[32]

In 1377 there were 46 poll-tax payers in Corston, a little below average for a place in Malmesbury hundred,[33] and Corston was of below average prosperity in the late 16th century.[34] Its population rose rapidly in the early 19th century, from 127 in 1801 to reach 171 in 1821 and 322 in 1851,[35] but had fallen to 304 by 1881.[36] Numbers increased again in the mid and late 20th century when married quarters were built for R.A.F. Hullavington and private and local authority houses were built in Corston village.[37]

The village lies beside Gauze brook at the north end of the chapelry. Its early focus may have been around a green where a road from Rodbourne joins the Malmesbury–Chippenham road; the church stands on rising ground in the north-eastern angle of the junction. In the early 18th century settlement extended north along the Malmesbury road to Gauze brook and Corston Mill, south to the farmstead later called Manor Farm, and east along the Rodbourne road to the farmstead later called Firs Farm.[38] Surviving buildings of that or earlier date include the possibly 17th-century Manor Farm, two stone cottages of 17th-century origin east of the main road, and the Hermitage, a 17th-century stone house south of the church. Only a few 18th-century cottages survive; some were rebuilt in the 19th century. The Radnor Arms west

30 *V.C.H. Wilts.* ii, p. 125; *Arch. Jnl.* lxxvii. 42–4, 88–90; W.R.O., tithe award; above, Brokenborough, manor.
31 *Reg. Malm.* i. 174.
32 *Inq. Non.* (Rec. Com.), 167; below, church.
33 *V.C.H. Wilts.* iv. 309.
34 *Taxation Lists* (W.R.S. x), 52.
35 *V.C.H. Wilts.* iv. 352.
36 P.R.O., RG 11/2025; RG 11/2027.
37 Below.
38 W.R.O. 490/774.

of the road was built and opened as an inn in the 1790s.[39] Firs Farm was largely rebuilt in the 19th century. The southern and eastern limits of the village remained unchanged until the 20th century. By 1828 settlement had spread north of Gauze brook to and beyond the boundary of the chapelry, mainly on the west side of the Malmesbury road.[40] There Newlands Cottage bears the date 1825; north of it Newlands Farm and Quarry House replaced other buildings in the later 19th century. The Bell inn, which stood west of the main road north of Gauze brook in 1881, had closed by 1899.[41] North of Gauze brook settlement also spread along Mill Lane in the mid and later 19th century when cottages and a nonconformist chapel were built west of the mill.[42] The Mill inn was open in 1910[43] and closed c. 1965.[44] Another chapel was built west and the vicarage house north of the church in the late 19th century; a reading room was built north-west of the church in 1904.[45] In 1933 three pairs of council houses were built 350 m. south-west of Manor Farm;[46] in the later 20th century a garage, on the site of a small group of gabled 17th-century cottages demolished in the 1960s,[47] and Kingway View, a row of bungalows, was built north of them. In the 1950s 22 council houses were built beside the Rodbourne road. Manor Park, a private estate of eight houses and bungalows, was built north-east of Manor Farm in the 1970s. Elsewhere in the village there has been infilling in the late 20th century. The bridge carrying the Malmesbury–Chippenham road over Gauze brook was rebuilt in 1984.[48]

There was no substantial building in the chapelry outside the village in the early 18th century.[49] By 1773 a farmstead called the Bell had been built beside the boundary with Stanton St. Quintin south-west of the village. Another, Kingway, was built east of the Chippenham road south of the village between 1773 and 1828.[50] After its land was

39 W.R.O. 490/706.
40 O.S. Map 1", sheet 34 (1828 edn.).
41 Ibid. 6", Wilts. XIII (1888 edn.), XIII. NW. (1900 edn.); P.R.O., RG 11/2027.
42 W.R.O., tithe award; O.S. Map 6", Wilts. XIII (1888 edn.).
43 W.R.O., Inland Revenue, val. reg. 9.
44 Wilts. Cuttings, xxii. 277.
45 Ch. Guide (1986).
46 Date on bldg.
47 Inf. from Co. Archivist, Co. Hall, Trowbridge.
48 Date on bridge.
49 W.R.O. 490/774.
50 Andrews and Dury, Map (W.R.S. viii), pl. 13; O.S. Map 1", sheet 34 (1828 edn.).

acquired for Hullavington airfield in 1935 Bell Farm was demolished and houses and other buildings for R.A.F. Hullavington were thereafter built on and around its site. They include 62 houses in Anson Place built in 1935–6 and 1948–9. In addition to the buildings the main north-east and south-west runway was built on the 115 ha. of Corston in the station, which also had land and buildings in Stanton St. Quintin and Hullavington.[51] Hangar Farm was built east of the Chippenham road near the airfield between 1959 and 1974.[52] The Plough, a small 19th-century stone building beside the Rodbourne road, was open as a public house in 1885;[53] it was closed in 1964.[54]

MANOR AND OTHER ESTATES. Corston seems to have been the 10-hide estate beside Gauze brook apparently granted by King Ine to Malmesbury abbey in 701.[55] Six hides in Corston, presumably the whole estate, were held of the abbey by Ranulph Flambard in 1086,[56] but later the abbey had no tenant in demesne. Corston passed to the Crown at the Dissolution[57] and in 1564 the manor of *CORSTON* was sold to Thomas Chadderton[58] (fl. 1567).[59] In 1569 it was bought from Thomas's creditors by his cousin William Chadderton,[60] who sold the lordship and most of the lands in 1573 to Sir Walter Hungerford.[61] Sir Walter (d. 1596)[62] was succeeded by his half-brother Sir Edward Hungerford (d. 1607),[63] whose relict Cecily, from 1608 wife of Francis Manners, from 1612 earl of Rutland, may have retained the manor until her death in 1653.[64] It was inherited by Sir Anthony Hungerford (d. 1657) and by his son Sir Edward,[65] who in 1682 conveyed the manor to his uncle Sir

51 Below, manor; O.S. Map 1/50,000, sheet 173 (1974 edn.); inf. from Defence Land Agent, Durrington.
52 O.S. Maps 1/25,000, ST 98 (1959 edn.); 1/50,000, sheet 173 (1974 edn.).
53 Ibid. 6", Wilts. XIII (1888 edn.).
54 Wilts. Cuttings, xxii. 277.
55 Finberg, *Early Wessex Chart.* p. 70.
56 *V.C.H. Wilts.* ii, p. 125.
57 P.R.O., SC 6/Hen. VIII/3986, rot. 115.
58 Ibid. E 318/Box 34/2307.
59 Ibid. C 3/201/11.
60 Ibid. REQ 2/178/30.
61 Ibid. CP 25(2)/239/15 & 16 Eliz. I Mich. no. 742.
62 Aubrey, *Topog. Coll.* ed. Jackson, 412.
63 P.R.O., C 142/306, no. 160.
64 *Complete Peerage,* xi. 262; W.R.O. 442/2.
65 Aubrey, *Topog. Coll.* ed. Jackson, 412; E. M. Oliver, *Memoirs of Hungerford Fam.* (priv. print. 1930), 15.

Giles Hungerford.[66] From Sir Giles (d. 1685) it passed like Stanton St. Quintin manor to his relict Margaret, to his son-in-law Robert Sutton, Baron Lexinton, and in the Bouverie family and with the viscountcy of Folkestone and the earldom of Radnor to Jacob, earl of Radnor (d. 1930).[67]

In 1905 Lord Radnor sold Manor farm, c. 330 a.,[68] probably to David Roberts, the owner in 1910[69] and 1912.[70] The farm was sold again in 1919,[71] and in 1927 belonged to Frank Sage.[72] In 1951 it was offered for sale as Manor farm, 155 a., and South Side farm, 143 a., by W. S. Tyler.[73] Since then those lands have been owned by members of the Eavis family, who held Manor farm, c. 330 a., in 1987.[74] Between 1910 and 1912 Lord Radnor sold Bell farm, 401 a., and 146 a., part of Lower Stanton farm based in Stanton St. Quintin, to Meredith Meredith-Brown (d. 1920), whose estate was broken up c. 1920. In 1919 or 1920 S. H. Jones bought Lower Stanton farm and 116 a. of Bell farm. Half those lands descended to his son Mr. S. Jones[75] who sold them as Hangar farm, 217 a., in 1989.[76] F. J. Huntley bought Bell farm in 1920, and in 1935 sold it to the state for Hullavington airfield.[77]

In 1575 William Chadderton sold the rest of Corston manor, c. 130 a. and rights of pasture, to Thomas Richman[78] (fl. 1576).[79] That estate was held c. 1580 by John Richman[80] (d. 1615), who was succeeded by his daughter Margaret, wife of Edmund James (d. 1620).[81] From Margaret (fl. 1664) it passed to her son Edmund James (d. by 1675) whose relict Anne married William Cole c. 1677. From Elizabeth, wife of Francis Goddard and a descendant of Margaret James's younger

66 W.R.O. 490/73, abstr. of title, 1718.
67 Below, Stanton St. Quintin, manor.
68 W.A.S. Libr., sale cat. xiv, no. 9.
69 W.R.O., Inland Revenue, val. reg. 9.
70 Ibid. G 7/500/1.
71 W.A.S. Libr., sale cat. xiv, no. 9.
72 W.R.O., G 7/515/9.
73 W.A.S. Libr., sale cat. xxixC, no. 19.
74 Inf. from Mr. J. Eavis, Manor Farm.
75 W.R.O., Inland Revenue, val. reg. 9; ibid. G 7/500/1; G 7/515/9; below, Stanton St. Quintin, manor.
76 Wilts. Times, 14 Jan. 1989.
77 Inf. from Defence Land Agent, Durrington.
78 W.R.O. 490/206, abstr. of title.
79 Taxation Lists (W.R.S. x), 52.
80 W.R.O. 442/1, f. 187v.
81 P.R.O., C 142/350, no. 44; C 142/401, no. 88.

daughter, Cole bought the reversion of a moiety in 1691, and from Edward Brown, grandson of Margaret's elder daughter Margaret, he bought the reversion of the other in 1700. The manor descended with Bradfield manor in Hullavington to Cole's daughter Anne Cale and to her daughter Anne, wife of the Revd. Anthony Whistler (d. 1719). The Whistlers' son John[82] sold it in 1771 to William, earl of Radnor,[83] and it was reunited with the manor.

The rectorial tithes from Corston were due to Malmesbury abbey, passed to the Crown at the Dissolution,[84] and were probably all granted in 1606 to Laurence Baskerville, William Blake, and Roger Rogers,[85] perhaps for a member of the Bridges family. In 1622 John Bridges conveyed the tithes to Robert Bridges and his wife Elizabeth,[86] and in 1653 they were settled on Richard Bridges and his wife Eleanor. Richard was apparently succeeded in turn by his son George and by George's son George, who in 1731 sold the tithes to Richard Bromwich. By will proved 1753 Bromwich gave them to his wife Susannah (d. 1764), who devised them to her nephew John Melhuish. In 1791 Melhuish sold them to R. H. Gaby and Walter Gaby (d. c. 1811)[87] and in 1822 R. H. Gaby sold them to Jacob, earl of Radnor.[88] Thereafter they were merged.[89]

ECONOMIC HISTORY. In 1086 Ranulph Flambard's estate had land for 5 ploughteams, but only 3 teams worked it; 2 *villani* and 2 coscets had 2 teams, and 2 *servi* and a third team were apparently on the demesne. There were 10 a. of meadow, 15 a. of pasture, and woodland 3 furlongs long and 1 furlong broad.[90]

Customary tenants may have cultivated much of Corston's land in the late 13th century.[91] In the late 16th century almost two thirds of the lands were arable. There were fields called Ham, Up, and Broad lying respectively east, south, and west of Corston village. Another, West field, was in the south-west corner of the chapelry; the location of a fifth field,

82 W.R.O. 490/206, abstr. of title; above, Hullavington, manors.
83 W.R.O. 490/206, deed, Whistler to earl of Radnor, 1771.
84 Above, Malmesbury, manors.
85 W.R.O. 490/13, abstr. of title.
86 P.R.O., CP 25(2)/372/20 Jas. I Mich.
87 W.R.O. 490/13, abstr. of title.
88 Ibid. 490/213, deed, Gaby to earl of Radnor, 1822.
89 Ibid. tithe award.
90 V.C.H. Wilts. ii, p. 125.
91 Reg. Malm. i. 174–7.

Old Lands, is not known. Most were presumably open fields, but all or part of Up field had been inclosed by the earlier 15th century. Most of the pasture lay in the south and beside the western boundary; there was presumably meadow land beside Gauze brook. Only *c.* 100 a. of pasture were common, and *c.* 200 a. of meadow and pasture were in closes; *c.* 60 a. of pasture, probably near the boundary with Hullavington, had been inclosed by the early 16th century. The tenants of both parts of Corston manor shared the common pasture; some also had grazing rights on 60 a. of King's Heath.[92]

The farm sold to Thomas Richman in 1575 was in 1574 a holding of 3 yardlands, including 34 a. of several pasture of which 12 a. had recently been inclosed, 90 a. of arable in the open fields, 6 a. of meadow, and rights of common pasture.[93] By 1691 most of the farm's arable had been converted to *c.* 160 a. of several pasture.[94] The copyholders of Corston owed cash payments instead of services of cutting and carrying hay from three meadows in Cole park,[95] and had earlier owed works of ploughing in Kemboro field in Burton Hill.[96] A leasehold comprised 98 a., including 80 a. of arable.[97]

By 1720 all Corston's lands had been inclosed.[98] Some were still copyhold in the late 18th century[99] but the larger holdings were probably leasehold. In 1800, by which date the two portions of the manor had been reunited, there were two large farms, of 354 a. and 409 a., and five of between 20 a. and 60 a. each.[1] In 1839 Manor farm was 484 a., mainly in the north, and Bell farm was 455 a., mainly in the south. The chapelry was then half arable and half pasture; most of the arable was in the south and centre. There were 16 a. of wood beside the boundary with Rodbourne.[2] Coarse heath, 17 a. lying 700 m. south of the village, was worked as 60 allotments in 1834,[3] but not in 1839.[4] Pasture in Corston

92 W.R.O. 442/1; 490/206, deed, Chadderton to Richman, 1574; 490/774; Eton Coll. Mun. 4/94; 4/234D.
93 W.R.O. 490/206, deed, Chadderton to Richman, 1574.
94 Ibid. 490/206, deed, Goddard to Skermer, 1691.
95 Ibid. 442/1.
96 *Reg. Malm.* i. 186.
97 W.R.O. 442/1.
98 Ibid. 490/774.
99 Ibid. 490/705.
 1 Ibid. 490/707.
 2 Ibid. tithe award.
 3 Ibid. 1553/105.
 4 Ibid. tithe award.

was used principally to graze sheep in the mid 19th century; there were over 1,100 in 1866.[5] In 1910 most of the land lay in four farms, Manor, 308 a., Bell, 401 a., Newlands, 119 a., and one of 146 a.[6] Manor farm was mainly pasture in the early 20th century.[7] It was later worked as two farms, in 1951 as Manor, 155 a., and South Side, 143 a., respectively north-west and south-east of the Malmesbury–Chippenham road. Both were mixed farms; there was more arable than pasture on Manor farm, more pasture than arable on South Side farm.[8] Thereafter the lands were again worked as a single farm. In 1987 Manor farm was a mixed holding; there was a dairy herd of 200, and wheat and barley were grown on *c.* 300 a., some of it in Hullavington parish.[9] Bell farm had been divided into holdings of 116 a. and 285 a. by 1927.[10] The larger portion, west of the Malmesbury–Chippenham road, went out of agricultural use in 1935.[11] The smaller, east of the road, was part of Lower Stanton farm; later, as part of Hangar farm, it was worked from a re-used hangar.[12]

There was a mill at Corston in 1086[13] and 1539.[14] A mill on Gauze brook was part of Corston manor in 1810.[15] It and the mill house were rebuilt in the early 19th century. The mill ceased working *c.* 1899.[16]

Stanton brickworks, east of the Malmesbury–Chippenham road 500 m. north of the boundary with Stanton St. Quintin, was probably open in 1861 and certainly in 1885; it was closed in the early 20th century.[17]

In 1834 there was a quarry, presumably for limestone, north of Corston church, and another at the north end of the village;[18] both had apparently been closed by 1885. Two more quarries were at the north end of the village, and another south of the brickworks, in 1899. By

5 P.R.O., MAF 68/73, sheet 12.
6 W.R.O., Inland Revenue, val. reg. 9.
7 W.A.S. Libr., sale cat. xiv, no. 9.
8 Ibid. sale cat. xxixC, no. 19.
9 Inf. from Mr. J. Eavis, Manor Farm.
10 W.R.O., G 7/515/9.
11 Above, manor.
12 *Wilts. Times,* 14 Apr. 1989; local inf.
13 *V.C.H. Wilts.* ii, p. 125.
14 P.R.O., SC 6/Hen.VIII/3986, rot. 115.
15 W.R.O. 212A/27/48, survey of Corston.
16 O.S. Maps 6", Wilts. XIII (1888 edn.), XIII. NW. (1900 edn.); *Kelly's Dir. Wilts.* (1899, 1903).
17 O.S. Map 6", Wilts. XIII (1888 and later edns.); P.R.O., RG 9/1278.
18 W.R.O. 1553/105.

1921 one of the quarries in the village had been closed.[19] The other and that near the brickworks remained open in 1927[20] but were disused in 1987.[21]

LOCAL GOVERNMENT. In the early 16th century and perhaps until the sale of the manor by the Crown in 1564, courts for Corston were held at a house in Cole park.[22] In 1561–2 the Crown held views of frankpledge and manor courts in spring and autumn.[23] Between 1712 and 1742 courts baron were usually held annually, in spring until 1718 and in autumn thereafter. From 1720 leet business was also transacted. A tithingman was appointed and the homage presented buildings to be repaired, watercourses to be cleaned, and the deaths of copyholders.[24] No court is recorded after *c.* 1790.[25]

Corston did not relieve its own poor, but in the later 18th century and the early 19th an overseer was appointed to deal only with Corston. In 1760–1 two people received regular relief totalling £7; occasional relief and other extraordinary costs amounted to £3. The number regularly relieved had risen to six by 1770–1, and £39 was spent on the poor in 1780–1.[26]

CHURCH. The shape of Corston church before it was rebuilt in the 19th century suggests that it was built in the 12th century.[27] A church at Corston may have been served from Malmesbury abbey until a vicarage of Malmesbury was ordained between 1191 and the mid 13th century, but none is recorded until 1341 when there was a chapel dependent on Malmesbury church.[28] Inhabitants of Corston had right of burial there in the 18th century,[29] and there is no evidence that they lacked it earlier. A recommendation in 1650 that Corston and Rodbourne should form a benefice[30] was apparently not implemented. In 1881 Corston with

19 O.S. Map 6", Wilts. XIII (1888 and later edns.).
20 W.R.O., G 21/501/1.
21 Local inf.
22 P.R.O., REQ 2/178/30.
23 Ibid. SC 2/209/16.
24 W.R.O. 212A/27/48, Corston manor ct. bk.
25 Ibid. 490/705.
26 Ibid. 1589/33.
27 Below.
28 *Inq. Non.* (Rec. Com.), 167; above, Malmesbury, churches.
29 W.R.O. 490/212.
30 *W.A.M.* xli. 5.

Rodbourne became a district chapelry, with an incumbent usually called a vicar. The advowson was assigned to Charlotte Kemble, patron of Malmesbury, and the vicar was apparently given part of the income of Malmesbury vicarage. In 1882 the advowson was given to the Crown in an exchange and the vicar's income was increased by £16 13s. 4d. from a private benefaction and by the same sum from the Ecclesiastical Commissioners.[31] A vicarage house was built in 1884.[32] The house was sold in 1985,[33] and in 1986 the benefice was united with the benefice of Great Somerford, Little Somerford, and Seagry: the Crown had the right to present at two of every five turns to the united benefice.[34]

Until 1881 vicars of Malmesbury usually appointed a curate to serve both Corston and Rodbourne churches.[35] In 1650 Simon Gawen served the two churches 'at the request of the greatest part of the inhabitants', who paid him tithes due to the vicar of Malmesbury.[36] In the late 18th century and the early 19th afternoon services were held on alternate Sundays at Corston.[37] The church was apparently served by the vicar of Malmesbury c. 1830.[38] On Census Sunday in 1851 a morning service at Corston was attended by 38 adults, a congregation said to be smaller than usual.[39] From 1951 the church, with that at Rodbourne, was held in plurality with the benefice of Foxley with Bremilham; the incumbent usually lived at Corston.[40] After 1983 there was no resident incumbent.[41]

ALL SAINTS' church, so called in 1763,[42] is built of limestone rubble with ashlar dressings and has a chancel and a nave with north transept and south porch. Only the south doorway and the octagonal west bellcot, both of which are probably 15th-century, survive from the structure of a single-celled church which was rebuilt in 1881. The old

31 *Lond. Gaz.* 11 Jan. 1881, p. 120; ibid. 19 May 1882, p. 2350; Bristol R.O., EP/A/3/ 127; EP/A/4/2/3.
32 Ch. Com. file, NB 5/86c.
33 *Ch. Guide* (1986).
34 Ch. Com. file, NB 5/86c.
35 *Cal. Pat.* 1385–9, 237; *W.N. & Q.* vii. 548; *Lond. Gaz.* 10 Feb. 1882, p. 536; W.R.O., D 1/43/1, f. 23v.; Bristol R.O., EP/A/4/2/3.
36 *W.A.M.* xli. 5.
37 *Vis. Queries, 1783* (W.R.S. xxvii), p. 150; Ch. Com. file, NB 5/116B.
38 *Rep. Com. Eccl. Revenues*, 840–1.
39 P.R.O., HO 129/252/1/18/24.
40 *Crockford* (1965–6 and later edns.); Ch. Com. file, NB 5/86c.
41 *Ch. Guide* (1986).
42 J. Ecton, *Thesaurus*, 404.

All Saints' church, mostly demolished 1881

church was a long narrow building, of similar size to the 12th-century nave of Rodbourne church.[43] A 15th-century screen, which divided the chancel and nave, a plain early 17th-century pulpit, and some wall tablets survive from its interior. The transept was added c. 1900 but other alterations which were proposed then, including the removal of a gallery, were not carried out until 1911 when the chancel was added.[44]

In 1553 plate weighing 2½ oz. was confiscated from Corston; a chalice weighing 8½ oz. was left. It was replaced in 1577 by another with paten cover for use at both Corston and Rodbourne. A paten of c. 1720, a flagon, and an almsdish were acquired by the chapels in the 19th century.[45] The chalice and the later plate were still held in 1987.[46]

43 Ch. Guide (1986); J. Buckler, watercolours in W.A.S. Libr., vol. vi. 32; see above, illus. on this page; below, Rodbourne, church.
44 Bristol R.O., EP/J/6/2/110, pet. for faculty, corresp., consecration papers.
45 Nightingale, Wilts. Plate, 195–6.
46 Inf. from the rector, Great Somerford.

There were two bells in 1553. A bell, said in 1927 to be ancient, and another, of 1884 by J. Warner & Sons,[47] were recast in 1930.[48] They hung in the church in 1986.[49]

NONCONFORMITY. A curate removed from Corston and Rodbourne in 1662, presumably for nonconformity, may have been the vicar of Malmesbury, Simon Gawen, or his nominee.[50] There were said to be many dissenters, including Quakers, in Corston and its neighbourhood in the late 17th century.[51]

A house at Corston was certified for Independent meetings in 1803[52] and a chapel was built north of the church in 1821. It was served in 1823 by John Evans, a minister from Malmesbury, who claimed that the congregation then numbered 200. In 1851 on Census Sunday 67 people attended the morning service, 127 the evening service.[53] The chapel was replaced by a new small Congregational chapel, of brick with stone dressings, built west of the church c. 1898; that chapel had been closed by 1921.[54] In 1825 a house at Corston was certified for meetings of Primitive Methodists.[55] The Zion chapel in Mill Lane was built in 1857[56] and opened in 1858 by Strict Baptists.[57] The small chapel, of stone rubble, had been closed by 1899.[58]

EDUCATION. There were two dame schools with a total of c. 20 pupils in Corston in 1858.[59] A school there in 1865[60] was presumably closed when the school at Rodbourne was extended to serve both villages in 1872.[61]

47 Walters, *Wilts. Bells,* 66.
48 *Kelly's Dir. Wilts.* (1939).
49 *Ch. Guide* (1986).
50 W.R.O., D 1/54/1/1, no. 70; above, church.
51 Aubrey, *Topog. Coll.* ed. Jackson, 266.
52 *Meeting Ho. Certs.* (W.R.S. xl), p. 59.
53 P.R.O., HO 129/252/2/5/3; O.S. Map 6", Wilts. XIII (1888 edn.); W.R.O. 1418/18, letter, Evans to Elliott.
54 A. Antrobus, *Wilts. Congregational Union,* 45; O.S. Map 6", Wilts. XIII. NW. (1925 edn.).
55 *Meeting Ho. Certs.* (W.R.S. xl), p. 109.
56 Date on bldg.
57 R. W. Oliver, *Strict Bapt. Chapels Eng.* (Strict Bapt. Hist. Soc.), v. 33.
58 O.S. Map 6", Wilts. XIII. NW. (1900 edn.).
59 *Acct. of Wilts. Schs.* 32.
60 *Harrod's Dir. Wilts.* (1865).
61 Below, Rodbourne, educ.

RODBOURNE

RODBOURNE is a village whose lands formed a long and narrow tithing and chapelry in the south-east corner of Malmesbury parish. The chapelry originated as an estate on the stream called Rodbourne given to Malmesbury abbey.[62] The stream was that south of Rodbourne village, joining the Avon at Great Somerford. The boundaries of Rodbourne's lands were described in the late 11th century or early 12th, when they were marked partly by the Rodbourne, Gauze brook, and the Avon.[63] Little Somerford was given land west of the Avon in 1281,[64] but Rodbourne's other boundaries had apparently been changed little by 1839. The chapelry then comprised *c.* 1,350 a. (546 ha.).[65] Rodbourne had a church from the 12th century or earlier.[66]

In 1334 Corston and Rodbourne were assessed together for taxation at the above average sum of 56*s*. Rodbourne may then have been more prosperous than Corston and in 1377 had 69 poll-tax payers, well above the average for Malmesbury hundred.[67] It may have been less prosperous in the late 16th century.[68] In 1801 the population of the chapelry was 108. Numbers rose in succeeding decades, with some fluctuations, and reached a peak of 173 in 1851.[69] By 1881 they had fallen to 143,[70] and the decline apparently continued in the 20th century.

The buildings of Rodbourne village are strung out along a street behind wide verges which in 1773 opened out to form a central green on which the church stood. Settlement then extended northwards along lanes forming the green's eastern and western edges, and southwards along the road later called Pound Hill. The oldest buildings in the village are at its east and west ends; Rodbourne House to the east and a cottage to the west are of 17th-century origin. Some houses beside Pound Hill had been demolished by 1828; those which survived, on both sides of the Rodbourne stream, form a hamlet called Rodbourne Bottom. North of the stream Bottom Farm and south of the stream cottages and farm

62 Below, manor.
63 *Arch. Jnl.* lxxvii. 88–90.
64 *Reg. Malm.* ii. 219–20.
65 W.R.O., tithe award.
66 Below, church.
67 *V.C.H. Wilts.* iv. 298, 309.
68 *Taxation Lists* (W.R.S. x), 52.
69 *V.C.H. Wilts.* iv. 352.
70 P.R.O., RG 11/2025.

buildings were rebuilt in the 19th century. A cottage on the west side of Pound Hill bears the date 1836. By 1828 the lane on the west side of the green had been closed and the green made smaller. It and the wide verges east and west of it survived in the late 20th century, when trees stood on much of them. Between 1773 and 1828 cottages or farmsteads were built on the south side of the street between the church and Rodbourne House,[71] but some of them had been removed by 1842.[72] Much of the village was rebuilt in the mid 19th century by members of the Pollen family which owned Rodbourne manor; some buildings bear their arms or initials. Roman Cottage south of the street was built in 1845; Parsloe's Farm north of it was extended in 1852.[73] Both are of stone with dressings of local brick. Also on the south side of the street Manor Farm and a school were built in the mid 19th century. Thereafter little new building took place in the village; a house and a bungalow were built north of Rodbourne House in the late 20th century, and a water tower was built west of the church in 1951.[74]

There was a farmstead called Rodbourne Cleeve, 1 km. south of the church, in 1773[75] and probably earlier. Cleeve House was built on its site in 1899.[76] From 1970 until 1985 it was used as a children's home by Wiltshire county council.[77] Angrove Farm north-east of the village was built between 1828 and 1842.[78] Angrove Cottages, south-west of the farmstead, were built in the early 20th century to replace others east of the farmstead apparently demolished when the railway line was built in 1903.[79]

MANOR AND OTHER ESTATE. The 10 *manentes* of Rodbourne were apparently granted to Malmesbury abbey by King Ine in 701, although the abbey later claimed to have been given them as part of its Brokenborough estate in 956.[80] Rodbourne belonged to the abbey until the Dissolution.[81] In 1544 the Crown granted *RODBOURNE* manor

71 *Andrews and Dury, Map* (W.R.S. viii), pl. 13; O.S. Map 1", sheet 34 (1828 edn.).
72 W.R.O., tithe award.
73 Dates on bldgs.
74 Inf. from Supply Controller, Wessex Water, Quay Ho., the Ambury, Bath.
75 *Andrews and Dury, Map* (W.R.S. viii), pl. 13.
76 Date on bldg.
77 Inf. from Co. Secretary, Co. Hall, Trowbridge.
78 O.S. Map 1", sheet 34 (1828 edn.); W.R.O., tithe award.
79 O.S. Map 6", Wilts. XIII (1888 and later edns.); above, Malmesbury, introduction.
80 Finberg, *Early Wessex Chart.* pp. 70, 91, 105–6; *V.C.H. Wilts.* ii, pp. 4, 88–9.
81 P.R.O., SC 6/Hen. VIII/3986, rot. 112.

to William Stumpe[82] (d. 1552). It passed to his son Sir James[83] (d. 1563) and to Sir James's daughter Elizabeth, wife of Henry Knyvett.[84] In 1573 Elizabeth and Henry conveyed the manor to Sir Giles Poole[85] (d. 1588). Poole was succeeded in turn by his son Sir Henry[86] (d. 1616) and Sir Henry's son Henry,[87] who sold it to Henry Danvers, earl of Danby, in 1642.[88] It passed with Malmesbury manor to the sisters of Henry Danvers (d. 1654), and with other Danvers lands may have been divided in 1673 when a moiety was probably assigned to Eleanor Lee, daughter of Danvers's sister Anne.[89] In 1683 Danvers's sister Elizabeth surrendered a moiety to James Bertie, earl of Abingdon, Eleanor's husband.[90] Abingdon was succeeded in 1699 by his son Montagu, earl of Abingdon,[91] who by 1720 had sold the whole manor to Walter Hungerford.[92] Walter (d. 1754) was succeeded by his nephew George Hungerford (d. 1764),[93] who devised a portion of Rodbourne to his wife Elizabeth and the rest to members of the Duke and Luttrell families.[94] On Elizabeth's death in 1816 all or part of the manor passed to her nephew Sir John Pollen, Bt., who held the whole manor in 1839.[95] From Sir John (d. 1863) the manor passed with the baronetcy to his nephew Richard (d. 1881), to Sir Richard's son Richard (d. 1918), and to that Sir Richard's sons Sir Richard (d. 1930) and Sir John.[96] About 1938 Sir John sold Angrove farm, 204 a. Thereafter the farm was held by members of the Palmer family until 1976 when it was bought by Mr. and Mrs. R. F. Parfitt, the owners in 1987.[97] The bulk of the estate passed from Sir John (d. 1959) to his kinsman Sir John Pollen, Bt., the owner in 1987.[98]

82 P.R.O., E 318/Box 20/1074.
83 W.N. & Q. viii. 389, 394.
84   Ibid. 446, 448.
85 P.R.O., CP 25(2)/239/15 Eliz. I East. no. 695.
86   Ibid. C 142/222, no. 45.
87   Ibid. C 142/365, no. 153.
88   Ibid. CP 25(2)/512/18 Chas. I East.
89   Above, Malmesbury, manors.
90 P.R.O., CP 25(2)/747/35 Chas. II Trin.
91   Complete Peerage, i. 46.
92 W.R.O. 130/76, survey, 1719–20.
93   W.N. & Q. viii, pedigree facing p. 300.
94 Aubrey, Topog. Coll. ed. Jackson, 280.
95 Burke, Peerage (1931), 1905; W.R.O., tithe award.
96 Burke, Peerage (1931), 1905–6.
97 Inf. from Mrs. C. Parfitt, Angrove Farm.
98 Who Was Who, 1951–60, 881; local inf.

Rodbourne House, formerly the home of the Pollens, is apparently of early 17th-century origin and consists of a main east–west range. It was given a new south front and a west wing with a bow window at its north end in the later 18th century. In the early 19th century the interior was refitted and a little later rooms were added to the north in the angle between the main range and the wing. A tower was built east of that extension in 1859;[99] at a similar or slightly later date some chimneys were rebuilt with alternating bands of red brick and ashlar. A ground-floor extension in red brick was built across the whole of the south front in the late 19th century. The gardens were extended between 1842 and 1885, when the road beside the south front was moved 50 m. further south.[1]

After the Dissolution tithes of grain, hay, wool, and lambs, arising in Rodbourne, probably in the whole chapelry, passed with tithes from Corston to Robert Bridges (fl. 1622) and his wife Elizabeth.[2] They were apparently bought by Henry Poole and were merged with Rodbourne manor.[3]

ECONOMIC HISTORY. Intercommoning of pastures beside the Avon between Rodbourne and Little Somerford was ended by an agreement of 1281. Most of the pastures on the right bank were allotted to the men of Rodbourne, but the lord and tenants of Little Somerford also retained meadow land there.[4] Rodbourne's pastures beside the river were apparently several in the mid 16th century when the only common pasture in the chapelry was the Heath, *c.* 60 a. south of the village. Open arable fields were then called East, West, and Park.[5]

There is no record of demesne land at Rodbourne. In the mid 16th century 15 copyholders held between them 29½ yardlands; none held more than 3 yardlands. Other holdings were of no more than a few acres each. Like those of Corston the tenants' obligations to cut and carry hay from Cole park and to plough in Kemboro field had been commuted for cash payments by the mid 16th century.[6]

99 Date on bldg.
 1 W.R.O., tithe award; O.S. Map 6", Wilts. XIII (1888 edn.).
 2 Above, Corston, manor; P.R.O., CP 25(2)/372/20 Jas. I Mich.
 3 P.R.O., CP 25(2)/512/18 Chas. I East.
 4 *Reg. Malm.* ii. 219–20.
 5 W.R.O. 88/2/4; cf. ibid. tithe award.
 6 *Reg. Malm.* ii. 186; P.R.O., E 318/Box 20/1074; above, Corston, econ. hist.

There were still open fields in Rodbourne in the early 18th century,[7] but common cultivation had ceased by the early 19th.[8] The Heath, apparently common pasture in 1820,[9] had by 1839 been inclosed and ploughed. Most of the chapelry was grassland in 1839; there were c. 250 a. of arable and 57 a. of woodland, including Angrove wood, 18 a. near the Avon, and Bincombe wood, 31 a. south-west of Rodbourne village. There were seven farms of over 80 a. each; 166 a., including the woodland, was in the lord's hand. Farms of 152 a., 179 a., and 82 a. worked from farmsteads in the village, and Bottom farm, 173 a., worked from a farmstead south of the village, were scattered holdings. Angrove farm, 208 a. in the north-east corner of the chapelry, and Cleeve farm, 264 a. in the south-west corner, were compact.[10]

Totals of stock in the chapelry in 1866, including 213 cattle, 322 sheep, and 105 pigs,[11] suggest that farming remained primarily pastoral. In the earlier 20th century most of the land was worked in farms of 100–200 a. In 1910 a farm of 308 a., called Godwins, worked from the village, may have included land formerly in Cleeve farm, the buildings of which had been removed, but by 1927 it had been divided into smaller holdings. In 1910 Parsloe's farm and Manor farm were also worked from the village, Angrove farm and Bottom farm from outside it.[12] Then, as later in the century, dairying and sheep farming predominated. Cattle reared for beef replaced some dairy herds in the late 1970s.[13]

There was a brickworks at the west end of Rodbourne village in 1839. Then and in 1848 Richard Tanner made bricks and tiles there. In 1867 George Tanner also produced pipes, and in 1911 Robert Tanner made bricks and tiles, burned lime, perhaps on the same site, and owned a quarry. In the 1930s he also produced small bricks for fireplaces.[14] The brickworks was closed c. 1940.[15]

LOCAL GOVERNMENT. Views of frankpledge and courts for Rodbourne manor were held in May or June and in December in the

7 W.R.O. 130/76, survey, 1719–20.
8 Ibid. tithe award.
9 Greenwood, *Map of Wilts.*
10 W.R.O., tithe award.
11 P.R.O., MAF 68/73, sheet 12.
12 *Kelly's Dir. Wilts.* (1911); W.R.O., Inland Revenue, val. reg. 9; ibid. G 7/515/9.
13 Inf. from Mrs. Parfitt.
14 *Kelly's Dir. Wilts.* (1848 and later edns.); W.R.O., tithe award.
15 Inf. from Mrs. S. Verity, Old Sch.

years 1544–6. Jurors presented public nuisances, such as the disrepair of a lane and a road, and the arrival of stray animals, and the homage presented the death of copyholders. A tithingman and a reeve were elected.[16]

Between 1559 and 1573 views and courts for Rodbourne were recorded with those for Burton Hill manor. From 1569 to 1572 a single view was held for both and the tithingman of Rodbourne presented. Separate courts baron were held for Rodbourne at which the homage presented and the tithingman was elected.[17]

Rodbourne did not relieve its own poor, but like Corston had its own overseer in the later 18th century and early 19th. Regular relief was received by five people in Rodbourne in 1760–1 and 1770–1. The cost was £16 in 1760–1 when a further £10 was spent on occasional relief; in 1780–1 a total of £21 was spent.[18]

CHURCH. Rodbourne church was built or replaced in the 12th century,[19] and, until a vicarage of Malmesbury was ordained between 1191 and the mid 13th century, may have been served from Malmesbury abbey.[20] Inhabitants may have had right of burial, as those of Corston had,[21] but marriages probably took place in the mother church until 1873 when Rodbourne chapel was licensed for their performance.[22] The institutional history of the church from 1881, and aspects of the earlier life of the church, are described with those of Corston.[23]

In the late 18th century and the early 19th services were held in Rodbourne church on alternate Sunday afternoons.[24] On Census Sunday in 1851 an afternoon service was attended by 80 adults, a congregation which was said to be larger than usual.[25]

The church of the *HOLY ROOD*, so called in 1763,[26] is built of stone rubble with ashlar dressings and has a chancel and a nave with

16 W.R.O. 88/2/6.
17 Ibid. 88/2/13; 88/2/29; above, Malmesbury, local govt. (manorial govt.).
18 W.R.O. 1589/33.
19 Below.
20 Above, Malmesbury, churches.
21 Ibid. Corston, church.
22 Bristol R.O., EP/A/23/8.
23 Above, Corston, church.
24 *Vis. Queries, 1783* (W.R.S. xxvii), p. 150; Ch. Com. file, NB 5/116B.
25 P.R.O., HO 129/252/1/19/26.
26 Ecton, *Thesaurus*, 404.

south porch, baptistry, and tower. The narrow nave is 12th-century and has two windows and two doorways of that date. Each doorway has a tympanum, the south carved with the tree of life, the north with a cross. Because it is small and almost square the chancel may also be 12th-century but otherwise its earliest feature is the late 13th-century east window. The chancel piscina is 14th-century and new windows were made in the south and west wall of the nave and the south wall of the chancel in the 15th century. The porch is of the later 15th century or the earlier 16th. The chancel was refitted in 1849, when a window in 14th-century style was made in its north wall. The tower and the baptistry which joins it to the porch were added in 1862;[27] there may earlier have been a bellcot. In 1865 glass designed by Ford Madox Brown and D. G. Rosetti and made by Morris & Co. was fitted in the east window. Extensive repairs, including the renewal of some roofs and the reflooring of the nave, were made in 1903.[28]

In 1553 a chalice weighing 7 oz. was left in Rodbourne and 2 oz. of plate were taken for the king.[29] Later plate was held jointly with Corston.[30]

A bell of 1654, probably cast at Bristol, hung at Rodbourne in 1987.[31]

NONCONFORMITY. A Quaker from Rodbourne was buried in 1669 and a Quaker family lived there in 1697.[32]

A house at Rodbourne was certified for Independent meetings in 1797.[33] An Independent chapel had been built by 1823 and on Census Sunday in 1851 an afternoon service in it was attended by 50 people.[34] No later reference to the chapel has been found.

EDUCATION. A school built at Rodbourne in 1851[35] was described as picturesque and commodious in 1858 when it had 20–30 pupils.[36] From

27 Wilts. Cuttings, ix. 32.
28 Ch. Guide (1987).
29 Nightingale, Wilts. Plate, 196.
30 Above, Corston, church.
31 Walters, Wilts. Bells, 163–4; inf. from the rector, Great Somerford.
32 W.N. & Q. iv. 26; v. 225.
33 Meeting Ho. Certs. (W.R.S. xl), p. 46.
34 P.R.O., HO 129/252/1/19/27.
35 Date on bldg.
36 Acct. of Wilts. Schs. 32.

1872 or earlier the school was a Church of England school and served both Rodbourne and Corston;[37] it was extended in 1872 and 1893.[38] The number of pupils fell from 82 in 1872[39] to *c.* 65 in 1908; until the 1930s average attendance remained between 50 and 65.[40] The school was closed in 1971.[41] In 1947–8 Rodbourne House was used as a private day and boarding school attended by 42 boys.[42]

37 P.R.O., ED 21/18532.
38 Dates on bldg.
39 P.R.O., ED 21/18532.
40 *Bd. of Educ., List 21, 1910* (H.M.S.O.), 509; *1912,* 553; *1919,* 363; *1922,* 362; *1936,* 426.
41 Inf. from the rector.
42 W.R.O., F 12, corresp. file, Rodbourne Coll.

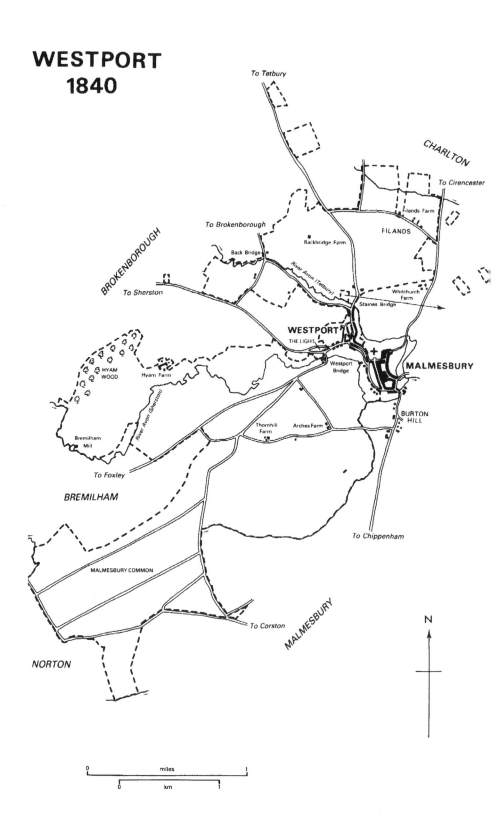

WESTPORT
1840

To Tetbury

CHARLTON

To Cirencester

To Brokenborough

BROKENBOROUGH

Filands Farm

FILANDS

Backbridge Farm

Back Bridge

River Avon (Tetbury)

To Sherston

Whitchurch Farm

Staines Bridge

WESTPORT

THE LIGHT

Westport Bridge

MALMESBURY

HYAM WOOD

Hyam Farm

River Avon (Sherston)

BURTON HILL

Bremilham Mill

Thornhill Farm

Arches Farm

To Foxley

BREMILHAM

To Chippenham

MALMESBURY COMMON

MALMESBURY

To Corston

N

NORTON

WESTPORT

WESTPORT was a separate settlement linked to Malmesbury by a short stretch of road along a narrow ridge and, as its name implies, it lay outside the west gate of Malmesbury.[16] It had a church in the late Saxon period, and later both Brokenborough and Charlton churches were dependent on Westport church.[17] Nearly all the land around the town of Malmesbury belonged to Malmesbury abbey, possibly from soon after its foundation in the 7th century, and, perhaps before the Conquest when St. Paul's church in Malmesbury may have been standing,[18] the abbey assigned some of the land to Westport church as a parish. Apart from Brokenborough and Charlton, the parish had an irregular shape almost like a figure 8 with the church and main settlement in the centre: it comprised land north, west, and south-west of the town and included the hamlets or farmsteads called Filands and Thornhill and possibly a hamlet called Walcot.[19] As a suburb of Malmesbury, part of the settlement called Westport was within the boundary of Malmesbury borough. The land owned by the borough, in the early 17th century called King's Heath, was added to Westport parish and extended the parish south-westwards: most of King's Heath, the south-west part, was later called Malmesbury common.[20] In 1840 the parish was 2,036 a. (824 ha.). For reasons suggested elsewhere much of the parish boundary was irregular and six small areas, mainly embraced by Malmesbury and Brokenborough parishes, were detached.[21] The Westport parish boundary followed a tributary of the Sherston branch of the Bristol Avon south of Malmesbury, both the Sherston Avon and the Tetbury branch of the Avon west of

16 This article was written in 1989. Maps used include O.S. Maps 1/50,000, sheet 173 (1974 edn.); 1/25,000, ST 98 (1959 edn.); 6", Wilts. VIII, XIII (1888–9 and later edns.).
17 Below, church.
18 Above, Malmesbury, introduction, manors.
19 W.R.O., tithe award; above, Malmesbury, introduction.
20 Below, manors; econ. hist.
21 W.R.O., tithe award; above, Malmesbury, introduction.

Malmesbury, and short stretches of road in several places. For a short distance the boundary was the town wall of Malmesbury. For most of its length, however, the parish boundary was not marked by prominent features, and to the west that with Brokenborough through Hyam park was defined only in 1838.[22]

Parts of Malmesbury common, a total of 16 a. belonging to the lord of Foxley manor and the rector of Foxley, were claimed by both Westport and Foxley c. 1840[23] and were in Foxley in 1885. Between 1840 and 1884 c. 13 a. in various fields north and north-west of the town were transferred from Westport to Brokenborough. Between 1882 and 1884 one of the detached areas of Westport was transferred to Brokenborough and five were transferred to Malmesbury, small exchanges were made between Westport and Malmesbury, and a detached part of Bremilham parish, 8 a. near the town, was transferred to Westport.[24] Most of the settlement was assigned to Malmesbury urban sanitary district when it was created in 1872 and was included in Malmesbury municipal borough in 1886.[25] The remainder of the parish, 1,961 a. (794 ha.), was added to St. Paul Malmesbury Without parish in 1896. In 1894 the Westport part of the municipal borough became the civil parish of Westport St. Mary Within. It absorbed the civil parish of Brokenborough Within in 1897 and thereafter measured 91 a. (37 ha.).[26] In 1934 it was merged with the other civil parishes of the borough to form a new Malmesbury parish. Lands west and north of the town and formerly in Westport parish were added to Malmesbury in 1984.[27]

Kellaways Clay outcrops over most of the former parish, especially in the south-west where Malmesbury common is flat and mostly below 80 m. Higher land lies at 91 m. in the north-east, where two areas of Oxford Clay outcrop, and in the west. Much of those areas of the parish was for long pasture. Both branches of the Avon and the south-east boundary stream have exposed terraces of Cornbrash and strips of clay of the Forest Marble: the Cornbrash favours tillage and limestone has been taken from quarries through the clay. Sand and gravel have been

22 W.R.O. 88/10/14.
23 Ibid. tithe award; Foxley tithe award.
24 Ibid. tithe award; *Census*, 1891; O.S. Maps 6", Wilts, VIII, XIII (1888–9 edns.).
25 Above, Malmesbury, introduction.
26 *Census*, 1891; 1901.
27 Above, Malmesbury, introduction; inf. from Chief Assistant (Environment), Dept. of Planning and Highways, Co. Hall, Trowbridge.

deposited in a small area near the northern boundary. The only steep slope in the parish is in the centre where the land rises from the rivers to the town wall. In the west Hyam wood, east of which was a park, was the only woodland.[28]

Two main roads from Malmesbury crossed Westport parish, that north to Tetbury (Glos.) and Gloucester and that west to Bristol via Sherston. Both were turnpiked in 1756.[29] Only a short stretch of the Sherston road, in the suburb of Westport, lay within the parish; it ran along part of the parish boundary further west, as did the Malmesbury–Cirencester road north-east of the town. The Tetbury road was disturnpiked in 1874, the Sherston road in 1876.[30] From the Sherston road a road ran north to Brokenborough, crossing the Tetbury Avon by Back bridge, apparently so called in 1478.[31] The settlements of Westport and Brokenborough were linked by a road which apparently forded the Tetbury Avon *c.* 500 m. north-west of the west gate:[32] by 1820 a new stretch of road had been made on the south bank and joined the road over Back bridge.[33] A road through Filands in use in 1773 carried much of the Chippenham–Tetbury traffic after an eastern bypass was built around Malmesbury in 1973.[34]

Before the Sherston road was turnpiked the main Malmesbury–Bristol road, part of an Oxford–Bristol road in the later 17th century, led through the south part of the parish towards Foxley: near Westport it crossed the Sherston Avon by a bridge, known in the Middle Ages as Turketyl and later as Westport bridge, and 400 m. south-west of the bridge a road diverged to Malmesbury common and Corston.[35] Both roads were in use in the late 20th century, when that to Corston was called Common Road. Lanes between Common Road and Burton Hill in Malmesbury, in use in the late 18th century, were not public roads in the late 20th. Others, across Malmesbury common, were replaced in 1832 by straight tracks, running north-east and south-west,[36] which were still in use in 1989.

28 Geol. Surv. map 1", solid and drift, sheet 251 (1970 edn.); below, econ. hist.
29 *Andrews and Dury, Map* (W.R.S. viii), pls. 13, 16; *L.J.* xxviii. 581.
30 *V.C.H. Wilts.* iv. 269, 271; 36 & 37 Vic. c. 90.
31 W.R.O. 88/1/16.
32 *Andrews and Dury, Map* (W.R.S. viii), pl. 16.
33 C. Greenwood, *Map of Wilts.* (1820).
34 *Andrews and Dury, Map* (W.R.S. viii), pl. 16; above, Malmesbury, introduction.
35 J. Ogilby, *Brit.* (1675), pl. 79; *Reg. Malm.* ii, p. xxxiii.
36 *Andrews and Dury, Map* (W.R.S. viii), pls. 13, 16; W.R.O., EA/142.

The suburb of Westport was the main settlement in the parish. Filands and Thornhill, hamlets in the Middle Ages, had each dwindled to one or two farmsteads by the late 18th century.[37] In 1801 the population of the parish was 702. It had risen to 1,023 by 1821 and continued to rise, with some fluctuations, until 1881, when it was 1,867. Although land and houses in Bremilham were added to Westport in the 1880s others were lost to Brokenborough, and by 1891, the last date for which a figure for the whole parish is available, the population had dropped to 1,669.[38]

Settlement had presumably extended from Malmesbury into the suburb of Westport by the late Saxon period.[39] Westport, so called in 1135,[40] is at the town's north-western corner and linked to it along the ridge by Abbey Row. Buildings on the west side of the town along lanes called Burnivale and King's Wall, between the town walls and the Sherston Avon, were also in Westport parish. In the 19th century the suburb comprised approximately a third of the borough's total area.[41] A guildhall stood in Westport c. 1200[42] and from the later 13th century until the 16th the parts of the borough in the two parishes were distinguished as Westport and Bynport.[43]

Most buildings of Westport were in King's Wall and Burnivale, in Abbey Row, in the Sherston and Tetbury roads leading respectively west and north from Abbey Row, and in the angle between the roads. In the late Saxon period the church was north of the Sherston road near what was until the 19th century the western edge of the settlement.[44] By the later 12th century the parish church had been built west of the Tetbury road, there later called Gloucester Road.[45] An open space south of the church, known from the 19th century as the Triangle, and another north-west of the church, called Horsefair from the 17th century, were presumably market places. A market for Malmesbury to be held in Westport was granted in 1252 and later markets and fairs were apparently

37 Below.
38 V.C.H. Wilts. iv. 360; above, Brokenborough, introduction.
39 Above.
40 Reg. Malm. i. 342.
41 Above, Malmesbury, introduction; Soc. Antiq. MS. 817, ix, f. 1.
42 Bradenstoke Cart. (W.R.S. xxxv), p. 76.
43 Above, Malmesbury, introduction.
44 J. M. Moffatt, Hist. Malm. 101.
45 Below, church.

held there.[46] From Horsefair a lane, called Mill Street in the late 18th century[47] and later West Street, ran south to the Sherston road, there called Bristol Street. Another, called St. Mary's Street, linked Horsefair to the Triangle. West Street and the Triangle were linked by Katifer Lane. In the late 17th century the buildings of Westport were probably clustered around those streets.[48] Early building in Burnivale and King's Wall included a chapel[49] and Postern Mill.[50]

Early 19th-century cottages in West Street

Probably in 1643, when there were both royalist and parliamentary attacks on Malmesbury, Westport suffered considerable damage, including the destruction of the parish church. Later 17th-century buildings to survive include the Three Cups in the Triangle and several cottages in Horsefair and Gloucester Road. In King's Wall a large house was built *c.* 1700,[51] and no. 22 Horsefair bears the date 1703. In the late 18th century

46 Above, Malmesbury, trade and ind. (mkts. and fairs).
47 Moffatt, *Hist. Malm.* 101. Westport's streets are named on the map above, p. 10.
48 Aubrey, *Topog. Coll.* ed. Jackson, pl. xxv.
49 Below, church.
50 Above, Malmesbury, trade and ind. (mills).
51 Ibid. Malmesbury, introduction.

lanes, later called Foundry Road and Harper's Lane, led respectively north from Horsefair to Gloucester Road and south-west from Bristol Street towards Westport bridge. By then settlement had spread north in Gloucester Road to Staines bridge and west in Bristol Street to the fork of the Foxley and Sherston roads.[52] In the late 18th century and the early 19th much of Westport was rebuilt.[53] A nonconformist chapel was built in Horsefair in 1788[54] and a double-fronted house of three storeys north of Abbey Row bears the date 1798, but most new building was of terraces of two-storeyed cottages with fronts of stone rubble.[55] A medieval range of building west of the church in St. Mary's Street, standing in 1809,[56] was apparently replaced soon afterwards. The increase in the population of Westport parish in the early 19th century[57] presumably resulted from new building in the suburb. There were c. 300 houses there in 1831;[58] most were apparently small, and in the 1840s it was reported that only one was occupied by a member of the professional classes.[59]

Another increase in population in the 1860s was ascribed to the sale of land and the building of new houses.[60] Some may have been built in Gastons Road, leading north from Bristol Street, where there were already a few houses in 1845,[61] and some in Burnham Road, which linked Gastons Road and Horsefair. Commercial and institutional building also took place in the later 19th century. A chapel was built in Bristol Street in 1856, a foundry was opened in Foundry Road c. 1870, and warehouses at the northern end of Gloucester Road and a hotel near Staines bridge may have been built in the 1870s.[62] Two large houses, Stainesbridge House and Verona House, were built near the bridge in 1871 and 1883 respectively,[63] and Euclid Villas, a pair of very tall Gothic houses south of Abbey Row, are of similar date. Cottages were replaced by new terraces in Bristol Street, where Avon Terrace bears the date

52 *Andrews and Dury, Map* (W.R.S. viii), pl. 16.
53 W.R.O. 212B/4362.
54 Below, nonconf.
55 See illus. on p. 121.
56 J. Buckler, watercolour in W.A.S. Libr., vol. vi. 19; see below, illus. on p. 142.
57 *V.C.H. Wilts.* iv. 360.
58 Soc. Antiq. MS. 817, ix, f. 1v.
59 *Recollections of W. H. E. McKnight,* ed. E. I. Thompson, 121.
60 *V.C.H. Wilts.* iv. 324, 360.
61 W.R.O. 815/27.
62 *Kelly's Dir. Wilts.* (1875, 1885); above, Malmesbury, trade and ind.; below, nonconf.
63 W.R.O. 149/101/2; date on bldg.

1888, and St. Mary's Street, where Mansfield Terrace bears the date 1899. In 1881 the population of the part of Westport which lay within Malmesbury urban sanitary district was 1,711; only 156 people lived elsewhere in the parish.[64]

In the mid 20th century most new building on the west side of Malmesbury was local authority housing in what had been Brokenborough parish. Within the former Westport parish a scattering of residential and industrial buildings grew up beside the Tetbury road, north of Staines bridge where it was called Tetbury Hill, and on the north side of Park Road west of Staines bridge. Two large estates of private houses were built, White Lion Park south-west of Park Road in the 1960s and Reed's Farm east of Tetbury Hill in the 1980s. A garage and light industrial and commercial buildings replaced earlier buildings north of Staines bridge in the 1970s and 1980s.

In 1620 four alehousekeepers were recorded in Westport.[65] One may have kept the Weaver's Arms, mentioned in 1666.[66] The Three Cups and the Castle, both in the Triangle, were open in 1822;[67] the Castle was closed after 1956,[68] the Three Cups was open in 1989. The Suffolk Arms, east of Tetbury Hill, was open in 1875 and 1989. The Bath Arms in Horsefair, the Railway hotel near Staines bridge, and the Plough beside the Sherston road, were opened between 1875 and 1885.[69] The Bath Arms was closed after 1956.[70] The Railway hotel, renamed the Flying Monk, was closed in the 1960s[71] and demolished c. 1980.[72] The Plough was closed in 1970.[73]

Thomas Hobbes (1588–1679), the philosopher, was born in a house near Westport church and received his schooling in Westport and Malmesbury. His father Thomas served Brokenborough church as curate in the early 17th century but lived at Westport: John Aubrey called him 'an ignorant Sir John' and wrongly described him as vicar of Westport.[74]

---

64 V.C.H. Wilts. iv. 353, 360.
65 Early-Stuart Tradesmen (W.R.S. xv), p. 30.
66 W.A.M. xxvi. 403.
67 W.R.O., A 1/326/3.
68 Ibid. G 21/516/4.
69 Kelly's Dir. Wilts. (1875, 1885).
70 W.R.O., G 21/516/4.
71 D. M. Fenton, Malm. Railway, 55.
72 O.S. Map 1/2,500, ST 9287–9387 (1981 edn.).
73 Wilts. Cuttings, xxiii. 300.
74 D.N.B.; Aubrey, Topog. Coll. ed. Jackson, 263–4; A. Rogow, Thomas Hobbes, 23–7.

Filands was probably a hamlet in the late 13th century.[75] It had 17 poll-tax payers in 1377.[76] Orchard Farm, north of the road through the hamlet, is of 17th-century origin, and in 1773 the hamlet consisted of that and another farmstead east of it.[77] Filands Farm was built west of Orchard Farm in Malmesbury parish in the early 19th century, and between 1840 and 1885 a brickworks was built further west.[78] Two houses were built near the Cirencester road in the early 20th century, in the 1930s four pairs of houses were built between Filands Farm and the brickworks, and in the later 20th century the brickworks was replaced by a new farmstead called White Lodge Farm. In 1964 a school was built south-west of White Lodge Farm.[79]

Thornhill, also apparently a hamlet in the 13th century,[80] had 12 poll-tax payers in 1377,[81] and in the Middle Ages Malmesbury abbey had a grange called Thornhill.[82] The farmstead called Archars Farm in 1773[83] may mark the site of Thornhill. It was rebuilt c. 1800 and renamed Thornhill Farm. By 1820 a new Arches Farm had been built east of it,[84] and cottages were built south-west of it beside Common Road in the late 19th century and the early 20th. Halcombe House, a substantial later 19th-century house, was built before 1885 north-east of Thornhill Farm near the junction of the Foxley road and Common Road,[85] and in the later 20th century houses and bungalows were built near the junction and along the north side of the Foxley road.

By 1538 a lodge had been built for the keeper of Hyam wood:[86] it was probably on the site of Hyam Park near the boundary between Westport and Brokenborough. Elsewhere in the parish, Bremilham Mill and a farmhouse called Back Bridge were standing in 1773[87] and survived in 1989. Between 1820 and 1840 a new Backbridge Farm was built

75 *Reg. Malm.* i. 156–7.
76 *V.C.H. Wilts.* iv. 309.
77 *Andrews and Dury, Map* (W.R.S. viii), pl. 16.
78 O.S. Map 6", Wilts. VIII (1889 edn.); W.R.O., tithe award.
79 Above, Malmesbury, educ.
80 *Reg. Malm.* i. 133–4.
81 *V.C.H. Wilts.* iv. 310.
82 P.R.O., E 134/2 Jas. I Mich./19.
83 *Andrews and Dury, Map* (W.R.S. viii), pl. 16.
84 Greenwood, *Map of Wilts.*
85 O.S. Map 6", Wilts. VIII (1889 edn.).
86 W.R.O. 88/1/24.
87 *Andrews and Dury, Map* (W.R.S. viii), pl. 16.

north-east of, and cottages were built south of, Back bridge.[88] A 'smallpox house' stood west of Thornhill Farm apparently in Westport parish in 1773,[89] a fever (isolation) hospital near Back bridge was in use from the 1890s to 1933, and a cemetery for Westport and Malmesbury parishes was opened west of Tetbury Hill in 1884.[90]

MANORS AND OTHER ESTATES. The lands which became Westport parish, like those which became Malmesbury parish, are likely to have been held by Malmesbury abbey from or soon after its foundation in the 7th century.[91] They belonged to the abbey in the early Middle Ages, when they were recorded as part of a large estate called Brokenborough,[92] and the abbey kept them until the Dissolution.[93]

In 1547 the Crown granted lands south-west of Malmesbury as *THORNHILL* manor to Sir William Herbert[94] (cr. earl of Pembroke 1551).[95] By 1551 the estate had passed, presumably by sale, to William Stumpe (d. 1552), who settled it on his wife Catherine for life. Catherine later married William Basely and died in 1556. Thornhill passed to her son William Stumpe,[96] who sold it in 1576 to William Grymer.[97] In 1582 Grymer sold it to John Snell (d. 1587) and Snell's son Thomas,[98] who was later knighted. Sir Thomas (d. 1612) was succeeded by his son Sir Charles, who, probably *c.* 1617 and according to John Aubrey to raise money to provide a ship for Sir Walter Raleigh's last expedition, sold Thornhill to John Langton. In 1625 Langton settled the manor on his son John. By will dated 1660 the younger John's son John may have devised it with Easton Piercy manor in Kington St. Michael to his wife Elizabeth and sister Joan Lewis for 80 years. Either by inheritance or, with Easton Piercy, by release from Elizabeth and Joan, Thornhill passed to John's brother Sir Thomas Langton (d. *c.* 1672), who was succeeded

88 Greenwood, *Map of Wilts.*; W.R.O., tithe award.
89 *Andrews and Dury, Map* (W.R.S. viii), pl. 16.
90 O.S. Map 6", Wilts.VIII (1889 and later edns.); above, Malmesbury, public services.
91 Above, Malmesbury, manors.
92 Ibid. Brokenborough, introduction, manor; *Arch. Jnl.* lxxvii. 42–8.
93 *Valor Eccl.* (Rec. Com.), ii. 119.
94 *Cal. Pat.* 1547–8, 193–4.
95 *Complete Peerage*, x. 406–7.
96 *W.N. & Q.* viii. 392–3, 481–4.
97 *Cal. Pat.* 1575–8, p. 143.
98 Glos. R.O., D 2697/17; P.R.O., C 142/221, no. 122.

in turn by his sons Thomas (d. *c.* 1696) and Robert.[99] In 1704 Robert sold the manor to Thomas Howard, earl of Berkshire (d. 1706).[1] It was conveyed by Joan Billers to William Robins and his wife Anne in 1758,[2] and by George Spackman to John Smith and his wife Elizabeth in 1767.[3] In 1788 the Smiths conveyed it to John Neate.[4] In 1827 it was apparently sold by Stephen Neate, and in 1839 Richard Blackford and Mary Garlick held Thornhill farm, 185 a. The farm was sold in 1869,[5] probably to C. W. Miles (d. 1892). It presumably passed with Miles's Burton Hill House estate in Malmesbury to C. N. Miles and A. C. Miles and was sold in 1919 by T. A. G. Miles. In 1921 Jesse Wootton sold the farm, 173 a.[6] R. S. Smith owned it in 1927 and 1931.[7] G. W. Sisum, the owner in 1939, sold the farm *c.* 1945. As a farm of 100 a. it was bought in 1962 by J. Neate and in 1969 by Mr. D. J. Grange, the owner in 1989.[8]

In the later 18th century there was a farm south-west of Malmesbury called *ARCHARS*.[9] At the Dissolution it is likely to have been granted by the Crown with Burton Hill manor in Malmesbury, which in 1577 was broken up by Adam Archard and Thomas Hall.[10] About 1800, when the farmstead was rebuilt and renamed Thornhill Farm,[11] it apparently belonged to the owner of Thornhill manor. In 1839 Arches farm, 100 a., belonged to Josiah Hanks.[12] With Thornhill farm it belonged to C. N. Miles in 1910, when it measured *c.* 150 a.,[13] and it was presumably sold like Thornhill farm in 1919. In 1927 Arches farm belonged to H. L. Storey[14] (d. 1933). Like Burton Hill House it was bought by the Shaftesbury Society, which sold it in 1948 to Percy Webb

99 *W.A.M.* iv. 45 and pedigrees at pp. 45, 77.
1 *Complete Peerage*, ii. 151; W.R.O. 212A/27/37, deed, Langton to earl of Berks., 1704.
2 P.R.O., CP 25(2)/1235/31 Geo. II Hil.
3 Ibid. CP 25(2)/1445/8 Geo. III Mich.
4 Ibid. CP 25(2)/1447/28 Geo. III East.
5 W.R.O. 374/130/66; ibid. tithe award.
6 Above, Malmesbury, manors; W.A.S. Libr., sale cat. xvii, no. 46.
7 *Kelly's Dir. Wilts.* (1931); W.R.O., G 7/515/9.
8 *Kelly's Dir. Wilts.* (1939); inf. from Mrs. J. D. Grange, Thornhill Farm.
9 *Andrews and Dury, Map* (W.R.S. viii), pl. 16.
10 Above, Malmesbury, manors.
11 Ibid. introduction.
12 W.R.O., tithe award.
13 Ibid. Inland Revenue, val. reg. 9.
14 Ibid. G 7/515/9.

(d. 1985). Webb's sons Mr. Allen Webb and Mr. Roy Webb owned the farm, 180 a., in 1989.[15]

After the Dissolution Malmesbury abbey's land called *HYAM*, later Hyam park and Hyam farm, was part of Brokenborough manor. The manor was granted in 1552 to John Dudley, duke of Northumberland, who sold it in 1553 to Sir James Stumpe. It passed to Sir Henry Knyvett and in the Howard family with the earldoms of Suffolk and Berkshire.[16] In 1839 Hyam farm included c. 240 a. in Westport parish.[17] It was sold by an earl of Suffolk after 1912,[18] and was bought in 1927 by T. L. Horn, who sold it in 1939 to his sister-in-law Ursula and her husband G. G. Cox Cox. In 1988 Mrs. Cox Cox owned Hyam farm which then included c. 150 a. of the former parish of Westport.[19] Hyam Park was built in the 17th century as a long north–south range with a main east front. In the 18th century a short west wing was added at the south end to make a new symmetrical south front, in 1922 a west wing was added at the north end, and in 1927 the south wing and south front were extended and other alterations were made to the house. Also in the 1920s a large cattle yard west of the house, bounded on the west by a stone barn probably of the 18th century, was made into gardens. Extensive 20th-century farm buildings are further west.

An estate called *FILANDS* was held in 1183–4 and in 1195 by Walter Mautravers (d. before 1201), presumably by knight service of Malmesbury abbey; it passed to his brother John (d. 1220),[20] and by 1248 may have reverted to the abbey.[21] In 1535 the abbey held lands in Westport formerly Mautravers's,[22] but after the Dissolution no separate estate was called Filands.

The land of Filands is likely to have been granted after the Dissolution as part of Whitchurch and Milbourne manor in Malmesbury, which included land in the north-east part of Westport parish. In 1782 William and Thomas Robins conveyed 42 a., formerly part of that manor, to John Jefferies, who devised them to Jane Coles. In 1820 she sold the

15 Above, Malmesbury, manors; inf. from Mr. A. Webb, Arches Farm.
16 Above, Brokenborough, manor.
17 W.R.O., tithe award.
18 Ibid. G 7/500/1.
19 Inf. from Mrs. U. Cox Cox, Hyam.
20 *Cur. Reg. R.* x. 17; *Pipe R.* 1195 (P.R.S. N.S. vi), 46; above, Great Somerford, manors.
21 *Reg. Malm.* i. 411–12.
22 *Valor Eccl.* (Rec. Com.), ii. 121.

land to Thomas Howard, Viscount Andover, later earl of Suffolk and of Berkshire,[23] and it was reunited with Whitchurch and Milbourne manor. Much of that manor descended with the Suffolk title and in 1989 belonged to Michael Howard, earl of Suffolk and of Berkshire,[24] but it is not clear whether the 42 a. were part of it. Another part of Whitchurch and Milbourne manor apparently passed with Whitchurch farm to Richard Kinneir, who in 1839 held 116 a. in Westport. That land passed with the farm to members of the Elwell family[25] who held 76 a. in Westport in 1927,[26] and to Mr. Edward Weaver, owner of Whychurch farm in 1989.[27]

In the Middle Ages the Crown held Malmesbury borough, including the part in Westport parish, and from 1215 to the Dissolution Malmesbury abbey held it in fee farm. The Westport part of the borough and the land adjoining it was from 1628 part of Malmesbury manor, sometimes called Malmesbury and Westport manor.[28] In 1839 the manor, then held by the Revd. George Rushout-Bowles, included c. 35 a. in Westport.[29] The lands passed to Elizabeth, Baroness Northwick (d. 1912), who in 1896 sold the reversion in lots.[30]

Malmesbury borough, which enjoyed certain privileges in or before the 11th century, may also have held lands; more land may have been granted by Malmesbury abbey after it became fee farmer of the borough in 1215,[31] and in the mid 13th century the guild merchant of Malmesbury received heath land south-west of the town from the abbey in an exchange.[32] The borough charter of 1381 ascribed a grant of 5 hides of heath near Norton, south-west of the town, to King Athelstan:[33] the charter clearly indicates that in 1381 the borough owned *KING'S HEATH*, but the claim that it had been given by Athelstan is implausible. In 1839 Malmesbury corporation owned Malmesbury common, 522 a., and c. 200 a. east and north-east of it.[34] In 1989 the burgesses and freemen

23 *Complete Peerage,* xii (1), 479–80; W.R.O. 88/5/18.
24 Above, Malmesbury, manors.
25 Ibid.; W.R.O., tithe award.
26 W.R.O., G 7/515/9.
27 Above, Malmesbury, manors.
28 Ibid.; P.R.O., PROB 11/1609, f. 232.
29 W.R.O., tithe award.
30 Ibid. 622/1; above, Malmesbury, manors.
31 Above, Malmesbury, manors, local govt. (boro. govt.).
32 *Reg. Malm.* ii. 150–60.
33 *Cal. Pat.* 1381–5, 54; above, Malmesbury, local govt. (boro. govt.).
34 W.R.O., tithe award.

of Malmesbury held a total of 718 a., of which *c.* 670 a. had been in Westport parish.[35]

In the 13th century Robert of Lea held 1 hide, apparently what later became *BACKBRIDGE* farm but then said to be in Thornhill.[36] The land probably passed with Lea manor in Lea and Cleverton parish until the later 16th century and with Boakley farm in Brokenborough until the early 19th.[37] In 1340 Sir John Mauduit and his wife Agnes conveyed 88 a. in Thornhill with Lea manor to their son-in-law John Moleyns.[38] The estate passed to Moleyns's son Sir William (d. 1381), who held it in 1370,[39] and probably thereafter in the Moleyns and Hungerford families and to members of the Hastings family, earls of Huntingdon. An earl of Huntingdon held an estate in Westport in the mid 16th century, part of which was sold in 1571 with Boakley farm by Henry Hastings, earl of Huntingdon, to Anthony Webb and in 1593 by Webb to William Bailey.[40] At his death in 1621 William held lands in Westport,[41] presumably the *c.* 130 a. held by his great-grandson Anthony Bailey (fl. 1655). As at Boakley farm, later owners were Giles Bailey, Daniel Bennett, Daniel's son Giles, and Giles Bailey Bennett. In 1822 Daniel's grandson Daniel Bennett sold Backbridge farm to Thomas Howard, earl of Suffolk and of Berkshire.[42] It passed with the earldoms to Henry, earl of Suffolk and of Berkshire, who owned the farm, 106 a., in 1912.[43] By 1927 it had been sold,[44] and it later had several different owners.

A small estate including Bremilham Mill passed with lands in Foxley from Thomas Bremilham to his son John, to John's son Richard (d. *c.* 1557), and to Richard's grandnephew Thomas Nicholas and great-grandnephew Robert Shipton. Thereafter it apparently passed with Player's farm in Foxley to Henry Vassall, Baron Holland,[45] who in 1839 held *c.* 70 a. and the mill in Westport parish.[46] The estate passed with

35 Inf. from the clerk to the burgesses and freemen, 1 Market Lane, Malmesbury.
36 *Reg. Malm.* i. 247.
37 Above, Brokenborough, manor; Lea and Cleverton, manors.
38 *Feet of F* 1327–77 (W.R.S. xxix), pp. 62–4.
39 *Cal. Close,* 1369–74, 175.
40 P.R.O., C 2/Eliz. I/E 4/68; above, Brokenborough, manor.
41 P.R.O., C 142/415, no. 89.
42 W.R.O. 88/5/24; above, Brokenborough, manor.
43 W.R.O., G 7/500/1.
44 Ibid. G 7/515/9.
45 P.R.O., C 3/167/52; ibid. CP 25(2)/81/695, no. 21; above, Foxley, manor.
46 W.R.O., tithe award.

Foxley manor to Maj. A. R. Turnor whose son Mr. R. W. C. Turnor owned the mill and 54 a. in 1989.[47]

Humphrey Bridges (d. 1598) and his son Humphrey held jointly an estate in Westport and adjacent parishes.[48] At the younger Humphrey's death in 1609 it comprised c. 100 a. and rights of common pasture. He was succeeded by his brother Anthony[49] (d. 1617), whose heirs were his sisters Elizabeth, wife of Robert Bridges, Margaret, wife of John Breath, and Jane, wife of Richard Stevens, and his nephew Anthony Bridges.[50] The later history of the estate has not been traced.

The endowment of a chantry, founded in Westport church by 1478,[51] included c. 70 a. in Westport.[52] In 1564 the lands were conveyed by Henry Knyvett and his wife Elizabeth to Matthew King.[53] In 1569 they were successfully claimed by Thomas Estcourt,[54] who in 1571 sold them to John Stumpe[55] (d. 1600). Stumpe was succeeded by his son James, who at his death in 1602 held c. 140 a. in Westport and other parishes and was succeeded by his son William.[56] No later record of the Westport part of that estate has been found.

Rents from Westport were given to Bradenstoke priory by Henry le Bret in 1232 and by Andrew son of John of Malmesbury in the later 13th century, and in the mid 13th century the priory held other land there.[57] In 1535 the priory received rents totalling 13s. 4d. from Westport.[58]

Malmesbury abbey was licensed to appropriate Westport church between 1159 and 1181; the licence was apparently confirmed in 1191.[59] Thereafter the abbey owned the RECTORY estate until the Dissolution,[60] and afterwards most rectorial tithes probably passed with the estates from which they were derived. In the later 16th century rectorial tithes from Thornhill were apparently leased by the Crown

47 Above, Foxley, manor; inf. from Maj. A. R. Turnor, Foxley Manor.
48 P.R.O., C 142/281, no. 82.
49 Ibid. C 142/310, no. 90.
50 Ibid. C 142/371, no. 102.
51 W.R.O. 88/1/16.
52 P.R.O., E 301/58, no. 36.
53 *Cal. Pat.* 1563–6, p. 135.
54 P.R.O., C 3/58/7.
55 *Cal. Pat.* 1575–8, p. 502.
56 *W.N. & Q.* viii. 533–4.
57 *Bradenstoke Cart.* (W.R.S. xxxv), pp. 76–8; *Cal. Chart. R.* 1226–57, 162.
58 *Valor Eccl.* (Rec. Com.), ii. 123.
59 *Reg. Malm.* i. 369–70, 374–5; below, church.
60 *L. & P. Hen. VIII,* xix (1), p. 649.

with those from Corston.[61] The lessees claimed payment of tithes from
the owner of Thornhill manor, apparently unsuccessfully.[62] Some tithes
from Thornhill did, however, pass with those from Corston to R. H.
Gaby.[63] In 1839 Gaby owned great tithes from 143 a. in Westport, the
earl of Suffolk and of Berkshire those from 89 a., the vicar of Malmesbury
those from 68 a., and the rector of Bremilham those from 10 a.: the
tithes were all commuted in 1840. King's Heath was tithe free, and tithes
from most other lands in the parish were merged.[64]

ECONOMIC HISTORY. Apart from King's Heath, which is treated
separately below, nearly all the agricultural land of the parish was worked
by Malmesbury abbey and its tenants in the Middle Ages. North of the
town inhabitants of Filands may have shared lands with those of
Whitchurch, as south of it those of Thornhill may have done with those
of Burton Hill. To the west the abbey had woods and possibly parkland
called Hyam in demesne.

In the late 13th century the abbey had 14 tenants at Filands and *c.*
12 at Thornhill; all were presumably customary tenants. Of those at
Thornhill, one held 60 a., probably arable in open fields, four others had
similar or greater holdings,[65] and all presumably had rights to common
pasture. In the late 15th century the abbey had a grange at Thornhill and
held demesne land there, apparently in hand. The land may have been
mainly pasture on which the abbey kept sheep and cattle to supply its
own larder.[66] In the 1530s the demesne, including arable in the open
fields and *c.* 50 a. of several pasture and meadow, was leased, perhaps as a
single holding.[67] In 1539–40 seven tenants shared 18 yardlands; another
held 30 a. of arable and the grange. Works of cutting and gathering hay
in meadows in Westport and Malmesbury parishes had been commuted,[68]
probably much earlier. Woodland and a warren at Hyam were leased
separately in 1538.[69] In 1340 Sir John Mauduit's 88 a. were shared by 5

61 *Cal. Pat.* 1560–3, 330; above, Corston, manor.
62 P.R.O., E 134/2 Jas. I Mich./19.
63 Above, Corston, manor.
64 W.R.O., tithe award.
65 *Reg. Malm.* i. 130–3, 156–7; ii. 386–7.
66 P.R.O., E 134/2 Jas. I Mich./19.
67 Ibid. SC 6/Hen. VIII/3986, rot. 115; *Valor Eccl.* (Rec. Com.), ii. 120.
68 P.R.O., SC 6/Hen. VIII/3986, rot. 115.
69 W.R.O. 88/1/24.

tenants; the largest holding was of 60 a. of arable and 3 a. of meadow.[70] Of Westport chantry's *c.* 70 a., a single tenant held 63 a. in the open fields in 1548.[71]

In the mid 16th century *c.* 40 a. of Westport parish north of Malmesbury were part of Whitchurch marsh, a common pasture presumably used mainly by the men of Whitchurch. South of Malmesbury, Kemboro field, partly in Malmesbury parish, was worked by tenants of both Burton Hill and Thornhill manors. Thornhill manor also included Quarry field, south of the Sherston branch of the Avon, and Brokenborough field, perhaps north of the river. Its common pasture, part of Awls or Alice heath, was probably to the south beside the parish boundary. Between the mid 16th century and the 19th both arable and pasture were inclosed, apparently piecemeal, and the number of farms was reduced. The Thornhill part of Alice heath had been inclosed by the mid 16th century[72] and the latest reference to open-field cultivation in Westport dates from 1628.[73] Except for part of King's Heath, lands in the north half of the parish may have been the last to be inclosed. The Westport part of Whitchurch marsh was not mentioned when the Malmesbury part was inclosed in 1792 under an Act of 1790 and had almost certainly been inclosed earlier.[74] Common pasture or open field between the suburb of Westport and Brokenborough village is likely to have been inclosed long before 1822 when lands of Backbridge farm were called new inclosures.[75] The land of Hyam, which may have been a park in the Middle Ages, is known to have been one in the 16th century,[76] and in 1649 comprised 201 a. in Westport and Brokenborough parishes.[77] The park had been extended to *c.* 400 a., half in each parish, by *c.* 1785.[78]

In the early 19th century most of the parish was worked in small farms with a high proportion of pasture. In 1839 *c.* 750 a. were in farms of *c.* 70 a. or more. Hyam farm, 441 a. including 201 a. in Westport, was

70 *Feet of F.* 1327–77 (W.R.S. xxix), pp. 62–4.
71 P.R.O., E 301/58, no. 36.
72 Ibid. SC 6/Hen.VIII/3986, rott. 113–14; W.R.O., tithe award; above, Malmesbury, agric.
73 *Wilts. Inq. p.m.* 1625–49 (Index Libr.), 72–3.
74 W.R.O., EA/34.
75 Ibid. 88/5/24.
76 Above, Brokenborough, econ. hist.
77 *Cal. Cttee. for Compounding,* iii. 1969.
78 W.R.O. 88/5/46/4.

worked from the farmstead on the boundary of Brokenborough and Westport, and 116 a. in the north of the parish were worked from Whitchurch Farm in Malmesbury with lands in that parish. Thornhill farm was 160 a., Arches and Backbridge farms were each *c.* 100 a., and the farm attached to Bremilham Mill was 69 a. Of the remaining lands, *c.* 700 a. were in farms of 20–50 a. each and some were in smaller farms. Most of the farms of less than 50 a. had land near Malmesbury and were presumably worked as smallholdings from within the town or the suburb of Westport. Hyam wood was then 40 a.[79]

The pattern of farming in the parish had apparently changed little by the early 20th century. A market garden on 6 a. beside Tetbury Hill in 1910[80] had expanded to occupy 11 a. by 1927.[81] In the 1930s most of the agricultural land of the former parish was still pasture although some south of the town was arable.[82] In the 1980s sheep and beef cattle were reared on Hyam farm, Arches was an intensive dairy farm, and the lands of Thornhill farm were permanent pasture;[83] factories were built on part of Backbridge farm.

In the south-west part of the parish the names of Cooks heath, Portmans heath, Alice heath, and Great heath suggest that most of the land was pasture, but in the mid 13th century Cooks heath and other lands were cultivated. Except for part of Alice heath, which was used by the men of Thornhill, from the mid 13th century nearly all that land belonged to the borough of Malmesbury:[84] it was later called King's Heath, and from the 18th century the low lying and badly drained south-west part of it was called Malmesbury common.[85] There is no evidence that either pasture or arable was inclosed in the Middle Ages. In the late 14th century rights to feed animals on and to cultivate the land apparently belonged to members of the guild merchant of Malmesbury and to members of other privileged groups in the borough, but the details of how they used the land are obscure.[86] By *c.* 1570 lands near the town

79 Ibid. tithe award.
80 Ibid. Inland Revenue, val. reg. 9.
81 Ibid. G 7/515/9.
82 [1st] Land Util. Surv. Map, sheet 103.
83 Inf. from Mr. A. Webb, Arches Farm; Mrs. U. Cox Cox, Hyam; Mrs. J. D. Grange, Thornhill Farm.
84 *Reg. Malm.* ii. 150–4.
85 B.L. Maps, M.T. 6e., 1 (2).
86 Above, Malmesbury, local govt. (boro. govt.).

had been inclosed and allotted, *c.* 1570 Cooks heath was similarly dealt with,[87] and in 1607 there were *c.* 100 a. in closes.[88] By 1610 more closes had been allotted[89] but most of the land was still subject to common grazing rights. In the early 19th century *c.* 210 a. were several and holdings varied from 1 a. to 15 a.[90] Closes were frequently broken in the late 16th century and the early 17th:[91] it is not clear how far the objection was to inclosure and how far the result of disputes about how the borough should be governed.[92]

Use of King's Heath was regulated by the borough court. Orders were made in 1620 for stinting on Hundred hill, and in the 1650s forbidding commoners to feed cattle not their own on the common pasture. In 1686 regulations for marking beasts and cutting gorse were issued and in 1691 it was agreed that winter grazing on the common pasture should be leased to the highest bidder. In 1669 a fine imposed on a capital burgess for ploughing his close was remitted because the change of use was to the general good. Under the terms of the borough charter of 1685 the alderman and 12 capital burgesses granted their closes on 21-year leases. The lessees improved the land by burnbaking and presumably brought them into cultivation and, when the leases were revoked under a charter restored in 1690, claimed compensation for the sums spent on improvement. In 1714 the borough court ruled that it was lawful for any close to be ploughed and sown providing it had been burned; there was to be a rotation of three crops, with clover sown in the fourth year.[93]

In 1760 and presumably earlier inhabitants of Foxley parish had the right to feed cattle on a small area of Malmesbury common near Foxley village.[94] In the early 19th century the common, described as a deplorable scene of waste and desolation, was overgrown with furze and gorse and so badly drained that it was impassable in bad weather.[95] Under an Act of 1821 *c.* 500 a. were inclosed and drained in 1832. All but 20 a.

87 P.R.O., E 134/9 Chas. I Mich./75.
88 Ibid. STAC 8/130/3.
89 Ibid. STAC 8/290/22.
90 *Rep. Com. Mun. Corp.* [C. 2490–1], p. 73, H.C. (1880), xxxi.
91 P.R.O., STAC 8/130/3; STAC 8/290/22.
92 Above, Malmesbury, local govt. (boro. govt.).
93 Hist. MSS. Com. 24, *12th Rep. VI, Ho. of Lords*, pp. 432–3; Malmesbury boro. rec., ct. bk. 1600–1721.
94 B.L. Maps, M.T. 6e., 1 (2).
95 *W.A.M.* li. 151–2.

were allotted either to Malmesbury corporation, presumably to be added to the holdings of those who already had some inclosed land, or to the trustees of King's Heath, who were drawn from the corporation and regulated the commoners' lands. The allotments to the corporation and trustees were divided into 280 holdings of between 1 a. and 3 a. each. The remainder was allotted to neighbouring landowners who had grazing rights on the common, including 15 a. to Henry Vassall, Baron Holland, lord of Foxley manor.[96] Thereafter part of what was still known as Malmesbury common was cultivated. In 1886 only 30 a. were pasture; the main crops were wheat, grown on 82 a., and potatoes, grown on 126 a. Stubble was still grazed in common, and 150–200 pigs were usually kept on the allotments between 1886 and 1906. By 1930, however, much of the land had passed out of use. Few commoners took up their rights to cultivate land themselves and much of the common was managed by the trustees, who let part of it to neighbouring farmers. During the Second World War the common was again drained and part was again ploughed.[97] In 1989 both Malmesbury common and the older inclosures, c. 700 a. in all, were let to neighbouring farmers.[98]

MILLS. In the 13th century Robert of Lea held a mill in Westport.[99] Postern Mill on the river below King's Wall was on a site used for a mill from the 12th century or the 13th.[1]

Bremilham Mill was probably standing in the 1550s and may have been on the site of a much earlier mill.[2] In the later 19th century it was apparently the site of a considerable business, but milling ceased there between 1885 and 1899. In 1925 the wheel raised water for domestic use.[3] The mill and its outbuildings were demolished after 1945.[4] The mill house, a 17th-century stone building of one storey with attics, was standing in 1989, and the mill wheel was *in situ*. Another mill in the parish may have stood near Back bridge.[5]

96 W.R.O., EA/142.
97 *Country Life*, 22 Mar. 1941; Wilts. Cuttings, xi. 172; P.R.O., MAF 68/1063, sheet 2; MAF 68/2203, sheet 14.
98 Inf. from the clerk to the burgesses and freemen, 1 Market Lane, Malmesbury.
99 *Reg. Malm.* i. 247.
1 Above, Malmesbury, trade and ind. (mills).
2 P.R.O., CP 25(2)/81/695, no. 21; above, Brokenborough, econ. hist.
3 Wilts. Cuttings, vi. 127; O.S. Maps 6", Wilts. VIII (1889 edn.), VIII. SW. (1900 edn.).
4 Inf. from Lt.-Col. J. H. Pitman, Foxley Ho., Norton.
5 Above, Brokenborough, econ. hist.

TRADE AND INDUSTRY. Stone quarrying and iron working may have taken place on the site of Postern Mill in the late Saxon period and there may have been a tannery near the mill in the later Middle Ages.[6] A tanner lived in Westport in 1729[7] and others are recorded there later in the 18th century.[8] A tanyard near Back bridge in 1798[9] was probably that between Park Road and the Sherston road in use in 1823 and 1839.[10] From 1865 the yard was held by members of the Thompson family who until the 1880s had another at the Light, the detached part of Bremilham parish south of the Sherston road. Tanning ceased in Westport between 1895 and 1899.[11]

In the mid 18th century shafts were sunk on Malmesbury common in the hope of finding coal. Only lignite was found[12] but mining rights on the common were still leased in 1812.[13] In 1885 and 1912 there was a brickworks west of Filands; it had closed by 1919. On the western edge of the suburb several quarries were opened after 1885 but were mostly disused in 1924.[14] What was said to be a quarry on Malmesbury common in the 1920s[15] was perhaps a clay pit.

Some businesses associated with the town of Malmesbury were carried on from premises in Westport, and new factories west of Tetbury Hill and small industrial units in Park Road were built in the 1980s.[16]

LOCAL GOVERNMENT. The part of Westport in Malmesbury borough was subject to the borough courts, which also regulated King's Heath. Courts held for Malmesbury manor also had jurisdiction in the parish, chiefly over the suburb of Westport. In the earlier 18th century two constables for Westport were appointed at the borough sessions, and

6 *Medieval Arch.* xxi, p. 167; inf. from Mr. C. K. Currie, 15 Claudeen Close, Swaythling, Southampton.
7 *Wilts. Apprentices* (W.R.S. xvii), p. 58.
8 W.R.O. 212B/3992; 212B/4027.
9 Ibid. 212B/4200.
10 Ibid. 212B/4332; ibid. tithe award.
11 *Harrod's Dir. Wilts.* (1865); *Kelly's Dir. Wilts.* (1875 and later edns.); above, Bremilham, econ. hist.
12 *W.A.M.* ii. 159.
13 W.R.O. 315/27/6.
14 O.S. Map 6", Wilts. VIII (1889 and later edns.); W.R.O., G 7/500/1.
15 Wilts. Cuttings, xi. 172.
16 Above, Malmesbury, trade and ind.

in the later 18th century two constables and two sidesmen were appointed at the manor court.[17]

Malmesbury abbey apparently held separate courts for Thornhill in the earlier 16th century.[18] No record of courts for Thornhill manor has been found.

In 1636 Malmesbury and Westport parishes disputed responsibility for relief of the poor living within the precinct of Malmesbury abbey. Westport was found to be responsible for those living in seven houses,[19] and a small part of the suburb was in Abbey parish which relieved its own poor in the later 18th century and the earlier 19th.[20] In 1648 Westport petitioned to set its own rates as other parishes did, giving as a reason the damage which had been suffered by the parish in military action and from the billeting of soldiers there. The petition may have been prompted by some alteration in the method of assessment following the garrisoning of Malmesbury in 1644; apparently before 1648 and certainly afterwards the parish set its own rates.[21]

In 1775–6 poor relief in Westport cost £125. Expenditure was £452 in 1802 when 53 adults and 90 children received permanent and 25 people occasional relief. The cost and numbers relieved were then approximately half those of Malmesbury parish. In 1813 permanent relief was given to 75 adults and occasional relief to 32; the total cost was £782. Expenditure was lower in the 1820s,[22] and between 1833 and 1835 the average annual cost was £408. In 1835 Westport became part of Malmesbury poor-law union.[23] In the late 18th century a building in Burnivale, which may have been St. Mary's chapel, was said to have long been used as a poorhouse.[24]

CHURCH. The church at Westport before the Conquest[25] may have been served by Malmesbury abbey. A new church had been built by the

17 Malmesbury boro. rec., sessions order bk. 1712–41; W.R.O. 212B/3977; 1165/3.
18 P.R.O., SC 6/Hen. VIII/3986, rot. 114v.
19 Hist. MSS. Com. 55, *Var. Coll.* i, pp. 100–1.
20 Above, Malmesbury, local govt. (par. govt.).
21 Hist. MSS. Com. 55, *Var. Coll.* i, pp.100–1, 116.
22 *Poor Law Abstract, 1804,* 566–7; *1818,* 498–9; *Poor Rate Returns, 1816–21, 189; 1822–4,* 228; *1825–9,* 219.
23 *Poor Law Com. 2nd Rep.* App. D, 559.
24 Moffatt, *Hist. Malm.* 95; below, church.
25 Above, introduction.

later 12th century, and between 1159 and 1181 the abbey was licensed to appropriate it. Until a vicarage was ordained in or before 1286 the abbey presumably served the cure.[26] From the later 13th century or earlier Charlton church and from 1341 or earlier Brokenborough church were dependent chapels of Westport.[27] A united benefice with Malmesbury was formed between 1650 and 1658 but the two were separated after 1660.[28] In 1879 Brokenborough and Charlton were separated from Westport,[29] in 1946 the vicarage was reunited with that of Malmesbury and Westport church converted to a parish hall, and in 1984 Malmesbury with Westport and Brokenborough benefice was formed.[30]

Malmesbury abbey was patron of Westport vicarage. In 1528 Sir Anthony Hungerford presented a vicar by a grant of a turn. From the Dissolution until the late 19th century the Crown usually presented.[31] A presentation by the alderman and burgesses of Malmesbury in 1586 or 1587[32] was probably made by a grant from the Crown, and in 1670 the bishop of Salisbury may have collated a vicar.[33] In 1882 the advowson was transferred by exchange to Charlotte Kemble.[34] It passed with that of Malmesbury vicarage to the Church Trust Fund, patron of the united benefices formed in 1946 and 1984.[35]

Westport vicarage was valued in 1291 at £4 6s. 8d., well below the average for a living in Malmesbury deanery,[36] and at £18 8s. 8d., over twice the average, in 1535;[37] both valuations presumably included income from Brokenborough and Charlton. The vicar's annual income from the three parishes between 1829 and 1831 was c. £312, a little below the average for a Wiltshire living.[38] In 1535 a yearly pension of £1 was payable from the vicarage to Malmesbury abbey;[39] the pension

26 *Reg. Malm.* i. 369–70; ii. 322–3.
27 Above, Brokenborough, church; Charlton, church.
28 Ibid. Malmesbury, churches; *Cal. S.P. Dom.* 1658–9, 220.
29 *Lond. Gaz.* 7 Mar. 1879, pp. 1957–60.
30 Ch. Com. file, NB 5/116B.
31 Phillipps, *Wilts. Inst.* (index in *W.A.M.* xxviii. 225).
32 P.R.O., IND 17004, Wilts. p. 16.
33 Ibid. IND 17007, p. 566; Phillipps, *Wilts. Inst.* ii. 31.
34 *Lond. Gaz.* 7 Mar. 1882, pp. 536–7.
35 Above, Malmesbury, churches.
36 *Tax. Eccl.* (Rec. Com.), 189.
37 *Valor Eccl.* (Rec. Com.), ii. 137.
38 *Rep. Com. Eccl. Revenues,* 852–3.
39 *Valor Eccl.* (Rec. Com.), ii. 137.

apparently passed with the lordship of Malmesbury borough[40] and *c.* 1830 the vicar paid £2 yearly to the lord of Malmesbury manor.[41] In the early 19th century John, earl of Suffolk and of Berkshire, informally augmented the vicarage.[42]

Although in 1341 Malmesbury abbey was said to receive all tithes from Westport,[43] the vicar had apparently been entitled to some in 1286[44] and was so in 1535.[45] He was entitled to small tithes from Brokenborough, Charlton, and Westport, except where the land was tithe free. In Westport, King's Heath may have been tithe free early, and by the early 19th century vicarial tithes from other lands belonging to Malmesbury borough had been compounded.[46] In 1784–5 the vicar successfully disputed other compositions but accepted moduses for what was thought to have been demesne land of Malmesbury abbey including one of £4 for the former Hyam park in Brokenborough and Westport.[47] In 1839 the vicar was entitled to small tithes from *c.* 800 a. in Westport. His tithes from Brokenborough, Charlton, and Westport were valued at £520 and commuted in 1840.[48]

The vicar had land and a house in Charlton, 46 a. in 1839,[49] but apparently neither in Westport or Brokenborough. In 1881–2 a house beside the Swindon road in Malmesbury parish was built for the vicar of Westport,[50] who was then and thereafter also vicar of Malmesbury. That house was sold in 1969.[51]

The small pre-Conquest church, of which the nave survives, stood north of Bristol Street. It was apparently known in the later Middle Ages as St. Helen's, and was presumably converted for other uses after the Dissolution.[52] A hermitage under the wall of Malmesbury borough in which Christine of Somerford was enclosed in 1250[53] may have been

40 *Cal. Pat.* 1563–6, pp. 463–4; above, Malmesbury, manors.
41 *Rep. Com. Eccl. Revenues,* 852–3.
42 Above, Charlton, church.
43 *Inq. Non.* (Rec. Com.), 167.
44 W.R.O. 88/5/46/4.
45 *Valor Eccl.* (Rec. Com.), ii. 137; *W.A.M.* lxxvii. 104.
46 W.R.O., tithe award.
47 Ibid. 88/5/46/4.
48 Ibid. tithe award.
49 Above, Charlton, church.
50 Ch. Com. file, NB 5/116B.
51 Above, Malmesbury, churches.
52 *Cal. Pat.* 1572–5, p. 478.
53 *Close R.* 1247–51, 314.

The Hermitage in Burnivale in 1809

St. Mary's chapel in Burnivale, recorded in the later 13th century[54] and the 16th.[55] A building in Burnivale, ecclesiastical in style and known as the Hermitage, was demolished in the early 19th century.[56] A chantry of St. Mary in Westport church had been endowed by 1478, when it had land in Brokenborough.[57] At its dissolution its total income was £6 9s. 3d., of which £3 18s. was from Westport and Malmesbury. Its priest, a former monk, was described as honest, learned, and able to serve a cure.[58]

In 1303 keeping of the vicarage was committed to a chaplain because of the vicar's incapacity;[59] probably in 1413, men were excommunicated for wounding the vicar;[60] and in 1438 the vicar apparently lived at Charlton.[61] Presentments were made in 1553 of

54 *Reg. Malm.* i. 121.
55 *L. & P. Hen. VIII*, xxi (2), pp. 241–2.
56 R. H. Luce, *Hist. Malm.* 38; Aubrey, *Topog. Coll.* ed. Jackson, 261; Buckler, water-colour in W.A.S. Libr., vol. vi. 35; see above, illus. on this page.
57 W.R.O. 88/1/16.
58 P.R.O., E 301/58, no. 36.
59 *Reg. Ghent* (Cant. & York Soc.), ii. 624.
60 *Reg. Hallum* (Cant. & York Soc.), pp. 119–20.
61 Above, Charlton, church.

parishioners who had not attended church or paid their dues, in 1565 of a parishioner who had not taken communion for five years, and in 1585 of another for sorcery.[62] A woman of Westport was tried with others from Malmesbury for sorcery in the 1640s.[63] John Pearte, curate of Westport in 1565, was said to be neither a preacher nor a graduate.[64] John Aubrey reported that an early 17th-century vicar, William Stumpe, destroyed many manuscripts of Malmesbury abbey's library, using them to plug barrels.[65] Among charges brought against Matthew Whitley, vicar from 1650 or earlier until 1670, was his failure in eight years to perform any clerical duty in Westport except two baptisms. Like most of his successors until the late 19th century Whitley lived at Charlton.[66]

In 1783 morning service was held at Westport on alternate Sundays. There was no weekday service and c. 12 people received communion when it was celebrated at Easter, Whitsun, Michaelmas, and Christmas.[67] Services were still held on alternate Sundays in the early 19th century, when Westport was among six churches served by a single curate. In the late 1840s morning and evening services were held each Sunday; the morning congregation usually included fewer than 10 adults.[68] On Census Sunday in 1851, however, 100 people attended morning and 280 people evening service in Westport.[69] G. H. H. Hutchinson, vicar 1837–76, was largely responsible for rebuilding the church and founding a school at Westport.[70] His work was interrupted in 1861 when he was licensed to be absent because his wife had become a Roman Catholic.[71] The vicarage was held in plurality with that of Malmesbury from 1879 until the two were united.[72]

The church of ST. MARY, standing and so called in the later 12th century,[73] was described by Aubrey as a pretty church with very good windows; it probably had a chancel, a nave with two aisles, and a tower

62 W.R.O., D 1/43/1, ff. 24v., 133v.; D 1/43/5, f. 22v.; D 1/43/6, f. 31Av.
63 W.A.M. xxix. 159–60.
64 W.R.O., D 1/43/5, f. 22v.
65 Aubrey, Nat. Hist. Wilts. ed. Britton, 78–9.
66 W.R.O., D 1/42/62; above, Charlton, church.
67 Vis. Queries, 1783 (W.R.S. xxvii), pp. 228–9.
68 Recollections of McKnight, ed. Thompson, 68–9.
69 P.R.O., HO 129/252/2/7/5.
70 Recollections of McKnight, ed. Thompson, 69; Alum. Cantab. 1752–1900, iii. 503; W.R.O. 1795/6.
71 P.R.O., PC 1/3966.
72 Clergy List (1892); Crockford (1907 and later edns.).
73 Reg. Malm. i. 369–70.

with a spire which may have been higher than that of St. Paul's in Malmesbury. It was destroyed during the Civil War, apparently by troops stationed in Malmesbury because it offered shelter to those attacking the town. A small church, with an undivided chancel and nave, was built after the war[74] and a north aisle was added later.[75] After it was rebuilt c. 1840,[76] in Tudor Gothic style of coursed rubble with ashlar dressings, it had an undivided chancel and nave with a south aisle of five bays and a western bellcot. A western gallery was later removed, and the arcade was blocked when the church was converted to a hall.

St. Mary's church, demolished c. 1840

In 1553 plate weighing 9½ oz. was taken for the king and a chalice of 5 oz. was left in the church. A chalice of 1654 and mid 19th-century plate including two chalices, a paten, two almsdishes, and a flagon, all belonging to Westport church,[77] were used in Malmesbury abbey church after 1946.[78]

74 Aubrey, *Topog. Coll.* ed. Jackson, 263.
75 Buckler, watercolour in W.A.S. Libr., vol. vi. 19; see below, illus. on this page.
76 W.R.O. 1795/6.
77 Nightingale, *Wilts. Plate,* 203; *W.A.M.* xxxvii. 334.
78 Inf. from the vicar, Malmesbury.

In 1553 three bells and a sanctus bell hung in the church. Five bells hanging there c. 1640 were either sold or melted down during the Civil War. A bell of 1739 hung in the church[79] until 1949, when it was melted down and the metal used for new bells for Malmesbury abbey church.[80]

Registers of baptisms and burials survive from 1678 and registers of marriages from 1685; those for some later years are missing.[81]

NONCONFORMITY. In 1676 there were 18 protestant nonconformists in Westport parish,[82] and until the late 18th century most nonconformists in Malmesbury apparently met in Westport. Presbyterian and Independent ministers in the town in the late 17th century probably preached in both Malmesbury and Westport.[83] William Conway, a Presbyterian expelled from Oxford university, was licensed in 1672 to preach in a barn in Westport and apparently continued to serve a congregation there until his death in 1694.[84] In 1689 two houses in Westport were certified for Presbyterian meetings,[85] and in 1715 the congregation numbered 160.[86] Although in 1783 the vicar of Westport reported that there was only one Presbyterian family in the parish,[87] a chapel was built in Horsefair in 1788. J. M. Moffatt, author of a *History of Malmesbury*, was minister from 1789 until 1804.[88] Probably from 1811 the church was Congregational. From 1812 until 1841 it was united with the Ebenezer chapel in Malmesbury.[89] In 1851 morning, afternoon, and evening services at the Westport chapel were attended by 178, 211, and 170 people respectively; congregations were usually larger, it was said.[90] A large new chapel, of stone, in Gothic style, and with a schoolroom, was built on a site adjoining that of the old chapel in 1867;[91] it remained

79 Walters, *Wilts. Bells*, 230; Aubrey, *Topog. Coll.* ed. Jackson, 263.
80 Inf. from the vicar, Malmesbury.
81 W.R.O. 1589/47–54; bishop's transcripts for some earlier and missing years are ibid.
82 *Compton Census,* ed. Whiteman, 129.
83 Above, Malmesbury, prot. nonconf.
84 *Calamy Revised,* ed. Matthews, 131.
85 *Meeting Ho. Certs.* (W.R.S. xl), p. 2.
86 Dr. Williams's Libr., Wilson MS. F i, p. 155.
87 *Vis. Queries, 1783* (W.R.S. xxvii), p. 229.
88 Moffatt, *Hist. Malm.* pp. xiii–xiv, 158.
89 G. L. Jenkins, *Nonconf. in Malm.* (1895), 15, 22; above, Malmesbury, prot. nonconf.
90 P.R.O., HO 129/252/2/7/6.
91 *Lond. Gaz.* 15 Nov. 1867, p. 6063.

open in 1989. Birth and baptism registers for the church survive from 1823.[92]

A house in Westport and another in Westport or Malmesbury were licensed for Baptist meetings in 1672.[93] By 1689 a pastor had been appointed,[94] and by 1695 a meeting house had been built in Abbey Row. It was a low stone building seating 60–70 and was replaced by a new Strict Baptist chapel, also of stone, built in 1802 and enlarged between 1814 and 1816. In the late 18th century baptisms took place in the Tetbury Avon north of the abbey church.[95] In 1851 services were usually held in the morning, afternoon, and evening on Sundays; on Census Sunday 208 people attended the morning service.[96] The chapel remained open in 1989. Birth and baptism registers survive from 1794.[97]

Methodists met in a barn said to be in St. Mary's Lane, possibly St. Mary's Street, in 1854. In 1856, when the church had 50 members, a Primitive Methodist chapel of red brick with stone dressings was built in Bristol Street.[98] Another small chapel was built of stone in a mixed Gothic style in the Triangle in 1899[99] and remained open in 1989.

EDUCATION. In 1547 the priest serving the chantry in Westport church kept a school.[1] In the later 16th century Thomas Hobbes, the philosopher, was taught successively at a school in Westport church, by a clergyman of either Westport or Malmesbury, and, with two or three other boys, by Robert Latimer, then living in Westport and later rector of Leigh Delamere.[2] J. M. Moffatt, Presbyterian minister of Westport 1789–1804, also kept a school.[3]

There was no day school in the parish in 1846–7.[4] From 1851 the children of Westport have attended the same schools as children from Malmesbury, some of which were in Westport parish.[5]

92 P.R.O., RG 4/2595.
93 *Meeting Ho. Certs.* (W.R.S. xl), pp. 174–5.
94 Jenkins, *Nonconf. in Malm.* 18.
95 R. W. Oliver, *Strict Bapt. Chapels Eng.* (Strict Bapt. Hist. Soc.), v. 27–9.
96 P.R.O., HO 129/252/2/7/7.
97 Ibid. RG 4/2238.
98 Jenkins, *Nonconf. in Malm.* 28–36.
99 Wilts. Cuttings, xxvii. 311.
 1 P.R.O., E 301/58, no. 36.
 2 Aubrey, *Topog. Coll.* ed. Jackson, 263; *Alum. Oxon. 1500–1714*, iii. 884.
 3 *V.C.H. Wilts.* iii. 123 n.; above, nonconf.
 4 Nat. Soc. *Inquiry, 1846–7*, Wilts. 12–13.
 5 Above, Malmesbury, educ.

Children were taught at a ragged school in Burnivale on Sundays and in the evenings from 1866 or earlier. From 1870 it was a day school; it had 53 pupils in that year and in 1873 a wooden schoolroom was built. In 1881–2 average attendance was 115. The school was closed in 1884.[6]

There was a private school in Westport in 1842;[7] another was attended by 57 boys and 49 girls in 1871.[8] In 1903 and 1927 Stainesbridge House was a girls' school.[9]

CHARITIES FOR THE POOR. Endowments, each yielding £1 a year, were provided for the poor of Westport by E. Waite (d. 1661) by will, and by Anne Rowles by deed in 1774. In 1904 the income from both was distributed to widows and others in need, each of whom received 6d. Residents of Westport were beneficiaries with those of parts of Malmesbury parish from Robert Cullerne's charity.[10]

6 W.R.O., F 8/600, Burnivale ragged sch.
7 Pigot, *Nat. Com. Dir.* (1842), 20.
8 *Returns relating to Elem. Educ.* 420–1.
9 *Kelly's Dir. Wilts.* (1903, 1927).
10 *Endowed Char. Wilts.* (N. Div.), 1017–19; above, Malmesbury, charities.

The nave of the abbey church, built in the 12th century

THE ABBEY OF MALMESBURY

Towards the middle of the 7th century, and perhaps in the year 637,[1] an Irish monk or hermit named Mailduib settled beneath the walls of a small stockade lying on the north fringe of Selwood Forest. The stockade crowned a hill whose steep sides sloped down to two streams which flowed to the north and south. The spot, later associated with stories of a heathen British king and a house of nuns,[2] appears then to have been almost deserted and Mailduib was attracted there in all probability by the solitude of the woodland which surrounded the place.[3] Of Mailduib little is known save his Irish descent, his monastic character, and his store of learning;[4] in the 13th century a stone cross associated with him stood in the cloister[5] at Malmesbury, though William of Malmesbury seems somewhat dubious about alleged remains of Mailduib's church.[6]

Mailduib had, however, no means of livelihood and necessity forced him to take pupils; in process of time his band of disciples took monastic vows[7] and formed a fair-sized community.[8] At an unknown

---

1 C. Plummer, *Baedae Opera Historica,* ii, 149, 'possibly... earlier than 640'; perhaps the Malmesbury author of the *Eulogium Historiarum* is recording a genuine tradition when he places it in 637; *Eulog. Hist.* (Rolls Ser.), iii, 279, or in 635: ibid. 328.

2 Leland, *Collectanea,* ed. Hearne, i (2), 302; Dugd. *Mon.* i, 253, 257. These accounts are taken from *Eulog. Hist.* i, 225 seq. and represent stories current at Malmesbury in the 14th cent. For origin and forms of the name Malmesbury see *P.N. Wilts.* (E.P.N.S.), 47–48.

3 William of Malmesbury, *De Gestis Pontificum Anglorum* (Rolls Ser.), 334.

4 Ibid. Most conjectures about Mailduib lack foundation; see R. Ehwald, *Aldhelmi Opera* (Mon. Germ. Hist. Auct. Ant.), xv (1), p. xi. For the various versions of his name see Plummer, *Baedae Op. Hist.* ii, 310–11.

5 A 13th-cent. note at the end of B.M., Cott. MS. Tib. A. XII. The MS. is damaged by fire.

6 These remains had disappeared in William's lifetime: *Gest. Pont.* 345. See below, p. 189.

7 Not all the pupils of Mailduib and Aldhelm took vows. Aldfrith, King of Northumbria (685–704) was probably educated at Malmesbury: Ehwald, *Aldhelmi Opera,* 61–62.

8 *Gest. Pont.* 334.

date a young man called Aldhelm joined the body and from that moment it grew in importance and influence. Of Aldhelm's ancestry little that is certain can be said beyond that he was Saxon by birth and was related to the line of Wessex kings;[9] William of Malmesbury is mistaken in supposing that he was first educated at Canterbury under Hadrian, Abbot of St. Augustine's.[10]

Aldhelm is said to have received the tonsure in 661[11] and to have remained at Malmesbury for ten years or so before setting out in 671 to study at the flourishing schools of Canterbury under Hadrian and Theodore, of whom he soon became the most illustrious pupil.[12] In the following year Aldhelm was forced by ill health to go back to Malmesbury, although he still hoped to return to Canterbury;[13] but Mailduib was now growing old, Aldhelm was himself becoming less inclined for secular learning,[14] and it was at this time that he was ordained priest.[15] He possessed indeed a singular combination of qualities: his love for learning and austerity[16] did not lessen his personal charm and talent for friendship, and his genuine holiness of life was of even greater influence than his powerful personality.[17] It was natural therefore that at Mailduib's death Aldhelm should be chosen to succeed him.

It is probable that Aldhelm was appointed in 675[18] and it is likely that Bishop Hlothere of Winchester marked the occasion by a charter

9 Ehwald, op. cit. x–xi; L. Boenhoff, *Aldhelm von Malmesbury,* 60; *Gest. Pont.* 332 seq. Wm. of Malm. says he came from Dorset, but this seems unlikely: *Gest. Pont.* 375.

10 *Gest. Pont.* 333; cf. Ehwald, *Aldhelmi Opera,* xi.

11 Dugd. *Mon.* i, 257; Leland, *Collectanea,* i (2), 302.

12 F. M. Stenton, *Anglo-Saxon Engl.* 180. See Aldhelm's letter from Canterbury to Bp. Hlothere of Winchester of Dec. 671: Ehwald, *Aldhelmi Opera,* 475–8; *Gest. Pont.* 341–3. (Wm. of Malm. incorrectly assumes that the letter was to Bp. Heddi.)

13 Letter to Hadrian of 675: Ehwald, *Aldhelmi Opera,* 478.

14 Letter to Wihtfrid, *c.* 675: ibid. 479–80.

15 Eleanor Duckett, *Anglo-Saxon Saints and Scholars,* 40.

16 The ice-cold spring into which he plunged was remembered at Malmesbury in the 12th cent.: *Gest. Pont.* 357.

17 *Gest. Pont.* 337 seq. 357 seq. Bede says he ruled his diocese *strenuissime*: Plummer, *Baedae Op. Hist.* i, 320. For the Irish influence upon Aldhelm's scholarship see Stenton, *Anglo-Saxon Engl.* 178 seq. He was also a skilled musician: Faricius, *Vita Aldhelmi,* ed. J. A. Giles, i, 357.

18 Appointment made by Hlothere (d. 676). Wm. of Malm. dates it in 675: *Gest. Pont.* 385, Florence of Worcester in 676: *Florentii Wigorniensis* (Engl. Hist. Soc.), ed. Thorpe, i, 27; see also Plummer, *Baedae Op. Hist.* ii, 309.

granting to the new abbot the lands upon which the abbey stood.[19] The reputation and distinguished connexions of Aldhelm soon attracted benefactors: in 680 Cenfrid, a noble of Mercia, granted land to Aldhelm at Wootton,[20] and in the following years Cadwalla, King of Wessex, gave land at Kemble (now Glos.), Crudwell, Charlton, near Malmesbury, and Purton.[21] Other benefactions included grants of land by King Ethelred of Mercia at Long Newnton[22] and at Tetbury (Glos.) in 681,[23] and by Ethelred's nephew Berhtwald at Somerford Keynes in 683.[24] Ine appears to have given land at Garsdon, and at Corston and Rodbourne, both in Malmesbury, in 701.[25]

At Malmesbury Aldhelm built a new and larger church in honour of our Saviour, St. Peter, and St. Paul, and composed verses for its dedication.[26] The monastery so flourished under his rule that Aldhelm was able to make two new foundations from it, one in honour of St. John the Baptist at Frome (Som.) and another in honour of St. Laurence at Bradford-on-Avon.[27] Aldhelm procured from Pope Sergius I for these

19 This supports Wm. of Malmesbury's date: *Registrum Malmesburiense* (Rolls Ser.), i, 280; *Gest. Pont.* 334; *Cart. Sax.* ed. Birch, no. 37; Ehwald, *Aldhelmi Opera*, 507–9. Ehwald follows Hahn and Boenhoff in thinking that, though interpolated, it represents a genuine original grant: H. Hahn, *Bonifaz und Lul*; Boenhoff, *Aldhelm von Malmesbury*, 60.

20 Ehwald, *Aldhelmi Opera*, 509–10; *Cart. Sax.* ed. Birch, no. 54; *Gest. Pont.* 349. Boenhoff and Ehwald again think that this, though altered, represents an original grant.

21 *Cart. Sax.* ed. Birch, nos. 63, 70; *Cod. Dipl.* ed. Kemble, no. 29. These charters are distinctly dubious, but cf. *Cart. Sax.* no. 50 which Ehwald appears to regard as genuine and W. H. Stevenson regards as possibly genuine: Ehwald, *Aldhelmi Opera*, 510–12; *E.H.R.* xxix, 691.

22 *Cart. Sax.* ed. Birch, no. 58, regarded as genuine by Sir Frank Stenton in *Anglo-Saxon Engl.* 68.

23 *Cart. Sax.* ed. Birch, no. 59.

24 Ibid. 65.

25 *Cod. Dipl.* ed. Kemble, no. 48; *Cart. Sax.* ed. Birch, no. 103; *Gest. Pont.* 354 seq. Levison regards it as genuine: W. Levison, *Engl. and the Continent in 8th cent.* 228 n. 1. The charter of 704 is spurious: *Reg. Malm.* i, 286. The complex question of the exchange of land with Baldred in 680 and Aldhelm's letter to Winberht of Nursling about it cannot be discussed here: *Gest. Pont.* 353–4; Ehwald, *Aldhelmi Opera*, 502–3; *Cod. Dipl.* ed. Kemble, no. 28; *Reg. Malm.* i, 284. The charter and letter refer to different pieces of land; neither may be genuine.

26 *Gest. Pont.* 345–6. He also composed verses for a church with altars for each of the twelve apostles; this may have been Malmesbury: Ehwald, op. cit. 19 seq.

27 *Gest. Pont.* 346. For Bradford-on-Avon see *V.C.H. Wilts.* vii, 23. Both foundations were later destroyed by the Danes: *Gest. Pont.* 346.

foundations and for Malmesbury itself a privilege which later was interpreted as placing them immediately under papal jurisdiction and exempting them from the control of the local bishop.[28] No mention is anywhere made of the date of the introduction of the rule of St. Benedict at Malmesbury and its dependencies, but Aldhelm's days at Canterbury, his interest in the monastic reforms of St. Wilfrid,[29] and his assumption that a religious community would be following that rule,[30] seem to indicate that it was introduced at Malmesbury during Aldhelm's abbacy; but of the circumstances or date nothing is known.[31]

The fame of Aldhelm spread far and wide; he had taken a prominent part in persuading the British king and clergy of Dumnonia[32] to keep Easter Day on the Roman date.[33] Ine, who had become King of Wessex about 689, had a great regard for the abbot's advice, and had rebuilt the monastery of Glastonbury at Aldhelm's instigation.[34] Aldhelm himself had built churches at Bruton (Som.)[35] and near Wareham (Dors.),[36] and at Malmesbury had completed churches in honour of the Blessed Virgin and of St. Michael.[37] It was natural therefore that Ine turned to Aldhelm when in 705 it came to the appointment of the first bishop of the new diocese of Sherborne.[38] Aldhelm was at first unwilling to accept the task on account of advancing years, but at length he agreed,[39]

28 R. Jaffé-Loewenfeld, *Regesta Pontificum Romanorum*, ed. Wattenbach, 2104; Ehwald, *Aldhelmi Opera*, 512–14 and refs. Aldhelm doubtless obtained the privilege when on a visit to Rome *c.* 695. See also Ehwald, op. cit. 494. In Wm. of Malm.'s version there is a marginal note (Magdalen Coll. Oxf. MS.) which hints that the privilege was obtained lest conflicts between the kings of Mercia and Wessex should jeopardize the future of the monastery: *Gest. Pont.* 374.

29 Ehwald, op. cit. 500–2.

30 Ibid. 268, 390, where a caution is given against assuming too much from Aldhelm's words.

31 Probably 675 or very shortly afterwards. Neither the privilege of Sergius I nor Aldhelm's instructions as to the choice of his successor mention St. Benedict's Rule. See also Ehwald, *Aldhelmi Opera*, 501 n. 3.

32 Devonshire preserves this name.

33 Ehwald, *Aldhelmi Opera*, 480–6.

34 *Gest. Pont.* 354; see also *Cart. Sax.* ed. Birch, no. 109, which may preserve traces of some genuine document. The part played by Aldhelm in founding the church of Wells (Armitage Robinson, *Saxon Bps. of Wells*, Brit. Acad. Suppl. Paper iv, 3) has no part in early tradition: *Collectanea*, iii (Som. Rec. Soc.), 53.

35 *Gest. Pont.* 374.

36 Ibid. 363–4.

37 Ibid. 361.

38 Ibid. 374.

39 Ibid. 376.

and was consecrated by Beorhtwald, Archbishop of Canterbury.[40] On his appointment Aldhelm desired to place abbots over his monasteries, but was opposed in this by the communities; reluctantly he yielded,[41] but, from fear lest future bishops should tyrannize over his monasteries, he granted them a privilege that, at his death, they should elect their own superiors freely.[42] After a short but active[43] pontificate of four years, he died in the little wooden church at Doulting (Som.) on 25 May 709.[44] His body was carried to Malmesbury and buried in the church of St. Michael, where it lay until 955.

Aldhelm was beyond comparison the most learned and ingenious western scholar of the later 7th century, and represented the 'culture of his age in its most developed form'.[45] His memory was always revered as that of a saint and miracle-worker.[46]

Aldhelm was apparently succeeded by Eaba, who is known only from a reference in a letter by an unknown English monk to Lull, Bishop of Mainz.[47] Both Lull and the monk were educated at Malmesbury under Abbot Eaba, perhaps about the year 730.[48]

The next abbot in whose existence any confidence can be placed was Ethelard,[49] Othelard,[50] or Aethelheard,[51] who is well attested, being mentioned by William of Malmesbury and by the unknown 13th-century compiler of a short history of the abbey found in a Cottonian manuscript.[52] There is also a charter which

---

40 A friend of Aldhelm: ibid.
41 According at least to Wm. of Malm.; see Stenton, *Anglo-Saxon Engl.* 159.
42 *Gest. Pont.* 378–80; *Cart. Sax.* ed. Birch, no. 114; Ehwald, *Aldhelmi Opera*, 514–16. Ehwald thinks it probably genuine as against Plummer, *Anglo-Saxon Chron.* ii, 38.
43 *Gest. Pont.* 382.
44 Ibid. 382, 385.
45 Stenton, *Anglo-Saxon Engl.* 182–3.
46 A Malmesbury calendar of 1521 kept his festival on 25 May and his translation on 3 Oct.: *Engl. Benedictine Kalendars after 1100,* ed. F. Wormald (Hen. Bradshaw Soc.), ii, 83, 88.
47 Letter of 755–86 in *Epistolae Merowingici et Karolini Aevi* (Mon. Germ. Hist. Epist.), iii, ed. Dümmler, 421; H. Hahn, *Bonifaz und Lul,* 237, 239.
48 *Epist. Merow.* ed. Dümmler, 421.
49 *Gest. Pont.* 389.
50 B.M., Cott. MS. Vit. A. X, f. 160. See also note 52.
51 *Flor. Wig.* (Engl. Hist. Soc.), i, 62 n. 2.
52 B.M., Cott. MS. Vit. A. X, ff. 158–60. This has been printed in *Jnl. of Brit. Arch. Assoc.* xxvii, 339. For comments on this list see p. 193.

has some genuine features which is witnessed by Aethelheard *economus atque abbas* in 749.[53]

The next abbot, Cuthbert, was appointed by Aethelheard on his accession to the see of Winchester.[54] There is a charter of Egfrith, King of Mercia, granting land at Purton to Abbot Cuthbert and the community of Malmesbury[55] in 796, and an Abbot Cuthbert of the Winchester Diocese was present at the council of Clofeshoh of 803.[56]

Of the period between 796 and 974 almost nothing is known. King Aethelwulf of Wessex (839–55) is said by William of Malmesbury to have made a rich shrine for St. Aldhelm's bones and to have granted lands and immunities from taxation.[57] It was between 824 and 867 that Eahlstan, the militant Bishop of Sherborne, committed many aggressions against Malmesbury, inspired, according to William, by avarice.[58]

At this time, about 870, according to the tradition recorded by William of Malmesbury,[59] John Scotus Erigena, the philosopher, at the instigation of King Alfred took up his residence at the abbey as a fugitive from the Continent; after some years he was murdered by his pupils. He was buried first in St. Laurence's Church, but the body was later translated to the left of the high altar of the abbey church, chiefly as the result of preternatural portents. The terms of the epitaph as given by William imply that the dead scholar was regarded as a martyr; and it seems clear that he bases the story on an old tradition and a tomb bearing an epitaph of a 'John the Wise' who is termed saint and martyr.[60] This John, however, almost certainly cannot have been the famous philosopher; he may possibly have been John the Old Saxon whose

53 *Cart. Sax.* ed. Birch, no. 179.
54 Stubbs, *Registrum Sacrum Anglicanum,* 8; Birch's identification of him with Aethel-heard, Abp. of Canterbury, though following Wm. of Malm., seems to lack foundation: Birch, 'Succession of Abbots of Malmesbury', *Jnl. Brit. Arch. Assoc.* xxvii, 318; *Gest. Pont.* 389. Later Wm. takes a less positive view and only says it was a matter of 'constant opinion': *De Gestis Regum Anglorum* (Rolls Ser.), i, 94. At this time, *c.* 777, Offa took away many townships belonging to the abbey: *Gest. Pont.* 388.
55 *Cart. Sax.* ed. Birch, no. 279; *Gest. Pont.* 388–9.
56 *Cart. Sax.* ed. Birch, no. 312. Wm. of Malm. mentions no other abbot until 974.
57 *Gest. Pont.* 389–92. See also *Cart. Sax.* ed. Birch, no. 481 (Tockenham), 457 (Dauntsey), 444 (Minety), 447 (freedom from taxation).
58 *Gest. Pont.* 176. In *Gest. Regum,* i, 109, Wm. accuses him of appropriating the whole monastery. Does this mark the real beginning of secular clerks at Malmesbury?
59 *Gest. Pont.* 392–4.
60 This tomb is mentioned *c.* 1060 in a list of burial places of saints in Engl.: F. Liebermann, *Die Heilingen Englands,* 18.

unfortunate régime at Athelney (Som.) nearly ended in murder.[61] John the Old Saxon escaped from Athelney, but when and how he died we do not know; it is possible that he is to be identified with the John the Wise of Malmesbury.

Between 871 and 899 King Alfred granted to Malmesbury the reversion of land in Chelworth, in Crudwell,[62] but the abbey had to wait 30 years for possession. Even then it was necessary to surrender land at 'Mehandun' in exchange.[63] In 909 the 'monastery' of Gloucester was founded, and may have been peopled with monks, or more probably clerks, from Malmesbury, with which it was for a long time closely connected.[64]

Throughout the Middle Ages the memory of King Athelstan was honoured at Malmesbury for his generous benefactions. He loaded the abbey with gifts,[65] which included a gold cross with a relic of the True Cross, which he used to wear in his battles,[66] and numerous relics of saints purchased from abroad.[67] He caused the bodies of his cousins Aethelweard and Aelfwine[68] to be buried in St. Mary's Church and his own body was later interred before the high altar.[69] William tells us that he gave a large number of estates to the abbey, but the only charter which he quotes[70] is a conflation of several others,[71] all of doubtful authenticity.[72]

Of the state of Malmesbury during the time of Athelstan and indeed for some decades before nothing is known. William writes that

61 *Asser's Life of King Alfred*, ed. W. H. Stevenson, 335–6.
62 *Gest. Pont.* 394–5; *Cart. Sax.* ed. Birch, no. 568.
63 *Gest. Pont.* 395–6; *Cart. Sax.* ed. Birch, nos. 584, 585. 'Mehandun' is identified by Birch as 'Manton'. In the same year (901) Edw. the Elder granted land near Hankerton to the abbey. The charters seem genuine in part: *Gest. Pont.* 396; *Cart. Sax.* ed. Birch, no. 589.
64 *Gest. Pont.* 293. At this time the abbey was burned by fire: ibid. 363.
65 Athelstan had a great devotion to St. Aldhelm and Wm. of Malm. suggests that he was related to him by blood: *Gest. Pont.* 396.
66 *Eulog. Hist.* (Rolls Ser.), iii, 10–11.
67 Including those of St. Pair of Avranches. For interesting letter from Prior of St. Samson's, Dol (Ille et Vilaine) concerning these relics see *Gest. Pont.* 394–400 and Armitage Robinson, *Times of St. Dunstan*, 73–74.
68 W. G. Searle, *Anglo-Saxon Bps., Kings and Nobles*, 343; *Gest. Pont.* 396.
69 *Gest. Pont.* 397–8, where his epitaph is given.
70 Ibid. 401.
71 Armitage Robinson, *Times of St. Dunstan*, 26.
72 Athelstan was also regarded as a great benefactor of the borough: *Cart. Sax.* ed. Birch, no. 720; Leland, *Itin.* ed. Hearne, vii, 96.

the abbey was turned into a 'sty of clerks' (*stabulum clericorum*) by King Edwy in 955,[73] but this date is almost impossible as the king did not ascend the throne until the November of that year and it is very probable that the *familia* of Malmesbury had not been monastic for many years.[74] There was, however, a tradition that Edwy granted land to the foundation,[75] while the secular clerks placed the body of St.Aldhelm in the shrine which had already been made for it.[76] If so doubtful a source as the pseudo-Ingulf is to be believed, Aio, a learned monk of Croyland, took temporary residence and refuge at Malmesbury from 941 to 946.[77]

The great revival, begun at Glastonbury about 943, which formed a turning-point in the history of English monastic life, appears to have reached Malmesbury in the reign of Edgar, and we may take William's word for it that it was St. Dunstan himself who rejected Edwy's clerks and put monks in their place.[78] The exact date at which the revival reached Malmesbury is doubtful; William places it in 974,[79] relying on a charter of Edgar to Abbot Aelfric who, the document says, had been appointed there to preside over the replacement of the secular clergy by monks.[80] Aelfric left many memories behind him at Malmesbury;[81] it was he who caused the Blessed Virgin to be regarded as the patron of the monastery in place of SS. Peter and Paul.[82] It was, however, as a

73 *Gest. Pont.* 403.
74 Prof. M. D. Knowles in *Monastic Order in Engl.* 34 thinks this certain. The author of the *Eulog. Hist.* (Rolls Ser.), i, 229, says, 'tempore Regis Edwi monasterium fuit desolatum a monachis per plura tempora'.
75 *Gest. Pont.* 403; *Cart. Sax.* ed. Birch, nos. 921, 922; *Reg. Malm.* (Rolls Ser.), 311–13.
76 *Gest. Pont.* 403, but the date is obscure, see *Eulog. Hist.* (Rolls Ser.), i, 227–8 and editor's notes.
77 T. Tanner, *Bibliotheca Britannico-Hibernica*, 14.
78 *Memorials of St. Dunstan* (Rolls Ser.), 301–2.
79 *Gest. Pont.* 404–5.
80 The document has some very doubtful features: *Cod. Dipl.* ed. Kemble, 584; *Gest. Regum*, i, 173–4; *Eulog. Hist.* i, 17; *Reg. Malm.* i, 316–18. Edgar calls him *custos*, a phrase reminiscent of the entrusting of Glastonbury to Dunstan which according to the Anglo-Saxon Chronicle preceded his appointment as abbot: *Angl. Sax. Chron. sub anno* 943. Prof. Knowles, however, dates the revival at Malmesbury *c.* 960: Knowles, *Mon. Order in Engl.* table after p. 71.
81 According to Hearne's list he was a monk of Winchester: *Chron. Edw. I and Edw. II* (Rolls Ser.), ii, p. cxviii. For the confusion between Aelfric of Malmesbury, Aelfric the author of the life of St. Ethelwold, and Aelfric the Grammarian see *Leechdoms, Wortcunning and Starcraft* (Rolls Ser.), iii, pp. xiv-xxix.
82 *Gest. Pont.* 405. Edgar's charter places the Blessed Virgin first among the abbey's patrons, another doubtful feature.

builder that he was chiefly remembered: he rebuilt or completely restored[83] St. Mary's Church, which now became the chief church of the monastery,[84] and also added various conventual buildings.[85] The church was furnished with an organ having brazen pipes[86] and a holy-water vat, both of which were connected with the name of St. Dunstan, and the saint was said to have hidden the body of St. Aldhelm in a vault to the right of the high altar in anticipation of a recurrence (which he prophesied)[87] of the Danish invasions.

Aelfric appears to have been succeeded by Aethelweard,[88] who in turn was succeeded by Cineweard, Beorhtelm, and Beorhtwold.[89] Of the last it is recorded that he alienated the lands of the monastery for small sums.[90] It was about this time that the Danes visited Malmesbury. They broke into the monastery and took everything except St. Aldhelm's shrine, which, according to William, was saved by a preternatural portent.[91]

Beorhtwold was followed by Abbot Eadric,[92] who is mentioned in 1012[93] and 1021–3.[94] Wulfsine, the next abbot, restored monastic observance, which had suffered from the effects of the Danish raids. He seems to have won the respect of the community, for more than 50 years after his name was revered by aged members of the house, who sometimes told anecdotes of him to the youthful William.[95] Wulfsine must have died in 1034 at the very latest.[96] Of Aethelweard II and

83 At least a tower remained of the earlier building: *Gest. Pont.* 397. See p. 190.
84 Ibid. 386, 405; *Gest. Regum,* 154. See p. 191.
85 *Gest. Pont.* 386, 405.
86 Ibid. 407; *Memorials of St. Dunstan* (Rolls Ser.), 301, where the organ is described as being harsh in comparison with those of the 12th cent.
87 *Gest. Pont.* 408.
88 Ibid. 411.
89 B.M., Cott. MS. Vit. A. X. Kineweard there appears as Cynewerd.
90 *Gest. Pont.* 411. Wm. of Malm. excuses him on account of the exactions of the Danes. An abbot of this name occurs in charters between 984 and 1012. Brihtwold II and Wulfsine II of Dugd. *Mon.* i, 255 are based on a misreading of Wm. of Malm. Wm. is not here introducing a fresh abbot but returning to speak more of one or two he has already mentioned.
91 *Gest. Pont.* 409–10. This was perhaps the great Danish raid of 1010: *Flor. Wig.* (Engl. Hist. Soc.), i, 163.
92 *Gest. Pont.* 411; Aethericus in B.M., Cott. MS. Vit. A. X.
93 *Cod. Dipl.* ed. Kemble, no. 719.
94 Ibid. 736, but this may be the first Abbot of Gloucester, who became abbot in 1022.
95 *Gest. Pont.* 411.
96 This date can be arrived at by calculating backwards from Beorhtwold II and Beorhtric.

Aelfwine, who succeeded him, almost nothing is known. Beorhtwold II, the next abbot, was a man of bad character who collapsed and died in the course of a drunken orgy in the town. William gives a somewhat spectacular account of the exhumation of his corpse from St. Andrew's Church after the intervention of evil spirits and its subsequent consignment to a malodorous bog.[97]

The internal history of the abbey during the first half of the 11th century is largely obscure: William relates several miracles worked at the shrine of St. Aldhelm[98] and tells of the unscrupulous acquisition of the head of St. Ouen.[99] It was at this time too that a Greek monk named Constantine took up his abode at Malmesbury: his charm of conversation, gentle behaviour, and holiness of life endeared him to all, and we get a delightful picture of him working in the vineyard, which he had constructed on the hill to the north of the monastery.[1] It is recorded that on his deathbed Constantine suddenly rallied, and, placing an archiepiscopal pall on his shoulders, led the monks to believe that the stranger who had lived among them was an archbishop. He was buried with the abbots of Malmesbury in St. Andrew's Church; later, when his remains were disturbed to make new buildings, the whiteness and fineness of his bones led the community to regard him as a person of no mean quality either of birth or holiness.[2]

The last pre-conquest Abbot of Malmesbury was Beorhtric. The story of his appointment, as related by William,[3] presents considerable difficulties. According to William's account, immediately after the death of Abbot Beorhtwold II, Bishop Heremann of Ramsbury attempted to move his bishopric to Malmesbury,[4] alleging that the endowments of his see were insufficient to support him.[5] Edward the Confessor at first consented to this project, but the monks, headed by their prior Beorhtric,[6] at once persuaded Earl Godwin and his son Harold to

---

97 *Gest. Pont.* 411–12. It was perhaps during this time that the abbey was again destroyed by fire: ibid. 363.
98 Ibid. 414–19.
99 Ibid. 419–20.
 1 By Wm.'s time the vine seems no longer to have been cultivated there: ibid. 415.
 2 Ibid. 415–16.
 3 Ibid. 182–3, 420.
 4 Heremann was Bp. of Ramsbury 1045– ?55.
 5 According to the author of the *Eulog. Hist.* i, 262, Heremann had built at his own expense a stone bell tower at Malmesbury: this was said to be in 1056.
 6 *Gest. Pont.* 420.

intervene.[7] This they did with success, and Heremann, enraged, left England. Thereupon Beorhtric became Abbot of Malmesbury, over which, according to William, he presided for seven memorable years.[8] It seems likely, however, that his abbacy was of longer duration. He was deposed by the Conqueror either late in 1066 or early in 1067 (see below) and may have become abbot immediately upon Beorhtwold's death, which must have been between September 1052[9] and April 1053.[10] At the latest he became abbot soon after Heremann's departure from England, which, according to Florence of Worcester, was in 1055.[11] It was during Beorhtric's abbacy, in 1065, that the Confessor granted Malmesbury a general confirmation of all its possessions, which it rated at 329 hides.[12]

It was about this time that Eilmar, a monk of Malmesbury, skilled in mathematics and astrology,[13] with, as William says, the rashness of youth in spite of his mature years, engaged upon a daring aeronautical experiment. He made himself wings which were worked by his hands and feet and threw himself into the air from the top of the tower. In the event his injuries were no more than a broken leg and, unabashed, he attributed his failure to fly solely to the fact that he had omitted to make himself a tail. The abbot, however, forbade a repetition of the experiment.[14]

Beorhtric's notable abbacy seems to have come to a sudden end in the closing month of 1066 or early in 1067, when he was transferred by the Conqueror to Burton (Staffs.)[15] to make way for Turold, a monk of Fécamp (Seine-Inférieure).[16] Turold appears to have been tactless

---

7 *summa celeritate*: ibid. 182–3.

8 *septem annis gloriosissimis cenobio prefuit*: ibid. 420.

9 Godwin, who intervened in the dispute which arose after Beorhtwold's death, returned from exile on this date: *Flor. Wig.* (Engl. Hist. Soc.), i, 208 seq.

10 Date of Godwin's death.

11 *Flor. Wig.* (Engl. Hist. Soc.), i, 214. Wm. stresses that the monks acted with speed: *Gest. Pont.* 183.

12 *Reg. Malm.* i, 321–5.

13 He was known as *Magus*. For his writings see Tanner, *Bibliotheca*, 561.

14 *Gest. Regum*, i, 276–7.

15 Leofric, Abbot of Peterborough and Burton, died 1 Nov. 1066: *Peterborough Chron. of Hugh Candidus*, ed. C. Mellows (Peterborough Nat. Hist. Scient. and Arch. Soc.), 75; *Two Sax. Chrons.* ed. Earle and Plummer, i, 198. *Ann. Mon.* (Rolls Ser.), i, 185 and Dugd. *Mon.* iii, 47 are in error here. It is, however, impossible to date the change of abbacy at Malmesbury with any certainty.

16 *Chron. Hugh Candidus,* ed. C. Mellows, 161. Here erroneously termed the Conqueror's nephew.

and overbearing[17] and was soon at loggerheads with his community, whereupon the Conqueror translated him to Peterborough with the remark that as the abbot had acted more like a knight than an abbot he would find there battles in plenty to fight.[18] This was in the early months of 1070.[19]

In Turold's place the Conqueror appointed[20] another Norman of forceful character,[21] Warin, a monk of Lyre (Évreux). An ambitious man, he did not hesitate to squander monastic revenues to make his way in influential circles, and William of Malmesbury rather acidly contrasts his later grand manner with his humble beginnings.[22] Warin caused indignation by making sarcastic witticisms about the bones of his precedessors. He turned their remains, including those of Mailduib and John Scotus, out of the church of St. Peter and St Paul and relegated them to a far corner of St. Michael's Church. He partly atoned, however, by the reverence which he showed to the body of St. Aldhelm, which he removed from the vault in which it had been hidden during the Danish raids. In 1078, assisted first by Serlo, Abbot of Gloucester, and later by St. Osmund, Bishop of Salisbury, he placed it in a magnificent shrine.[23] Two years later the startling cure of a poor deformed lad took place, and was reported by the monks to Warin, who was at court with Lanfranc. The archbishop immediately ordered Aldhelm to be venerated as a saint.[24]

Warin appears to have used his influential connexions to some purpose. Though the grant of 1081 in which the Conqueror confirmed Edward the Confessor's general grant of liberties is probably spurious,[25] Queen Maud gave 3 hides at Garsdon in that year[26] and in 1084 Godwin

17 Though Wm. of Malm. accuses him of toadying to the Conqueror (*Gest. Pont.* 420) he is called *swiðe styrne* in the *Anglo-Saxon Chron. sub anno* 1070.
18 *Gest. Pont.* 420.
19 *Chron. Hugh Candidus,* ed. Mellows, 161. His predecessor at Peterborough had died at end of Nov. 1069: ibid. 77.
20 In 1216 Innocent III speaks of him as having been intruded by lay power: *Reg. Malm.* ii, 7.
21 *vir efficax: Gest. Pont.* 425.
22 Ibid. 421.
23 *Gest. Pont.* 424–5.
24 At this time a fair was granted by the Conqueror on St. Aldhelm's Day, the day before, and three days after: *Gest. Pont.* 428; *Reg. Malm.* i, 329.
25 H. W. C. Davis, *Regesta Regum Anglo-Normannorum,* p. 35; *Reg. Malm.* i, 325–6.
26 *Reg. Malm.* i, 326–8.

granted to Warin and the monks the London church of St Nicholas Acon.[27]

It was during Warin's time that the Domesday Survey was made and in it we find the following properties belonging to the abbey. In Wiltshire: Highway (11 hides), Dauntsey (10 hides), Somerford Keynes (5 hides), Brinkworth (5 hides), Norton, near Malmesbury (5 hides), Brokenborough with Corston (50 hides), Kemble (30 hides – now in Glos.), Long Newnton (30 hides), Charlton (20 hides), Garsdon (3 hides), Crudwell (40 hides), Bremhill (38 hides), Purton (35 hides);[28] in Gloucestershire: Littleton-upon-Severn (5 hides);[29] and in Warwickshire: Newbold Pacey (3 hides).[30] These lands were valued at £188 14s. in all and were assessed as 3 knights' fees.[31]

Abbot Warin died sometime between September 1087[32] and June 1091[33] and was succeeded a fortnight later by Godfrey, a monk of Jumièges (Seine-Inférieure)[34] who had been steward and guardian of the vacant abbey of Ely for several years.[35] This abbot was active in adorning the church and increasing the goods of the monastery[36] and he gained William of Malmesbury's gratitude by building up a fine library in place of the former meagre collection of volumes,[37] a task in

27 Ibid. i, 328.
28 V.C.H. Wilts. ii, pp. 125–7.
29 Dom. Bk. (Rec. Com.), i, 165.
30 Ibid. 239.
31 This was a conventional book assessment of a very complex situation, see J. H. Round, 'The Knight Service of Malmesbury Abbey', E.H.R. xxxii, 249–52. Prof. Knowles gives the gross income of Malmesbury at this time as £178 10s.: Knowles, Mon. Ord. in Engl. 702.
32 He died tempore Villelmi iunioris: B.M., Cott. MS. Vit. A. X, and Hearne list in Chron. Edw. I and Edw. II (Rolls Ser.), ii, pp. cxviii–cxix.
33 Jan. 1091 seems to be the first recorded date of the next abbot, see p. 160, note 39.
34 Gest. Pont. 431.
35 Thomas of Ely in his History of Ely says he became abbot in 1081: H. Wharton, Anglia Sacra, i, 610–11 (see also V.C.H. Cambs. ii, 202). This seems unlikely and conflicts with Godwin's grant and the statements in B.M., Cott. MS. Vit. A. X and the Hearne list. Thomas is 10 years out with the intervention of William in Ely affairs and may be 10 years out here. 1091 seems most probable date.
36 Innocent III was told a different story: Reg. Malm. ii, 7.
37 Remains of the early library still exist however; e.g. the 10th- to 11th-cent. Prudentius in C.C.C. Libr., Camb. and the 9th-cent. Philo in Bodl. (MS. Marshall 19). A bible supposed to have belonged to Aldhelm was shown in Wm. of Malm.'s day: Gest. Pont. 378, and some alleged gifts of Athelstan in Leland's time: Tanner, Bibliotheca, 267. For an historical work attributed to Abbot Godfrey see Tanner, op. cit. 329; T. Duffus Hardy, Descript. Cat. of Materials, i (2), p. 667. Tanner is, with some reason, doubtful.

which the historian himself took part. In Godfrey firmness was combined with kindness; though irascible by nature, he was easily placated with a soft answer and was noted for his sobriety and frugality. In spite of all his work for the monastery he was criticized for the readiness with which he parted with the treasures of the church of Malmesbury at a price below their market value in order to aid Rufus in raising the money required for pawning the Duchy of Normandy in 1096; William gives an account of preternatural warnings and of the loathsome disease which attacked the abbot in consequence of his bad stewardship.[38] When Godfrey died a bronze ring was found encircling his stomach, a phenomenon attributed by some to austerity, by others to a desire to hide from the public eye his increasing girth. One of the critics of the late abbot composed verses in this strain which were rebutted in verses, equally inept, probably composed by William himself.[39] Rufus granted Godfrey the custody of his own woods at Bratton in 1094[40] and between August 1100 and April 1101 Henry I renewed the Conqueror's grant of a five-day fair in Malmesbury town.[41]

Abbot Godfrey died in 1105 or 1106 and was succeeded by Eadwulf, a monk of Winchester.[42] Eadwulf is one of the most obscure of the abbots of Malmesbury. He is not mentioned by William of Malmesbury. Perhaps William did not get on with his superior and found it inexpedient to make any comments in chronicles which would almost certainly be seen by the abbot. In fact, beyond the reference in the Winchester annals we find Eadwulf mentioned only twice: once in a document by which Malmesbury granted a corrody in exchange for a hide of land at Kemble;[43] and again, although not by name, by Faricius, Abbot of Abingdon, who wished news of his forthcoming death to be sent to the Abbot of Malmesbury.[44] Faricius had left Malmesbury, where he was cellarer, in 1100 to become Abbot of Abingdon.[45] He died in 1117.[46]

38 *Gest. Pont.* 431.
39 Godfrey occurs on 27 June 1091 as a witness to Rufus's charter to John Bp. of Bath: Davis, *Regesta,* pp. 81–82.
40 Davis, *Regesta,* p. 90. From this and a document ordering a land-holder to restore land to the abbey (ibid. p. 108) it is possible that Rufus had at one stage taken the lands of the abbey into his hands.
41 *Reg. Malm.* i, 333.
42 *Ann. Mon.* (Rolls Ser.), ii, 42.
43 *Reg. Malm.* ii, 3–4.
44 *Chron. Abing.* (Rolls Ser.), ii, 290.
45 For Faricius see *Chron. Abing.* (Rolls Ser.), ii, *passim* and esp. pp. 44 seq. and 285 seq.
46 *Chron. Abing.* (Rolls Ser.), ii, 290.

According to the annals of Winchester, Bishop Roger of Salisbury took over the abbey in 1118, expelling Abbot Eadwulf.[47] William of Malmesbury hints at a violent usurpation,[48] but the Cottonian writer states that at Eadwulf's death Roger stepped in.[49] The classical description of Bishop Roger is given by William in his *Historia Novella*[50] where he records his humble beginnings, his financial ability, his progress from the office of chancellor to that of Bishop of Salisbury, his love of splendour and magnificent buildings,[51] his successful efforts to promote the fortunes of his relations and, in the end, his fall, misfortune, and unlamented death. It was not until September 1131 that Roger obtained royal permission for his seizure of Malmesbury and its endowments, and it was some five years later that he obtained the borough of Malmesbury for himself.[52] This was a time of trouble and confusion in which Malmesbury was more than once involved in the strife between the parties of Stephen and Maud. At Malmesbury, close to the abbey church, Roger began to build a castle in the abbey graveyard,[53] and this, and other buildings at Malmesbury, were highly praised by William for their excellence of design and construction.[54] After the arrest of Roger in 1139[55] Malmesbury was seized by Stephen,[56] recaptured on 7 October 1139 by Robert FitzHubert with great violence,[57] and retaken by Stephen a fortnight later.[58] Hardly were

47 *Ann. Mon.* (Rolls Ser.), ii, 42. The date may well be correct; there was certainly an abbot at Malmesbury in Feb. 1117. See above, note 44.

48 *Gest. Regum*, ii, 559; cf. i, 109. The Evesham chronicler hints much the same: *Chron. Evesham* (Rolls Ser.), 139–40.

49 So also the compiler of the Hearne list: *Chron. Edw. I and Edw. II* (Rolls Ser.), ii, pp. cxviii–cxix.

50 *Gest. Regum*, ii, 557–60.

51 He is called *pontifex magnanimus*; ibid. ii, 484.

52 *Sar. Chart. & Doc.* (Rolls Ser.), 7–8. In 1126 Honorius II confirmed to Roger the churches of Malmesbury, Abbotsbury (Dors.), and Horton (Glos.): Holtzmann, *Papsturkunden in England*, ii, 141–2.

53 *Gest. Regum*, ii, 547.

54 Ibid. 484.

55 Ibid. 549. That Roger was at Malmesbury just before his arrest is confirmed by the rather doubtful authority of the interpolator of Florence of Worcester: *Flor. Wig.* (Engl. Hist. Soc.), ii, 107. He issued a charter from there 4 years before. *Anc. Chart.* (P.R.S. x), 38–39.

56 *Gest. Regum*, ii, 549.

57 Ibid. 556, 563–4.

58 Ibid. 556–7.

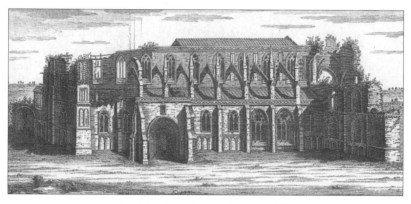

The abbey from the south-west in 1732

these tumultuous events over when Roger died on 11 December 1139.[59]

At Reading, shortly after Christmas 1139, Stephen invested John, a monk at Malmesbury, with the abbacy,[60] at the same time restoring the monastic estates which Roger had seized. As abbot, John made a journey to Rome and his friend William of Malmesbury drew up an account of his travels entitled apparently *Itinerarium Johannis abbatis Malmesburiensis versus Romam.*[61] Unfortunately this work no longer exists. John was a man of exemplary character, liberal and kindly, although his election had been opposed by Henry of Blois, who thought that the abbot had parted with money to the king for his election.[62] William, however, assures us that he paid only a small sum and that to secure the liberties of the abbey alone. John died on 19 August 1140[63] within a few months of taking office, leaving behind him an 'unfading memory'.[64]

59 *Gest. Regum,* ii, 557. The interpolator of Florence of Worcester dates it 4 Dec.: *Flor. Wig.* (Engl. Hist. Soc.), ii, 113.
60 *John of Worc.* ed. Weaver, 69 (as usual a year out). Wm. of Malm. says he was elected by the monks: *Gest. Regum,* ii, 560. The election may have taken place as soon as Roger was imprisoned: B.M., Cott. MS. Vit. A. X, although the author of the *Gesta Stephani* (Rolls Ser.), iii, 61, makes it take place after Roger's death.
61 Leland, *Collect.* ii, 272.
62 *Gest. Regum,* ii, 560. Wm. stresses that this was on account of the alleged irregularity, not on personal grounds.
63 *John of Worc.* ed. Weaver, 59 n. 1.
64 *Gest. Regum,* ii, 560.

The next abbot was Peter Moraunt,[65] a native of Bourges,[66] appointed early in 1141 by Henry of Blois, Bishop of Winchester and legate.[67] Peter had been a monk of Cluny,[68] and had been for a time Prior of La Charité and then superior of the monastery of St. Urban near Joinville (Haute-Marne). He had troubles to face there and at the request of Henry of Blois he came to England.[69] Peter was a man of learning and education;[70] he composed verses[71] and had accompanied Abbot John on his journey to Rome.[72] William tells us, not without a certain complacency, that he had himself been offered the abbacy – not for the first time – but had declined in favour of his friend Peter.[73]

The new abbot succeeded in the midst of the turmoil of the Anarchy, and Malmesbury again played a prominent part in the conflict. In 1144 William of Dover attacked Malmesbury, which was blockaded by the Earl of Gloucester until relieved by the king.[74] In the following year Malmesbury was again harassed by William of Dover, who seized the castellan of the castle and sent him to the empress. The empress in return attempted to win the garrison over by every possible means, only to find it reinforced by Stephen.[75] Comparative peace then followed for some years, though, as at Salisbury, there was friction between the military guarding the castle and the religious. This friction forced Pope Eugenius III in April 1151 to order the military[76] not to molest the monks. The capture of Malmesbury Castle in 1153 by the young Henry of Anjou in his bid for power was the final incident in the Anarchy.[77]

65 This is the surname given in *Reg. Malm.* ii, 222.
66 Leland, *Collect.* ii, 272.
67 *Flor. Wig.* (Engl. Hist. Soc.), ii, 129. He was present as abbot at the reception of the empress at Winchester in Mar. and Apr. 1141: *Gest. Regum,* ii, 573.
68 B.M., Cott. MS. Vit. A. X.
69 *Flor. Wig.* (Engl. Hist. Soc.), ii, 129.
70 Ibid.
71 He is probably the versifier *Petrus sodalis meus* of Wm. of Malm.: *Gest. Pont.* 192–3.
72 Leland, *Collect.* ii, 272.
73 From extracts made by Leland from preface of Abbot John's *Itinerarium*: Leland, *Collect.* ii, 272. See also letter of Wm. of Malm. to Peter *frater amantissimus*: *Gest. Regum,* i, pp. cxliii–cxlvi.
74 *Gesta Stephani* (Rolls Ser.), 109.
75 Ibid. 113–14.
76 *Castellani: Reg. Malm.* i, 381–2. Later, probably in 1173, Alexander III empowered the abbot to excommunicate, among others, any of the garrison of Malmesbury Castle who molested the abbey: ibid. 367–8.
77 *Ann. Mon.* (Rolls Ser.), i, 47.

With the help of Stephen and of Henry of Blois, Peter early obtained a bull of Pope Innocent II reiterating Malmesbury's exemption from episcopal control and confirming its possessions.[78] This was confirmed by Eugenius III (1151), Anastasius IV (1153), and Adrian IV (1156).[79] Little is known of the internal working of the abbey during the time of Abbot Peter. Some land was granted away in fee farm[80] and the vill of Chelworth and 15 hides of land were acquired. This acquisition was in exchange for the *fraternitas* of the abbey, a corrody, a special collect to be said daily at Mass, and the promotion of the grantor's three sons to Holy Orders.[81] It is possible that Peter entertained Henry II and Archbishop Theobald when they were at Malmesbury in September 1157.[82]

It was early in the abbacy of Peter, perhaps in 1143, that William of Malmesbury died. He had been born about 1095 and had spent most of his life in the monastery, first as a student and then as librarian and precentor successively. The fine qualities displayed in his historical writings justify his own claim to be the first monastic historian since Bede. A great debt is due to him for his contributions to historiography in general, and for the history of his own house and that of Glastonbury his work is invaluable. It may safely be claimed that in his calm maturity and sober judgement he stands far above the chroniclers of his period, and after Aldhelm he must remain the greatest glory of Malmesbury.[83]

According to Hearne, Peter died on 5 February 1159.[84] This, however, is subject to doubt and perhaps the royal writ of between April 1155 and 1158, requesting the abbey's tenants to do service to their abbot as their ancestors had done, indicates the date of Gregory's accession.[85] Little is known of Gregory except that he was educated at

---

78 *Reg. Malm.* i, 346–8.
79 Ibid. 348–52, 355–8, 363–6.
80 Ibid. 443, 459. This is what we should expect at a time of falling land values.
81 *Reg. Malm.* ii, 323–6.
82 *Sar. Chart. and Doc.* (Rolls Ser.), 24–25.
83 For details of his life and work and a list of his books, see preface by Stubbs to *Gest. Regum*, i and Knowles, *Mon. Ord. in Engl.* (2nd ed.), 499–501. Some of Wm.'s holograph MSS. remain, see N. Ker, 'William of Malmesbury's handwriting', *E.H.R.* lix. 371–6.
84 *nonas Feb. anno Dni. MCLX* in Hearne list, but he adds that it was in 7 Hen. II, which is impossible unless he is reckoning his years of Grace from 1 Jan.: *Chron. Edw. I and Edw. II* (Rolls Ser.), ii, p. cxix.
85 *Reg. Malm.* i, 334–5.

Westminster Abbey[86] and took part in various important events outside Malmesbury in 1163.[87] During his abbacy, in 1163, Pope Alexander III confirmed the exemption of the abbey.[88] Half a hide of land in Sutton Benger was leased out for a rent and reduced services.[89] Gregory appointed a master cook[90] and also a master porter. This porter, Reynold FitzSimon, was disseised during the next abbatial vacancy[91] and was only finally restored by Abbot Osbert.[92]

The death of Gregory, which must have taken place sometime in 1168, was followed by a vacancy which lasted until late 1171 or early 1172.[93] Robert, the next abbot, is said to have been a physician to Henry II and was surnamed 'de Venys'.[94] His appointment or election was the signal for a dispute between the abbots of Malmesbury and the bishops of Salisbury which lasted for nearly half a century. Fortified by the long series of papal confirmations of exemption obtained by his predecessors, Abbot Robert refused to take the oath of obedience to Jocelin, Bishop of Salisbury, which the latter demanded before giving him the abbatial blessing. Jocelin then refused to perform the ceremony and Robert appealed to Rome and received the blessing from another bishop.[95] Thereupon Bishop Jocelin refused to allow clergy presented by the abbot to churches in his diocese to be inducted. In 1174 Pope Alexander III ordered the bishops of London and Worcester to investigate the dispute, and in a bull of the following year he stated that, as the Bishop of Salisbury still troubled the monks on account of the profession of obedience, the Bishop of Exeter and the Abbot of Ford were to inspect the privileges of Malmesbury and, if satisfied, to inhibit the

---

86 *Spicilegium Liberianum,* ed. Liverani (Florence, 1863), 673, reading Gregorius for Gulielmus, which is out of the question.
87 *Cal. Chart. R.* 1327–41, 149; Eyton, *Itin.* 59; *Reg. Antiquissimum of the Cath. Ch. of Lincoln,* ed. C. W. Foster (Linc. Rec. Soc.), i, 65, ii, 12; *Ricardi de Cirencestria Speculum Historiale* (Rolls Ser.), 326.
88 *Reg. Malm.* i, 352–5.
89 Ibid. ii, 395.
90 Ibid. 298.
91 Ibid. 318; *Pipe R.* 1168–9 (P.R.S. xiii), 22.
92 *Reg. Malm.* ii, 318.
93 *Pipe R.* 1168–9 (P.R.S. xiii), 22; 1170 (xv), 65; 1171 (xvi), 24; 1172 (xviii), 128. Eyton, *Itin.* 94 must, therefore, be wrong in dating the protection of Hen. II to this abbot in June 1166: *Reg. Malm.* i, 335.
94 Hearne list in *Chron. Edw. I and Edw. II* (Rolls Ser.), ii, p. cxix.
95 *Reg. Malm.* i, 371–2.

Bishop of Salisbury from such action in the future.[96] The Pope, in further bulls of 1175 and 1177, ordered Jocelin to admit clerics of suitable character to the Malmesbury benefices when presented by the abbot.[97]

Abbot Robert had other troubles as well. Discord broke out between him and certain of the brethren, and in 1176 (probably) the bishops of Exeter and Worcester visited the abbey at the papal behest to take measures to ease the situation.[98] According to Gerald de Barry,[99] Robert was accused of illiteracy by the monks and Gerald tells an amusing story of his mis-reading of a Latin word when examined by the papal commissioners. John Cumin, afterwards Archbishop of Dublin, however, intervened and related an anecdote of an even more illiterate abbot in Rome. It was decided that as Abbot Robert was a good steward and guardian of his monastery he should remain in office, but that the prior and sub-prior should 'supply his defects' where spiritual issues were concerned.[1] Upon Robert's death, which appears to have been in 1176,[2] Osbert Foliot, who had been Prior of Gloucester,[3] was elected abbot, and, as before, Bishop Jocelin claimed obedience. Osbert apparently refused, and Richard, Archbishop of Canterbury, intervened in the dispute that followed. Early in 1177 while the issue was still *sub judice* Osbert went secretly to Wales, where he received the abbatial blessing from Bishop Nicholas of Llandaff. According to a report that he made to the Pope, the archbishop, for his part, suspended the Bishop of Llandaff, called the disputants together, and found against Malmesbury's claim to exemption.[4] About the same time Bishop Nicholas wrote a letter of abject apology to Bishop Jocelin.[5] Early in 1177 Osbert appealed to the Pope, who thereupon appointed judges delegate. The delegates were to

96 *Reg. Malm.* i, 371.
97 Ibid. 268–9.
98 Ibid. ii, 15.
99 *Giraldi Cambrensis Opera* (Rolls Ser.), ii, 346.
 1 A. Morey, *Bartholomew of Exeter*, 61, regards the story as 'more than unlikely in the case of a house such as Malmesbury', but it fits in so well with the charter of Bp. Roger of Worcester in the cartulary that it may be substantially true: *Reg. Malm.* ii, 15.
 2 He is mentioned in Aug. 1175: *Gesta Reg. Hen. Secundi Benedicti Abbatis* (Rolls Ser.), i, 99, and in Mar. 1176: *Reg. Malm.* i, 433.
 3 'Annals of Winchcombe' in B.M., Cott. MS. Tib. E. IV *sub anno* 1180 (in error); cf. B.M., Cott. MS. Faust. B. I, f. 22*b*.
 4 Haddan and Stubbs, *Councils*, i, 385.
 5 *Sar. Chart. & Doc.* (Rolls Ser.), 41–42.

inspect the privileges of Malmesbury and if they found them to comprise exemption were to restrain the diocesan and others from meddling.[6] The decision of the delegates is not known, but it may be inferred that it was in Malmesbury's favour, for shortly afterwards the Pope granted or confirmed to the abbey various rights and privileges – a course which he could hardly have taken if he had been lending his support to Jocelin. Thus the abbey was confirmed in its right to present incumbents to livings[7] and was licensed to appropriate the churches of Westport (Malmesbury) and Purton – the one to find lights burning day and night before St. Aldhelm's altar, the other to provide for a weekly commemoration of the Blessed Virgin:[8] the churches of Colerne and Dauntsey which had been usurped by vicars, who had refused to move *pendente lite,* were restored,[9] and the monks were protected from dishonest merchants, who had falsely accused them of contracting debts while at the papal court.[10]

Abbot Osbert granted ½ hide at Foxham[11] (in Bremhill) at a rent of 14s. and for service on onerous terms and another 2 hides in Swindon at a rent of 40s.[12] He also appointed a second master-cook and reinstated Reynold FitzSimon in his hereditary portership.[13] The abbot died on 17 March 1182.[14]

In 1183 Master Nicholas,[15] a monk of St. Alban's, succeeded to the abbacy.[16] Nicholas had been Prior of Wallingford and had come more than once into public notice.[17] Of his career as abbot, which lasted until 1186 or possibly 1187,[18] we know nothing save that he was

---

6 *Reg. Malm.* i, 370.
7 Ibid. 369.
8 Ibid.
9 Ibid. 372–4.
10 Ibid. 374.
11 Ibid. 459; ii, 180.
12 Ibid. ii, 4.
13 Ibid. 298, 318.
14 *Ann. Mon.* (Rolls Ser.), i, 52; ibid. iv, 385. The Annals of Winchcombe give his death as 17 Mar. 1181: B.M., Cott. MS. Tib. E. IV *sub anno.* The Pipe R., however, records a half-year vacancy between autumn 1181 and 1182 which would date his death in Mar. 1182: *Pipe R.* 1182 (P.R.S. xxxi), 88.
15 Hearne list calls him *Doctor Theologiae: Chron. Edw. I and Edw. II* (Rolls Ser.), ii, cxix.
16 *Ann. Mon.* (Rolls Ser.), i, 53; ii, 243.
17 *Giraldi Cambrensis Opera* (Rolls Ser.), viii, 195.
18 He was called *quondam abbas* between 1186–7: *Pipe R.* 1187 (P.R.S. xxxvii), 182. We notice the sale of wool, cheese, and hides at Malmesbury during the vacancy: ibid.

deposed after having been accused before the king and archbishop for running into heavy debt and having refused to amend.[19] A bull of Celestine III[20] states that Abbot Nicholas had promoted immature and unsuitable candidates to the sub diaconate and diaconate, having them ordained by some 'unknown' bishop on St. Stephen's day.[21] Further, he forbade them either to exercise their orders or to proceed to the priesthood. The significance of this apparently unintelligible procedure seems to be that Abbot Nicholas wished to show his independence of the diocesan by taking action which had no purpose other than to flout the authority of the Bishop of Salisbury.[22]

For most of 1187–9 the abbey was in the king's hands,[23] and Robert of Melûn, sub prior of Winchester, must have succeeded in the latter year.[24] Early in his abbacy, in 1191, he obtained a grant of exemption from Celestine III,[25] a dispensation for irregularities committed by Abbot Nicholas,[26] and papal confirmation of the appropriations of the churches of St. Mary's Westport, Crudwell, Kemble, Purton, and Bremhill.[27] About the same time Richard I granted him a charter of protection, describing him as *specialis clericus noster.*[28] Robert was much in public affairs and between 1194 and 1199 was employed as a justice.[29] He was also employed as a papal delegate in a number of cases, of which the most famous was that at Evesham in 1202–3.[30] It was

---

19 B.M., Cott. MS. Faust. B. I, f. 20a. This dates his deposition in 1185 but seems, as usual, to be a year out. According to the annals of Tewkesbury he died in 1205: *Ann. Mon.* (Rolls Ser.), i, 57.

20 *Reg. Malm.* i, 375–6.

21 This is not one of the days on which orders could be given.

22 There is one charter of Abbot Nicholas in the cartulary: *Reg. Malm.* ii, 323.

23 *Pipe R.* 1188 (P.R.S. xxxviii), 139.

24 The annals of Winchester date his succession wrongly in 1187: *Ann. Mon.* (Rolls Ser.), ii, 63; see B.M., Cott. MS. Faust. B. I, f. 21b.

25 *Reg. Malm.* i, 259–63.

26 Ibid. 375–6.

27 Ibid. 374–5.

28 Ibid. 337.

29 At Reading in Sept. 1194: B.M., Cott. MS. Vesp. B. xxiv, f. 21b; *Pipe R.* 1195–9 (P.R.S. N.S. vi–x), *passim.*

30 *Chron. Abbatiae de Evesham* (Rolls Ser.), 123. Samson, Precentor of Malmesbury, occurs at this time: Hist. MSS. Com. *D. and C. Wells,* i, 525, 526. Doubtless he was the same as the Samson, monk of Malmesbury, who with Richard, a fellow monk, is found in Oseney documents of 1200–5: *Oseney Chart.* ed. Salter (Oxf. Hist. Soc.), v, 6–7.

doubtless at this time that the bond of union between the abbeys of Malmesbury and Evesham was drawn up. Under this agreement monks of either house had full right of entry into choir or chapter of the other, and mutual prayers for the living and dead of both houses were arranged for in detail.[31] Abbot Robert, like his predecessors, continued to let out land for cash rents[32] and also granted a corrody.[33]

Robert of Melûn died on 24 May 1206[34] and the vacancy lasted until September 1208, when an abbot-elect is first mentioned.[35] The new abbot, Walter Loring, had been a secular clerk in the entourage of Abbot Robert I,[36] and was a monk for 30 years before he became abbot.[37] His abbacy was marked by a renewal of the conflict with the Bishop of Salisbury. Richard Poore, on his translation from Chichester to Salisbury in 1217, determined to end the exempt position of Malmesbury. Accordingly he wrote to Honorius III explaining that this exemption injured his authority, and the Pope, in June 1218, appointed the abbots of Waverley and Durford to examine the whole situation.[38] At the subsequent proceedings Malmesbury was represented by John Walsh;[39] the bishop argued for a return to the situation in Bishop Roger's time; Pandulf, the legate, and King Henry, however, favoured a compromise, and so it was agreed. Under this the monastery was to remain totally exempt,[40] but the bishop was to receive the manor of Highway and the advowsons of Bremhill[41] and Highway. The documents issued by past popes were to be deposited at Cirencester Abbey until it was seen whether the Pope would confirm the decision

---

31 Dugd. *Mon.* ii, 19. See also B.M., Cott. MS. Vesp. B. xxix, ff. 11a–12b. Malmesbury also had a union with St. Swithun's, Winchester, and 22 others: B.M., Add. MS. 29436, ff. 44b–45a. For close bond between Malmesbury and St. Oswald's Priory, Gloucester, see *Gest. Pont.* 293.

32 *Reg. Malm.* i, 254, 452; ii, 13. He later got into debt: ibid. ii, 81.

33 Ibid. ii, 221–3.

34 *Pipe R.* 1206 (P.R.S. N.S. xx), 201. He is last mentioned in Aug. 1205: Madox, *Formulare Anglicanum,* 25–26.

35 *Pipe R.* 1208 (P.R.S. N.S. xxiii), 195.

36 *Reg. Malm.* ii, 5; cf. i, 251.

37 Ibid.

38 Ibid. i, 401; *Sar. Chart. & Doc.* (Rolls Ser.), 88–91, but see Hist. MSS. Com. *Var. Coll.* i, 341.

39 Afterwards abbot.

40 The abbot was, however, to be blessed by the Bp. of Salisbury, who was also to confer holy orders and receive 1 oz. gold yearly as tribute.

41 The monks were to retain the manor of Bremhill.

of the commissioners. If he did so, the documents were to be returned to Malmesbury forthwith;[42] if he did not they were to remain at Cirencester with the proviso that they might be removed to Salisbury if trouble should break out again. Copies of the documents were to be deposited at Waverley. There is no evidence that the Pope confirmed Malmesbury's exemption, but the bishop did so.[43]

Walter was an energetic superior in many ways. In 1215 he secured from King John the borough of Malmesbury and the three hundreds belonging to it,[44] and in the following year Malmesbury Castle, with permission to destroy it if the monks wished to use the site.[45] Reference about this time to new methods of cultivation and inclosures at Ashley[46] suggest that Walter was an enterprising agriculturist. Other of his services to the abbey are recorded in an undated charter.[47] Among the changes made was the assignment of three manors to the conventual cook.[48] This is said to have been done to stifle certain complaints. Walter repaid £160 which his predecessor had borrowed from the Jews and 100 marks owing to the king, and he restored the church and sacristy.[49] A little later he secured the consent of the Bishop of Salisbury to the appropriation of Crudwell church, alleging the expenses of hospitality as a justification of the need for this extra source of income.[50] Perhaps more worldly wise than spiritual, he had during the years of his abbacy received monks whose illiteracy or ill fame caused scandal. In 1216 Innocent III forbade him to do this in the future, but the Pope followed

---

42 *Reg. Malm.* i, 404–7; *Sar. Chart. & Doc.* (Rolls Ser.), 93–95. There are also subsidiary documents in *Reg. Malm.* i, 391–5.

43 *Reg. Malm.* i, 395–8. No final papal confirmation appears to exist. The Bull of Honorius III refers only to minor causes of dispute: ibid. 378.

44 *Reg. Malm.* i, 339–40. Both grants were confirmed by Honorius III in 1217: ibid. 379–80. For the abbot's dealings with the borough see ibid. 446. The liberty of Malmesbury Abbey and the borough of Malmesbury are to be dealt with elsewhere in *V.C.H. Wilts.*

45 *Reg. Malm.* i, 340–1. It cost him 600 marks to the king and 37 marks to the queen: ibid. ii, 81. It is described as being *in atrio monasterii*, and an endless source of trouble to the monks: ibid.

46 Ibid. i, 445.

47 Ibid. ii, 80–82.

48 Ibid.

49 Ibid.

50 *Sar. Chart. & Doc.* (Rolls Ser.), 119–21. The pension of 2s. to the abbey infirmarian was still to be paid.

his rebuke a few days later by a general confirmation of the abbey's privileges.[51]

Loring died in 1222,[52] and his successor, John Walsh or Welsh, was a monk of Malmesbury.[53] His election received the royal assent on 10 November 1222.[54] He appears to have taken some part in public life both in church and state.[55] He acquired land in 'Scirmore' for repairing roofs and for other expenses,[56] made inclosures at Brokenborough,[57] and in 1230 obtained the consent of the Archbishop of Canterbury to the acquisition of tithes and lands for the maintenance of hospitality.[58] According to Matthew Paris he was suspended in 1244 by the papal legate for opposing the latter's extortionate financial demands.[59] During his abbacy Henry III twice visited the monastery.[60]

On John's death in late February or early March 1246,[61] Geoffrey, sacristan[62] of Malmesbury, succeeded.[63] The Bishop of Salisbury arranged for him to be blessed as abbot in Salisbury Cathedral on Sunday, 29 April, but the convent, alleging Geoffrey's physical weakness, urged that he should be blessed at Potterne without prejudice to the bishop's rights in the future.[64] Of Geoffrey's abbacy little is worthy of record. In 1247 he appropriated the church of Brinkworth.[65] In 1252 he obtained a royal grant of a weekly market at Westport and a fair at Whitchurch,[66]

51 *Reg. Malm.* i, 376–7.
52 *Ann. Mon.* (Rolls Ser.), iii, 77.
53 He was called John *Walensis.*
54 *Cal. Pat.* 1216–25, 351.
55 *Ann. Mon.* (Rolls Ser.), i, 232; *Cal. Close,* 1237–43, 162; *Royal Letters of Hen. III* (Rolls Ser.), 373; *Acta Stephani Langton* (Cant. & York Soc.), App. v, 171; the latter probably refers to Abbot John, for William's failing health from 1219 onwards would have made the task unlikely for him.
56 *Reg. Malm.* i, 380–1.
57 Ibid. ii, 185–7.
58 Ibid. i, 264–7. Confirmed by Peckham in 1285: ibid. i, 267–8.
59 *Chronica Majora* (Rolls Ser.), iv, 285. In 1238 the abbot's servants were outlawed for theft and for hiding thieves: *Cal. Close,* 1237–42, 147.
60 In 1235 and 1241: *Cal. Pat.* 1232–7, 115, 225; *Cal. Close,* 1234–6, 125; ibid. 1237–43, 317–18. On the latter occasion wine was sent ahead of the king from Bristol to Malmesbury: *Cal. Lib.* 1240–5, 65.
61 *Cal. Pat.* 1232–47, 475.
62 B.M., Cott. MS. Faust. B.VIII, f. 142*a.*
63 *Cal. Pat.* 1232–47, 476.
64 *Sar. Chart. & Doc.* (Rolls Ser.), 301.
65 *Cal. Papal Reg.* i, 249.
66 *Reg. Malm.* i, 341–2.

both in Malmesbury. The market and fair may have done something to relieve the debts which we find mentioned in the following year,[67] though Geoffrey left debts of £147 to be paid off by his successor. In general Geoffrey does not seem to have been a particularly energetic superior,[68] perhaps because of his ill health.

The election as abbot of William of Colerne, monk of Malmesbury, received the assent of Henry III on 20 April 1260[69] and was the signal for an era of vigorous rule and forceful administration. As a financier and agriculturist William was outstanding: his financial skill is illustrated by his action in buying a wardship and the manor of Weston (Herefs.) at Easter 1283 for 55 marks[70] and selling it in June for 70 marks.[71] There is a long list of this abbot's acquisitions in the cartulary;[72] he obtained the churches of Purton and Kemble and a large number of parcels of land, including the manors of Blackland near Calne, Colerne, and Fowlswick in Chippenham. The yearly value of these estates was worth £183 5s. and we are told that he spent £753 13s. 4d. on their purchase, an investment yielding the enormous return of approximately 25 per cent. on his capital.

It was during the abbacy of William of Colerne that the Taxation of Pope Nicholas IV was made:[73] from it, and from a rent roll of the manors of Malmesbury, probably made at about the same time,[74] we can get a picture of the properties owned by the abbey at the end of the 13th century. They comprised the churches of St. Mary Westport and St. Paul in Malmesbury, Kemble, Crudwell, and Purton, and pensions in the churches or chapels of St Nicholas Acon, London, Llanfihangel (Mon.), Foxley, Brinkworth, and Lyneham; also the

---

67 *Cal. Pat.* 1247–58, 230. There was also trouble over the perquisites of the master-cook in Oct. 1252: *Cal. Close,* 1251–3, 265.

68 For grants by the abbot see *Reg. Malm.* ii, 201–4, 319–20, 362, and index. Licence to elect a new abbot on the death of Geoffrey was given on 7 Apr. 1260: *Cal. Pat.* 1258–66, 120.

69 *Cal. Pat.* 1258–66, 122.

70 *Reg. Malm.* ii, 246–7, 248–9.

71 Ibid. 249–50. He also, early in his abbacy, bought up the office of hereditary porter: ibid. 111–15.

72 Ibid. 358 seq.

73 Probably in 1291: *Tax. Eccl.* (Rec. Com.). For useful map and account of Malmesbury estates see *Archaeologia,* xxxvii, 257–315.

74 *Reg. Malm.* i, 138 seq.; *Archaeologia,* xxxvii, 273 seq. Dated '12 Edward', who is either Edw. I (Nov. 1283 to Nov. 1284) or Edw. II (July 1318 to July 1319), probably the former.

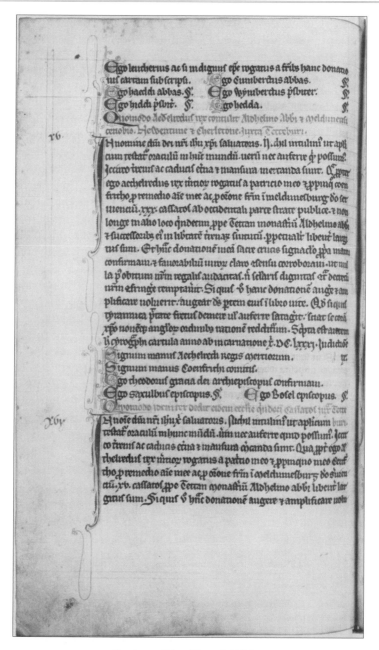

Register of the abbey, f. 122 *b*

manors of Littleton-upon-Severn, Bremhill (with Hazeland, Bremhill Wick, Spirthill, Hanger Park, Foxham, and Avon), Blackland (Calne), Brokenborough (with 'Kynegareshay', Thornhill, Burton, and Cleverton), Charlton, Cole Park (Malmesbury), Colerne, Euridge (Colerne), Norton, Garsdon, Long Newnton, Kemble, Brinkworth, Grittenham (Brinkworth), Sutton Benger, Fowlswick (Chippenham), Whitchurch (Malmesbury), Crudwell (including West Crudwell, Chelworth, Murcott, Eastcourt, 'Shortway', 'Ykemree', Hankerton, and Cloatley), and lands in the parish of St. Nicholas Acon (London) and at Sherston Pinkney.

Certain estates were allotted to various obedientiaries: the cook had a mill at Cole Park, part of the profits of three mills at Brokenborough, and incomes from Kemble and Crudwell; the pittancer had moneys coming from Kemble and Crudwell and the sacrist an income from Crudwell. The annual income of Malmesbury at this time as given in the *Taxatio* was £325 19s. 11d. The rental shows money rents paid to the value of £177 7s. 11½d.

William of Colerne pursued a vigorous agricultural policy. At Brinkworth[75] he made extensive inclosures and at 'la Rowmershe' in the valley of the By Brook near Yatton Keynell[76] he drained a large area of land, surrounding it with hedges and acquiring for the abbey all necessary rights of approvement from neighbouring landholders. A sum of no less than £1,315 1s. 1½d. was spent on stocks of corn,[77] doubtless sold at very considerable profit.

A large proportion of the money gained from this progressive agricultural policy was discharged on building operations. To the abbey buildings he added two large stone halls[78] and a kitchen, he rewalled and reroofed with stone the larder which lay near the abbot's garden, he filled that garden with vines and apple-trees, he planted a vineyard and a herb-garden, and he rewalled and reroofed the infirmary and chapter-house. He also erected a chapel dedicated to St. Aldhelm in the convent garden and three ovens near the convent kitchen. On the manors he built many farm buildings, including fourteen barns in various manors,

---

75 *Reg. Malm.* ii, 141–2.
76 Ibid. 262 seq., 307–9, 367.
77 Ibid. 364.
78 He also made various repairs and alterations in the presbytery of the church and put in a reredos (*magna tabula*) for the High Altar: ibid. 376.

stables, and a mill at Purton. Finally he rebuilt the churches of Crudwell and Kemble.

Abbot William rendered many other material services to the convent. He assigned a great number of estates and tithes to provide alms for the poor, to augment the pittances of the convent, to provide lights in the Lady Chapel and a mass in the charnel-house chapel. He increased the almoner's income and augmented the funds of the kitchen.[79] Further, he spent £47 13s. 4d. on elaborate copes and vestments for the church,[80] and £100 in laying on water to the abbey: it was at Martinmas 1284 that the water first flowed into the troughs.[81] Nor was the abbot behindhand in paying feudal dues, debts,[82] or necessary legal expenses: £140 was spent at the time of the *quo warranto* inquests;[83] he acquired a licence in mortmain for obtaining the legacy of a house in Fleet Street, London,[84] he paid 40 marks arrears of tribute due from Malmesbury to the Pope,[85] and spent considerable sums in the king's service before the battle of Evesham and in the Welsh, Scottish, and Gascon wars.

Of the purely spiritual side of the abbot's rule we are less well informed. He was clearly a conscientious disciplinarian and his decrees made in 1293 regulating the monks' food[86] show a desire to avoid all forms of singularity and disorder. The times and places when flesh was to be eaten were clearly stated, and were to be the same for all; meals in the *misericordia* were to be eaten in a silence interrupted only by the voice of the reader, all were to be present at grace after dinner and to go quietly and together to bed after compline. It is perhaps not surprising that a monk of Winchester petitioned to join the community.[87]

Abbot William took some part in public affairs, though it seems that domestic administration was his main interest. He entertained Henry

79 *Reg. Malm.* ii, 368–71, 371–8. He granted a tun of high quality wine to the convent on his anniversary: ibid. 300. He also increased the rents of the hostillar: ibid. 342–3.
80 Including a cope embroidered with scenes from the Old and New Testaments and another adorned with leopards. The pair cost £22 6s. 8d.: *Reg. Malm.* ii, 361.
81 The water was brought by pipes apparently from Long Newnton, or possibly from the Newnton Brook, farther upstream than Malmesbury: ibid. 376.
82 This was in Sept. 1262 and to Jewish creditors: B.M., Add. MS. 15667, f. 11a.
83 'In itinere Salomonis de Roffa et sociorum suorum anno regni regis E. nono': *Reg. Malm.* ii, 362. Again at Wilton, 17 Edw. I: ibid. 362.
84 Ibid. 381–2.
85 Ibid. 362.
86 *Reg. Malm.* ii, 382–4.
87 *Cal. Close,* 1259–61, 70.

III at Malmesbury on 1 September 1265[88] and Edward I on 23 March 1283.[89] It was, however, at this time that the king began to pension off aged retainers upon the abbey,[90] a practice against which later abbots were to protest in vain. Archbishop Peckham caused Abbot William some anxiety by apparently questioning the immunity of the abbey, though in the event we find a document of April 1282[91] in the archbishop's register admitting its exemption.[92]

By 1287 the abbot's health was failing and he was too ill to attend the Parliament of that year or the one of August 1296.[93] At the latter date the life of the abbot was drawing to a close and in September 1296 he died.[94] He was by far the most imposing of the later medieval abbots of Malmesbury, a brilliant financier, a lover of discipline, a keen realist and possibly a patron of learning,[95] he is perhaps not unworthy to stand beside an Amesbury of Glastonbury or an Eastry of Canterbury as typical of the best 13th-century monastic superior.

William of Badminton, whose election received the royal assent on 25 October 1296,[96] was in some ways a not unworthy successor to William of Colerne: but, whereas Colerne found his chief work in acquiring and improving monastic estates and in maintaining discipline at home, Badminton occupied himself far more in public affairs and identified himself in particular with the general interests of the English Black Monk Congregation. He was one of the presidents of the

88 *Cal. Pat.* 1258–66, 446; *Cal. Close,* 1264–8, 70, on which occasion the sacrist was granted 4 oaks by the king for the work at Malmesbury church.
89 *Cal. Pat.* 1281–92, 13.
90 In Mar. 1293 and Aug. 1297: *Cal. Close,* 1288–96, 279; ibid. 1296–1302, 127.
91 Cant. Reg. Peckham, f. 60a. The document is cancelled, but probably because addressed wrongly to Bp. of Worcester as diocesan. The finances at Malmesbury seem to have been in such good order that there was no need here, as elsewhere, for reforms.
92 This was the result of Abbot William's efforts; it cost £20 and entailed following the abp. round during the course of his metropolitical visitation: *Reg. Malm.* ii, 363.
93 Ibid. ii, 460–1. The abbot is here described as a 'royal chaplain'.
94 *Cal. Pat.* 1292–1301, 205.
95 A list of ornaments and books acquired by Wm. Favel, one of his monks, is given in *Reg. Malm.* ii, 379–80. They included works of Augustine and Aristotle, vestments and £1 spent on painting a retable to St. Mary Magdalen's altar. It was during Colerne's abbacy, in 1270, that Walter Clive, the prior, was conducting researches into the history of Mailduib: B.M., Cott. MS. Tib. A. XII, at end (MS. damaged by fire).
96 *Cal. Pat.* 1292–1301, 208.

congregation from 1298 to 1310 or 1311[97] and appears to have carried out his duties with regularity and precision.

It was in 1298, during the abbacy of Badminton, that a committee of the General Chapter[98] of the Black Monks decided to establish a house of studies for the Black Monks of southern England.[99] This foundation was in Stockwell Street, Oxford, in what had formerly been a cell to Gloucester Abbey.[1] Malmesbury was chosen to provide the prior and monks, probably because Sir John Gifford, the founder, was now living in retirement at the abbey and doubtless under the abbot's influence. Though the college was never completely controlled by Malmesbury, it was inevitable that the abbey should exercise a very considerable influence over it. It was in November 1298 that three Malmesbury monks were sent there to take over the establishment,[2] and Abbot Badminton was present at Oxford that year for the inception of the first Black Monk who had studied theology there.[3]

In his dealings with the general chapter we get the impression of a busy man of affairs, quick to seize the opportunity whether great or small, and it was perhaps no accident of chance that a Malmesbury monk, Philip Dentesey (or Dauntsey), was appointed chapter's representative at the Council of Vienne in 1311.[4]

Less is known of Badminton's administration at home: he appears as a rule merely to have taken over Colerne's financial and agricultural heritage without further exploiting it. We hear of large supplies of corn being bought in the first years of his abbacy;[5] on the other hand, he complained of serious financial difficulties in the winter of 1323. It is possible, however, that here the abbot was merely making excuses in an attempt to protect himself and his community against the fifth aged royal retainer to be planted on them in the space of a few years.[6] As

---

97 *Chapters of Engl. Black Monks,* ed. W. A. Pantin (Camd. Soc. 3rd ser. xlv, xlvii, liv), see index in liv.
98 Badminton was of course president by this time.
99 After 1338 for the rest of England also.
 1 For history of early days of Gloucester College see V. H. Galbraith, 'New Doc. about Gloucester College', *Snappe's Formulary,* ed. Salter (Oxf. Hist. Soc.), lxxx, 318 seq. and W. A. Pantin, 'Gloucester College', *Oxoniensia,* xi and xii, 55–74.
 2 *Ann. Mon.* (Rolls Ser.), iv, 539.
 3 *Hist. et Cart. Monast. Glouc.* (Rolls Ser.), i, 35.
 4 *Chapters of Black Monks* (Camd. Soc. 3rd ser. xlv), 169, 171, 172.
 5 £88 18s. 2d. worth in 1299: *Reg. Malm.* ii, 364.
 6 *Cal. Chanc. Warrants,* 1244–1336, 547.

most of these pensioners were retired musicians[7] — a temperamental race — it was perhaps not unnatural for the abbot to allege financial difficulties following upon pestilence and floods. In 1304 Mary, daughter of Edward I, was entertained at Malmesbury.[8] The abbot was away in Rome in late 1300 or early 1301[9] and again between 1309 and 1314. In 1316 there was trouble when three Malmesbury monks castigated a clerk of Rodborough (Glos.) with a sapling *(cum virga flexibili)* for an unnamed crime. Bishop Roger Mortival of Salisbury gave the abbot power to remove their excommunications.[10]

Abbot William of Badminton was perhaps prominent rather than great; he moved in important social events and forwarded the interests of Malmesbury by the adroit use of such machinery as came to hand. Of his inner character and feelings we know nothing, but we cannot resist the conclusion that his career was such as to afford a dangerous precedent in that he devoted too much attention to public rather than domestic concerns. He died in May 1324 after an abbacy of nearly 30 years.[11]

Badminton was succeeded by Adam de la Hoke, a monk of Malmesbury,[12] and Adam by John of Tintern.[13] Both abbots were deeply implicated in the civil wars of Edward II's reign.[14] It appears that Tintern was the ringleader and he did not extricate himself from his troubles until 1347.[15] Nothing is known of their government of the convent[16] or their care of its interests, save that de la Hoke was involved in a lengthy dispute with the Crown over the advowson of Brinkworth church.[17] It

7   *Cal. Close, passim.*
8   E 101/365/21.
9   *Reg. Simon de Gandavo* (Cant. & York Soc.), i, 50.
10 Sar. Reg. Mortival, ii, f. 17a.
11 *Cal. Pat.* 1321–4, 416.
12 Ibid. 423.
13 Ibid. 1338–40, 452.
14 Ibid. 1317–21, 294–5; cf. 1334–8, 111; 1343–5, 131; *Cal. Close,* 1337–9, 253; 1343–6, 235. The Despensers had apparently close connexions with the abbey and encaustic tiles with their arms were found on site of church: *W.A.M.* viii, 101.
15 *Cal. Pat.* 1345–8, 558. He had been arrested in 1337 for 'certain misdeeds': *Cal. Close,* 1337–9, 253.
16 The *Vita Edwardi II* was attributed by Hearne to a monk of Malmesbury, but Stubbs thinks this unlikely: *Chron. Edw. I and Edw. II* (Rolls Ser.), ii, p. xxxi seq.
17 *Cal. Pat.* 1330–4 *passim; Cal. Close,* 1337–9, 613. The dispute continued in Tintern's time: *Cal. Pat.* 1345–50 *passim.*

may be that de la Hoke's projected journey to Rome just before his death was connected with this dispute.[18]

The election of Simon de Aumeney, a monk of Malmesbury recently made prior of the Malmesbury cell at Pilton (Devon)[19] and whose surname was apparently Seagre,[20] received the royal assent on 19 August 1349.[21] His rule presents no striking features, though there are indications that all was not going well with the abbey. A former Prior of Malmesbury who later became superior at Pilton had an illegitimate daughter;[22] and a monk, Andrew of Tiderinton, apostatized from religion in 1353.[23] Abbot Simon died in October 1361.[24]

Walter de Camme, who was elected on 31 October 1362,[25] was of completely different calibre from his three immediate predecessors. Vigorous, enterprising, and efficient, he was perhaps made in the pattern of William of Badminton. Of a Gloucestershire family which had important connexions in London, he had made his mark as a competent, if not always tactful, Prior of Gloucester College,[26] and had played some part in Malmesbury affairs during the rule of his, possibly somewhat effete, predecessor.[27] He always displayed a keen interest in the Oxford college and had proved a tireless upholder of the Malmesbury interests there.

At Malmesbury perhaps the most important memorial of de Camme's abbacy was the acquisition, largely by the help of William de Camme his brother, of a very large property at Lincoln's Inn in Holborn. This property, together with other revenues from nearer home, formed

18 *Cal. Close,* 1337–9, 613; *Cal. Pat.* 1338–40, 161. De la Hoke died 25 Mar. 1340: *Eulog. Hist.* (Rolls Ser.), iii, 204. Tintern died 8 Aug. 1349: ibid. 214, possibly from the Black Death.
19 The first reliable reference to Pilton Priory occurs *c.* 1261: Dugd. *Mon.* iv, 443–5. According to tradition at Malmesbury, the Pilton estate was given to the abbey by King Athelstan: Leland, *Itin.* iii, 131. De Aumeney became prior in 1349: G. Oliver, *Mon. Dioc. Exon.* 245.
20 *Cal. Papal Letters,* iii, 473. Aumeney or Ampney is the name of the village from which he came.
21 *Cal. Pat.* 1348–50, 366.
22 Ibid. 1358–61, 583.
23 *Cal. Papal Letters,* iii, 575.
24 *Cal. Pat.* 1361–4, 85.
25 *Eulog. Hist.* (Rolls Ser.), iii, 313. As usual, the author is a year out; cf. *Cal. Pat.* 1361–4, 93.
26 *Chap. of Black Monks* (Camd. Soc. 3rd ser. liv), 25–27.
27 *Cal. Pat.* 1350–4, 456.

a foundation for the Lady Chapel, with its daily sung mass. Six candles were to burn there daily at mass and there was to be a daily private mass for the abbot's soul.[28] A new obedientiary was created for the important foundation, the warden of the Lady Chapel.

There had been some renewal of the ancient dispute with the bishops of Salisbury; what the occasions of it were is not known, but in 1364 Abbot Walter achieved a satisfactory agreement with Bishop Robert Wyville. By this the so-called customary payment to the bishop was not to be revived and the monks of Malmesbury were to be ordained by any bishop according to earlier custom. With regard to the appropriation of churches, a further single appropriation was to be allowed. For this grant the abbot paid altogether £22.[29] A more important concession was obtained from Pope Urban VI and Archbishop Simon of Sudbury. Abbot Walter and the convent had petitioned for the use of *pontificalia* on the ground that Malmesbury was an exempt abbey worth no less than 6,000 florins annually. Urban VI instructed the archbishop to investigate these claims, and the abbot's proctor was able to show that pontifical ornaments were used in other exempt monasteries. Accordingly in 1379 the archbishop granted permission for the abbot and his successors to wear mitre, gloves, sandals, tunic, dalmatic, and other pontifical ornaments on appropriate occasions in the monastery and its dependencies: also to give the solemn blessing during mass, evensong, and lauds and at table, provided no archbishop, bishop, or legate was present.[30]

Abbot Walter died in February 1396[31] after an abbacy of 35 years, in the earlier part of which he had displayed vigour and initiative. Royal assent to the election of Thomas Chelworth (or Chelesworth), said to have been 'provided to the abbey'[32] by the king, was given on 18 March 1396. On election he was induced by the community to take an oath to observe certain statutes and ordinances drawn up by it, apparently with

28 B.M., Cott. MS. Faust. B.VIII, ff. 163*a*, 191*b*, 192*a*, 193*a*. The elaborate transaction began in 1367 and was not completed until 1381, when it had been confirmed by Abp. Courtenay and a licence in mortmain granted: *Cal. Pat.* 1367–70, 233. This property was known as the 'Castell' in the latter part of the 16th cent.: Hist. MSS. Com. *Middleton, 322.*

29 *Reg. Malm.* ii, 421.

30 Cant. Reg. Simon of Sudbury, ff. 56*b*–57*a*; cf. Wilkins, *Concilia,* iii, 142–4.

31 *Cal. Pat.* 1392–6, 661.

32 His own phrase.

the knowledge and approval of the late abbot. For some six or seven years the new abbot submitted to this yoke, but in 1403 he appealed against it to Rome. The Pope instructed the Abbot of Stanley to investigate the matter and, if the facts were as alleged, to release Abbot Thomas from his oath on performance of a suitable penance.[33] Who the ringleaders were in this conciliar movement at Malmesbury and what was their precise purpose is not known. It seems likely that Abbot Walter de Camme's displays of authority were not always prudent or tactful, and doubtless dissentient members of the community had gained the consent of the abbot to the oath when he was in his dotage.

Little is known of the régime of Abbot Thomas at home. He took some part in outside affairs.[34] At the chapter of 1423, when he was represented by his prior, he was admonished for not sending monks to study at Oxford.[35] In 1412 he transferred to Worcester Priory certain of the outlying property in Stockwell Street, Oxford,[36] and in 1421 he gave the Rector of Somerford Keynes a corrody in return for an undertaking by the rector to attend to Malmesbury business when required.[37] He died towards the end of March 1424.[38]

The election of the next abbot, Roger Pershore, Prior of Malmesbury, received the royal assent on 5 May.[39] Shortly after, the Bishop of Salisbury sat in the episcopal chapel at Ramsbury to hear a protest from Malmesbury against the bishop's action in making inquiries about the fitness of the new candidate for office.[40] The abbey, it was pointed out, was subject immediately to the Holy See and was not in any way under the bishop's jurisdiction, and though in fact the abbots were blessed by the diocesan there was no need for this to be so.[41] The bishop replied that he had not intended to derogate from Malmesbury's privileged position. Of Pershore's abbacy nothing is known. He died on 26 March 1434.[42]

33 *Cal. Papal Letters,* v, 546–7.
34 *Reg. Chichele* (Cant. & York Soc.), iii, 37.
35 *Chap. of Black Monks* (Camd. Soc. 3rd ser. xlvii), 138, 150, 152.
36 Hist. MSS. Com. *14th Rep., D. and C. Worc.* 182.
37 *Cal. Pat.* 1422–9, 263.
38 Ibid. 199.
39 Ibid. 194.
40 Sar. Reg. Chandler, f. 43a. The author's interpretation of a rather obscure account of the proceedings.
41 This was not actually the case, see above, p. 169, n. 40.
42 Sar. Reg. Neville, f. 16a.

The *congé* for the new election was given on 13 April,[43] and on Saturday the 17th, after a mass of the Holy Ghost, the convent met to elect a new abbot. The occasion was an unusual one in that there appears to have been a genuine election by ballot. There were 26 electors, 23 of whom were priests. Three scrutators were appointed and it was decided that two named apostates should have no vote by proxy. Of the votes cast, Thomas Bristow obtained 13, William Aust 11, William Wolpen 1, and Robert Upton 1. In the evening Thomas Bristow accepted office in the infirmary chapel.[44]

Bristow had been ordained priest by Bishop Mascall of Hereford at Leominster in September 1406,[45] so he was probably in the middle fifties when he was elected. His abbacy is notable merely for the beginnings at Malmesbury of an abuse that was to become so common later as to acquire a certain respectability, that of monks leaving the monastery to take on the cure of souls. Thus in 1450 John Brystow received papal permission to take a benefice,[46] and William Avenyng obtained a similar dispensation in 1453.[47] In 1452 the Bishop of Salisbury renewed the claim renounced by his predecessor to ordain all Malmesbury monks,[48] but it is unknown whether the claim was admitted or not. Thomas Bristow died in late November or early December 1456.[49]

On 14 December John Andever S.T.P. was elected by 'inspiration'[50] after a meeting at which 23 were present in the chapter-house.[51] The new abbot was the illegitimate son of a priest and an unmarried woman, and in 1437 had received a dispensation to hold any ecclesiastical dignity.[52] He was then a bachelor of theology: by about 1439 he was a doctor and Prior of Gloucester College,[53] and in 1446 had become prior of the

43 *Cal. Pat.* 1429–36, 338.
44 Sar. Reg. Neville, f. 16a.
45 *Reg. Mascall* (Cant. & York Soc.), 133.
46 *Cal. Papal Letters,* 70.
47 Ibid. 252.
48 Sar. Reg. Beauchamp, f. 26b.
49 *Cal. Pat.* 1452–61, 331.
50 Or unanimous accord. Doubtless he was appointed by the Crown. He was probably at Pilton during the election.
51 Sar. Reg. Beauchamp, ff. 26b–27a.
52 *Cal. Papal Letters,* viii, 641.
53 *Chap. of Black Monks* (Camd. Soc. 3rd ser. liv), 105–8.

cell at Pilton.[54] A man of some learning,[55] he did not live to hold the abbey long. In 1459 he obtained permission to be away for two years with 24 servants in order to visit Rome and the holy places on business connected with the monastery.[56] Doubtless he was back at Malmesbury to entertain Edward IV when he spent two days there in September 1461.[57] He died in September 1462.[58]

Twenty-nine electors assembled[59] to choose the new abbot on 15 October, when John Ayly was elected by 'inspiration'.[60] In 1476 the king took Malmesbury under his protection for five years, on the ground that the abbot was blind and incapable of government.[61] How far this was true is doubtful: the abbot could hardly have been 70 years old at this date,[62] and if he were so old and incapable it is difficult to see why the king thought him fit to receive the obedience of the new Abbot of Cirencester in 1478.[63] It is possible that the monastery had again become involved in politics. It is perhaps significant that the Duke of Clarence wrote from Malmesbury for military aid in March 1471, just before deciding to make his submission to the king on the eve of the battle of Barnet.[64]

Abbot Ayly died in April 1480,[65] and the next abbot, Thomas Olveston,[66] received the temporalities from the king in the following June.[67] The next election, held on 4 March 1510, was attended by 18 electors.[68] It is interesting to note that not only had the community reached this low level (it was up again to 32 in 1527),[69] but nearly all its

---

54 G. Oliver, *Mon. Dioc. Exon.* 245.
55 His main interest was biblical study, see Tanner, *Bibliotheca,* 41.
56 *Cal. Pat.* 1452–61, 529.
57 Ibid. 1461–7, 40, 99.
58 Ibid. 210.
59 Sar. Reg. Beauchamp, f. 112a.
60 Royal assent given on 25 Oct.: *Cal. Pat.* 1461–7, 228.
61 Ibid. 1476–85, 12.
62 He was a sub-deacon in 1424: Sar. Reg. Neville, f. 16a.
63 Ibid. 131.
64 Hist. MSS. Com. *12th Rep. App. IV, Rutland,* p. 4. Clarence just then was on the Lancastrian side.
65 *Cal. Pat.* 1476–85, 190.
66 He had been made Prior of Pilton in 1472: Oliver, *Mon. Dioc. Exon.* 245.
67 *Cal. Pat.* 1476–85, 202.
68 Sar. Reg. Audley, ff. 135a–6a.
69 *Chap. of Black Monks* (Camd. Soc. 3rd ser. liv), 134–5.

members held offices, many of them in duplicate. The course of this election was not straightforward. Part of the community apparently wished for Richard Frampton as abbot, while an equally strong party led by the prior was violently opposed to him. Indeed the prior withheld the common seal of the abbey and the petition for royal confirmation had to be sealed with another seal borrowed for the occasion.[70] Although the king gave his assent to Frampton's election on 28 June 1510,[71] it was not until over a year later that a commission set up by the Bishop of Salisbury and meeting at Marlborough decided finally in his favour,[72] and the abbot took his oath of fealty to the Crown on the following day.[73] Less than four years later, in February 1515, Frampton died.[74]

Richard Camme, who had been cook and steward in 1510, was elected abbot in March 1515.[75] On 20 December 1527[76] the Abbot of Gloucester carried out a visitation of Malmesbury on behalf of the president. Abbot Camme deposed that many of the monks rebelled against all authority and that he had been unable to repress even grave crimes; that at 7 p.m. on 10 November eight[77] of the monks fully armed had broken into his quarters, threatened him with physical violence and removed two monks who were in his prison for evil behaviour; that of these insurgents, Thomas Gloucester had often cast away his habit, had climbed over the walls and consorted with harlots, and had seized the possessions of others for his own use, and John London was nearly as bad, and had apostatized and offered violence, and Robert Ciscetur was frequently drunk. Other monks, continued the abbot, were little better: several had broken out at night, the prior, John Codryngton, was remiss and openly admitted it in light-hearted fashion, the sub-prior was equally weak, there was no reading in the refectory, soft garments were worn, and women of doubtful reputation were received in the infirmary. The complaints of the rest of the community follow and charges both grave and slight were alleged freely. It appears clear that the abbot had allowed the community to become completely out

70 Sar. Reg. Audley, *in loc.*
71 *L. & P. Hen. VIII*, i, p. 175.
72 Sar Reg. Audley, *in loc.*
73 *L. & P. Hen. VIII*, i, p. 292.
74 Ibid. ii (1), p. 62.
75 Ibid. p. 91.
76 *Chap. of Black Monks* (Camd. Soc. 3rd ser. liv), 124–36.
77 *Sic*, but 10 are named: ibid. 126.

of hand: he was violent tempered, even hitting the brethren with his stick,[78] and he was under the influence of a local woman called Alice Taylor who spent a good deal of time with him gossiping and retailing information about the behaviour of the community.[79] The general impression conveyed is one of sordidness and neglect, of services sung late because there was no clock, of ill-cooked food, neglect of the sick, inadequate plumbing, absence of mass-servers, brawling, grumbling, and disorder. The Abbot of Gloucester promptly excommunicated six of the monks[80] and issued a lengthy series of injunctions which included reform in the infirmary, the provision of a new water-supply within three years at most, the purchase of a clock, the finding of two boys to serve mass, and instructions to the abbot to learn self-control and to be more kindly and considerate.

The abbot was dead by 13 May 1533[81] and a complex series of events followed. Cromwell, who had been appointed Secretary of State just over a month before, clearly wished Robert Frampton, the chamberlain, to succeed to the abbacy. He therefore wrote on 13 May to the prior desiring the chamberlain to be one of those sent to certify the death of the late abbot to the king. The prior had, however, forestalled Cromwell and two of the brethren had already been sent for the purpose.[82] Meanwhile a party in support of the candidature of Walter Jay or Bristow[83] was springing up, and Rowland Lee hastened to Malmesbury on 17 June to carry out Cromwell's wishes in the matter of the election.[84] When he got there, he found letters to him from Cromwell[85] stating that the king wished to have an election by compromise;[86] this, however, proved difficult as Bristow's party insisted on an election by ballot, saying that they had the king's licence for a free election. As Bristow's faction was more than double that of Frampton, Lee could get no farther and therefore postponed the election until 17

---

78 *Cum baculo suo.* Can this actually mean his crozier?
79 There is no hint of any improper relationship.
80 All named.
81 *L. & P. Hen. VIII*, vi, p. 218.
82 Ibid.
83 Ibid. pp. 218, 305. The matter is complicated by the fact that many of the documents are wrongly dated by the editor with regard to the year.
84 Ibid. v, p. 141.
85 Ibid. vi, pp. 304–5.
86 i.e. by a few chosen representatives whose vote would stand for the others.

July. His visit, however, was not fruitless, for he acquired from the Abbot of Gloucester the *comperta* of the visitation of 1527,[87] which furnished more than enough information to discredit Bristow, though unfortunately many of Frampton's party were also deeply compromised and Lee marked their names with a cross so that this information should be concealed.[88] The next step was the dispatch of a letter of 3 July from John Codryngton, the prior, and others of Bristow's party, stating that they had heard from the king that he had been told that there were great dissensions at Malmesbury and was sending Dr. Lee to the abbey. The writers further pointed out that Lee had been there twice already and that in any case they would be quite content to send the king the names of four brethren to choose from. Frampton's would doubtless not have figured among them. In spite of this, Lee was soon back at Malmesbury and on 12 July acquainted Cromwell with his failure, after three days of argument, to persuade Bristow's party to give way.[89] On 17 July, however, Lee managed to become one of two arbitrators, the election was made by compromise and both Frampton and Bristow came to court to present the result.[90] As an inevitable consequence, on 22 July the king gave his assent to Frampton's election as abbot.[91]

The days of the abbey were now numbered. Already the new abbot had found it hard to pay all the dues demanded of him, stating that his predecessor had left little money and that during the vacancy part of the plate and cattle had been embezzled and the abbey was 'sore decayed'.[92] Cromwell was now demanding receiverships and rights of pannage for his friends,[93] though the abbot alleged that nearly all the demesnes had been leased out in his predecessor's time and that notwithstanding the resources of his two parks, which were still in hand, he had to spend 200 marks a year on grain and stock. The king's visitors were also busy: Ap Rice was at the abbey in August 1535,[94] and Dr. Petre on his arrival there in the following January stated that he had done nothing, as the abbot was in London, but observed that the house

87 This was sent to Cromwell and so found its way into the Public Records: otherwise, doubtless, nothing would have now been known of the visitation of 1527.
88 *L. & P. Hen. VIII*, vi, p. 305.
89 Ibid. p. 364.
90 Ibid. p. 374.
91 Ibid. p. 404.
92 Ibid. v, p. 724.
93 Ibid. p. 462; ibid. xiv (2), p.122.
94 Ibid. ix, p. 39.

was well stocked with cattle, the shrine well kept, and all the demesne lands in the hands of the monastery.[95]

The *Valor Ecclesiasticus*[96] gives a detailed picture of the assets of the monastery on the eve of the Dissolution. The large proportion of rents assigned to the *camera abbatis* or abbot's exchequer shows that most of the assets of the house were in the hands of the abbot and his immediate advisers to administer freely, and the *Valor* notes that the abbot could dismiss obedientiaries at will.

Most of the spiritualities were assigned to various obedientiaries: the cook received tithes in Corston, Rodbourne, Thornhill, and Burton (all in Malmesbury), in Brokenborough and Brinkworth, and was given an annual pension by the Vicar of Kemble. The chamberlain had tithes in Milbourne (Malmesbury), Long Newnton, Charlton, Cleverton, Garsdon, and Tockenham, and had pensions from the churches of Brinkworth and Garsdon. The sacrist had tithes at Brokenborough, Long Newnton, Charlton, Thornhill, Burton, Cleverton, and Lea, and pensions from the Malmesbury churches of St. Paul and St. Mary Westport and from the churches of Long Newnton and St. Nicholas Acon, London. The warden of the Lady Chapel had tithes at Tockenham and the precentor a pension from Beckhampton church. Certain tithes at Milbourne, Charlton, Hankerton, Yatton,[97] Colerne, and Broughton do not appear to have been appropriated to any particular obedientiary. Other unappropriated spiritualities are Oaksey chapel, offerings made to St. Aldhelm's image at Malmesbury, to the images of St. Leonard at Euridge (Colerne) and St. James at Whitchurch (Malmesbury), and moneys received in St. John the Baptist's Chapel at Malmesbury. Finally there are small funeral and Easter offerings at Malmesbury.

Among the temporalities in the hands of the abbot and convent were the monastery buildings and environs, covering about 6 acres; also the convent garden *cum cuniculis*,[98] streams, ponds, fishery, and fruit-trees, covering about 43 acres and kept for the abbot and convent to walk in. Near by was a water-mill and a dovecote, the latter at that time in complete decay.

95 Ibid. xiv (1), p. 32. This is contradicted by the abbot's statement and by the evidence of the *Valor*.
96 *Valor Eccl.* (Rec. Com.), ii, 118–22.
97 This appears to be in Colerne, and is not Yatton-Keynell.
98 Rabbits or even possibly arbours.

To the abbot's exchequer went the Malmesbury stallage-dues, fair tolls, profits of shire aud hundred courts, and the amercements of the borough brewers. The abbot's exchequer also received rents in Brokenborough, Sutton Benger, Crudwell, Bremhill, Kemble, Long Newnton, Charlton, Rodbourne, Burton, Corston (including grazing receipts from West Park, which was largely overgrown with thorns and thickets), Cole Park (including grazing receipts), Purton, Lea, Norton, Hankerton, Foxham, Thickwood (Colerne), and Littleton-upon-Severn.

The cook was well endowed. He received rents in Malmesbury borough, other dues called 'burgable and longable',[99] market-dues and rents from pitches in the market-place, hundred-silver paid by the tenants of Dauntsey, Little Somerford, and Cowage to the hundred of Malmesbury Without, the profits of the courts and sheriff's tourns in that hundred, and dues payable to the hundreds of Startley and Chedglow. The cook further received rents at Brokenborough, Kemble, Long Newnton, Charlton, Thornhill (which included the farm of a water-mill at Mill Bridge and that of a mill at Cow Bridge), Purton, Brinkworth, the farm of the manor of Blackland, a rent called 'Matravers Fee', and the farm of a mill called Winyard Mill in Whitchurch (Malmesbury), and rents at Swindon and Littleton-upon-Severn. The cook formerly received a rent from a fishery in the Wye near Tintern, but this had been destroyed at the king's order, probably at the dissolution of Tintern Abbey.

The chamberlain drew his revenues from rents in Malmesbury borough, the farm of Purton manor, rents at Norton, Grittenham, Euridge (including the farm of the site of the manor), and Whitchurch.

The sacrist had rents in Malmesbury borough and Garsdon, and the almoner received rents in the borough and in Whitchurch. The pittancer had rents at Bimport and Westport in Malmesbury, and at Brokenborough, Crudwell, Kemble, Long Newnton, Charlton (to provide 1 lb. of pepper), Corston, Lea, Hankerton, Brinkworth, Colerne, Stanton St. Quintin, Seagry, and Littleton-upon-Severn.

The warden of the Lady Chapel received rents in Malmesbury borough, Bremhill, Hankerton, Brinkworth, Sherston Pinkney, and from various houses and buildings in Fleet Street and Holborn in London. The infirmarian drew rents in Malmesbury borough, Brokenborough,

99 i.e. *burgh-gafol* and *land-gafol.*

Kemble, Foxham, and Bristol. The refectorian received rents in the borough and the prior rents at Purton.

At the time of drawing up the *Valor*, of eighteen manors or sites of manors, seventeen were at farm and the demesne of the eighteenth was also let out to farm. It is difficult to estimate the exact state of the finances as there was an elaborate system of internal debts owed by one obedientiary to another. The total coming from all sources of income was £890 13s. 9¼d., of which about five-eighths went to the abbot's exchequer, one-quarter into the hands of the cook, and the remaining eighth went to the other obedientiaries. Fifteen stewards are mentioned, many of them being persons who later acquired monastic lands. There were two corrodies.

The end of the abbey was now at hand and on 15 December 1539, London, Ap Rice, and others received the surrender of the house, which they valued at £830 1s. 3½d. a year.[1] Yearly pensions were awarded to the abbot and 21 monks.[2] The abbot received 200 marks yearly, the prior and sub-prior £10, and the rest of the convent between £6 and £7 apiece. Walter Jay, who was the steward of the lands and chamberlain, received £13 6s. 8d. Besides the obedientiaries mentioned in the *Valor* a sub-prior, a third prior, a steward of the lands, an abbot's steward, and a sub-sacrist also occur. Seven monks are described as seniors and one as a student. Over and above his pension the abbot was given a holding in High Street, Bristol, and a garden near the Red Cross on the outskirts of that city. Unless the number of monks had fallen sharply since 1527, when there were 32 excluding novices, it is clear that some must already have apostatized from religion or alternatively have refused pensions on conscientious grounds.

The history and sequence of the churches and monastery buildings at Malmesbury are not easy to make out, especially as William of Malmesbury is not infrequently ambiguous.[3] Of Maildulib's small church (*parva basilica*) there were supposedly some remains which had disappeared by the 12th century.[4] St Aldhelm built three new churches:

---

1 *L. & P. Hen. VIII*, xiv (2), p. 255. But see *Valor*, First Ministers' Accts. (SC 6/Hen. VIII/3986/m. 96 and E 315/494/34–44.)
2 *L. & P. Hen. VIII*, xiv (2), p. 255.
3 An excellent account with plan is given by H. Brakspear in *Archaeologia*, lxiv, 399–436. See also *W.A.M.* viii for articles by J. E. Jackson and E. A. Freeman, and *Architect. Rev.* ix, 63 seq.
4 *Gest. Pont.* 345.

one in honour of our Saviour, St. Peter, and St. Paul which was regarded until Abbot Aelfric's time as the chief church of the monastery.[5] It was probably this church which had remained until William's time and which he praises as being second to none for its workmanship.[6] St. Aldhelm also built 'in ambitu...cenobii' a church in honour of St Mary,[7] and against St. Mary's a church of St. Michael,[8] 'the remains of which we have seen', says William. St. Mary's Church appears to have been rebuilt in part by Abbot Aelfric in the days of Edgar. William argues, however, that the tower, which still existed in his days, was older, because there was record of King Athelstan having been buried beneath it.[9] A church of St. Laurence is mentioned as the first burial-place of John Scotus,[10] while Constantine and Abbot Beorhtwold II were buried in St. Andrew's Church which adjoined the *major ecclesia*. It was in St. Andrew's Church that succeeding abbots were buried. The building was later pulled down to provide space for new buildings and had clearly disappeared by the time of William of Malmesbury.[11]

We know little more of the pre-conquest buildings. Abbot Aelfric in the 10th century built domestic quarters for the monks,[12] and about the same time the monastery and church were restored and the latter fitted with bells and organs.[13] There was a cloister, for the unfortunate Elfildis was buried there at a slightly later date,[14] and in 1056 Bishop Heremann built a bell-tower.[15]

5 *Gest. Pont.* 345, 386.
6 *nostro perstitit aevo*: ibid. 361–2. Presumably the church had already gone, for otherwise Wm. would have used some phrase like 'is still to be seen'. Most writers, including Brakspear and Freeman, regard this as referring to St. Mary's Church. From the context it could well do so (it is called *major ecclesia* and it is ambiguous whether the earlier *major ecclesia* of St. Saviour or the later one of St. Mary is meant); but if this line is taken a mesh of contradictions follows.
7 *Gest. Pont.* 361.
8 Ibid. In which St. Aldhelm was first buried.
9 *Gest. Regum*, i, 154; *Gest. Pont.* 397. It is not easy to reconcile all these statements. Thus in *Gest. Regum* Wm. says that Abbot Aelfric rebuilt the church, but in the *Gest. Pont.* he appears to modify this statement (p. 397) and further points out that part of St. Mary's survived the fires of the times of Alfred and Edw. the Confessor: ibid. 362–3.
10 *Gest. Pont.* 394.
11 Ibid. 411, 416. Note phrase *quia tunc erat*.
12 *Officinas monasterii*: *Gest. Pont.* 405.
13 Ibid. 407.
14 Ibid. 415.
15 *Eulog. Hist.* (Rolls Ser.), iii, 294.

Thus by the 12th century Mailduib's alleged church and St. Andrew's Church had already disappeared; Aldhelm's church of our Saviour was standing at least up to William's time,[16] as was St. Mary's Church (portions of which were Aldhelm's work but mainly of the time of Abbot Aelfric) which appears to have been rebuilt by the early part of the 12th century. Some portions of St. Michael's Church remained up to William's time. Leland, in his description of the abbey written shortly after the Dissolution, says: 'Ther was a litle Chirch joining to the South side of the *Transeptum* of thabby Chirch, wher sum say *Johannes Scotus* the Great Clerk was slayne... Wevers hath now lomes in this litle Chirch, but it stondith and is a very old Pece of Work.'[17] This was almost certainly St. Laurence's Church.[18]

In the 12th century St. Mary's Church was replaced by a nave of nine bays,[19] transepts with an eastern chapel on either side, and a choir of four bays terminating in a round apse, at the apex of which stood the shrine of St. Aldhelm and a chevet of three chapels. These buildings appear to have been in progress in William of Malmesbury's time.[20] In the 13th century the choir was lengthened and an eastern Lady Chapel added: the latter encroached on the graveyard, and a charnel-house with a chapel was made for the disturbed bones and endowed in 1267.[21] In the following century the tower was heightened and a spire of timber and lead higher than that of Salisbury was added. This fell either just before or just after the Dissolution.[22] In the tower were 10 bells, including

16 Was this on the site of the present ruined church of St. Paul, which stands at the SW. of the abbey precincts?

17 Leland, *Itin.* ii, 25.

18 It is usually supposed to have been St. Michael's: *Archaeologia,* lxiv, 402, but Wm. of Malm. says of this *cuius vestigia vidimus* as if the remains were no longer there, and Aubrey says that St. Michael's was to the west of the abbey church, though this seems difficult as St. Michael's was contiguous to St. Mary's, see *Gest. Pont.* 361 and Aubrey, *Topog. Coll.* 260. It seems much more probable that it was St. Laurence's Church where John Scotus was first buried; in Leland's time the legend was that Scotus was killed there, and this is supported by Wm. of Malm.'s letter to Peter where he says that Scotus *iacuit aliquamdiu in ecclesia illa quae fuerat nefandae caedis conscia,* see *Gest. Regum,* i, p. cxlvi.

19 With elaborate south porch.

20 By 1080 there was apparently some kind of retrochoir: *Gest. Pont.* 427. There is no reason to suppose, as does Freeman, that Roger built much more at Malmesbury than a castle: *W.A.M.* viii, 83–84.

21 *Reg. Malm.* ii, 123, 125.

22 Leland, *Itin.* ii, 25; Aubrey, *Topog. Coll.* ed. Jackson, 256.

The abbey from the north-east in 1809

a great one dedicated to St. Aldhelm.[23] In the 14th century also the wooden roofs of nave and transepts were replaced by vaulting in stone and the clerestory of the nave was remodelled. About the year 1400 a large square tower with two bells was built over the two western bays of the nave. In the 15th century a new building was erected over the south side of the nave and an organ chamber constructed in the triforium. Finally, in the 16th century, a screen was built at the crossing beneath the central tower.

The cloisters, as at Gloucester and Canterbury, stood to the north of the nave; built in the 12th century, they were elaborately remodelled and vaulted in the fifteenth after the manner of those of Gloucester, and paved with encaustic tiles.[24] In the east walk was the chapter-house, of 12th-century date but heightened and vaulted by Abbot William of

---

23 Aubrey, op. cit. 255; B. Willis, *Mitred Abbeys*, i, 136, where inscription on bell is given. For account of church and buildings see *Itineraria Symonis Simeonis et Willelmi de Worcestre*, ed. J. Nasmith, 83.

24 From lettering on the tiles they can be attributed to the times of the abbots from Wm. of Colerne to Thos. Bristow: *Archaeologia*, lxiv, 428.

Colerne.[25] To the north was the frater with the kitchens to the west of it.[26] To the east of the frater was the dorter and farther east still the 13th-century rere-dorter of the monks.

To the east of the chapter-house stood the infirmary, and south-eastwards the abbot's house with its gardens and chapel.[27] On the west side of the cloisters was the guest-house of 13th- and 14th-century date. On the north side of the monastic buildings and sloping down steeply to the river and beyond it was the convent garden of over 40 acres with its streams and fruit-trees.[28] There were gate-houses on the south opening out of the end of the High Street and on the west nearly opposite the west front of the church.[29]

ABBOTS OF MALMESBURY

Several names have been rejected from the usual list of abbots of Malmesbury for the following reasons. William of Malmesbury has little to say about the period following upon the death of Aldhelm, and what he does say is often contradicted by the unknown 13th-century historian of the abbey whose short history is now among the Cottonian manuscripts (see p. 151, n. 52). The compiler uses William extensively but corrects him without comment.[30] It seems clear that Malmesbury's method of working was to search the muniments for ancient charters and to build up his story around them; thus he is sometimes misled by forged or interpolated documents. The list in the Cottonian manuscript seems to represent in its earlier stages merely a list of names copied indiscriminately from a *Liber vitae.*[31] Many persons listed as abbots of Malmesbury undoubtedly existed, but there is no reason to suppose that their connexion with the abbey was anything more than an inclusion in its list of benefactors or as sharing in the prayers of the community.[32]

---

25 *Reg. Malm.* ii, 365.

26 The kitchen was standing in Aubrey's time: Aubrey, *Topog. Coll.* ed. Jackson, 260.

27 *Reg. Malm.* ii, 365.

28 *Valor Eccl.* (Rec. Com.), ii, 119.

29 Ibid.

30 Birch in his article 'On Succession of Abbots of Malmesbury' in *Jnl. Brit. Arch. Assoc.* xxvii, 314–42, 446–8, does something to clear up the confusion.

31 i.e. a list of abbots like the *Nomina abbatum* of the *Liber Vitae* of Durham; see facsimile, Surtees Soc. cxxxvi, f. 17a.

32 This view is supported by the fact that the spelling of these names in the Cotton MS. is of decidedly antique character.

A list similar to the Cottonian one, transcribed by Hearne from a manuscript, now lost, of the *Vita Edwardi Secundi*, is even more unreliable and appears to be a separate recension from the same *Liber Vitae*.[33] This has been referred to in this article as the Hearne list.

After Aldhelm, the Cottonian list records an Abbot Daniel; this is undoubtedly the same as the Bishop of Winchester from 705 to 744. William of Malmesbury says that he retired and lived as a monk at Malmesbury,[34] though he nowhere calls him abbot, and there is no reason to think that he ever assumed that office.

William, relying on a spurious charter of Cuthred,[35] makes an Abbot Aldhelm II succeed in 745,[36] though an apparently genuine charter of Cynewulf of 758[37] granting Marden and Rodbourne to Malmesbury makes no mention of any abbot. The Cottonian list does not record Aldhelm II, and it seems that William was misled by the phrasing of Cuthred's charter – *Aldhelmo abbati familieque sub illius regiminis degenti* – which probably means no more than the rule and way of life introduced by St. Aldhelm.

Megidulfus,[38] the next abbot of the Cottonian list, is clearly a confusion with Mailduib the founder. The same may be said of his successor Forthere, who has doubtless been confused with the Bishop of Sherborne who died about 737.[39] The next two abbots in the Cottonian list are equally unsatisfactory. The first is Aeambriht; it is true that Aethelbald of Mercia at some date between 755 and 757[40] granted

33 *Chron. Edw. I and Edw. II* (Rolls Ser.), ii, pp. cxviii–cxix.
34 *Gest. Pont.* 160. A spring in which he bathed was remembered there in the 12th cent. ibid. 357–8. *Anglo-Sax. Chron.* ed. Plummer, i, 47, says he retired in 744–5, as does Florence of Worc. *Flor. Wig.* (Engl. Hist. Soc.), i, 55. Plummer, *Baedae Op. Hist.* ii, 308, seems too cautious here.
35 Spurious at least in its present form: *Cart. Sax.* ed. Birch, no. 170.
36 *Gest. Pont.* 387. This doubtless to fit in well with Daniel's death, but in any case Daniel is numbered among the witnesses of the charter of Cuthred: *Cart. Sax.* ed. Birch, no. 170.
37 *Cart. Sax.* ed. Birch, no. 185. Wm. of Malm. says 'it is reported' that Aldhelm II was a nephew of St. Aldhelm: *Gest. Pont.* 388. See Haddan and Stubbs, *Councils,* iii, 396, for grant by Cynewulf to Malmesbury.
38 This name is not found in Wm. of Malm. but occurs in the Hearne list as 'Migidulphus': *Chron. Edw. I and Edw. II* (Rolls Ser.), ii, cxviii.
39 It was not an uncommon name, cf. Wessex priest of that name mentioned *c.* 742–6 in a letter of St. Boniface to Daniel, Bp. of Winchester, *Epist. Merow.* ed. Dümmler, i, 329.
40 *Cart. Sax.* ed. Birch, no. 181.

an Abbot Eanberht land in a wood called *Toccan sceaga* which may
have been in Wiltshire,[41] but Eanberht cannot have been Abbot of
Malmesbury for his dates conflict with the genuine Abbot Aethelheard.
The second abbot, Sigibriht, has a not uncommon name and there is
no evidence for his existence as Abbot of Malmesbury.[42]

In place of Cuthberht the Cottonian list gives Wlfred as the next
abbot, and perhaps he may be identified with the 'Waerfrid abbot' who
is found as witness in a charter of 854,[43] but there is no evidence that he
was Abbot of Malmesbury. The next two abbots are 'Athelmodus' and
'Hetheredus'. These again probably represent only the bishops of
Sherborne (766–78) and of Worcester (780–800) taken from a *Liber
Vitae.*

The dates of Abbot Aelfric and his successor are hard to determine.
William of Malmesbury identifies Abbot Aelfric with the Aelfric who
became Bishop of Crediton in 977[44] and says he was succeeded by
Aethelweard. In support of this he quotes a charter of 982[45] in which
King Ethelred grants Rodbourne to the monks 'living under the rule
of abbot Aethelweard' and Aethelweard appears in the Cottonian list.
On the other hand, Dean Armitage Robinson identifies the Aelfric of
Crediton with an ex-abbot of Westminster[46] and two charters, of 993
and 998 respectively, the second regarded as genuine by Stenton,[47] quote
'Aelfric abbot of Malmesbury' among the witnesses. It seems likely that
Robinson is in error, for it appears impossible that any Abbot of
Westminster could be promoted to a bishopric at this time, for Flete,
upon whose statement Robinson is building, in reality appears to be

---

41 Stenton, *Anglo-Saxon Engl.* 203.

42 The ingenious supposition of Birch does not bear close inspection: *Jnl. Brit. Arch.
Assoc.* xxvii, 315.

43 The *Anglo-Saxon Chron.* sub anno 855 states that Aethelwulf, the grantor of this
charter, gave a tithe of his lands to the glory of God. The series of charters in *Cart.
Sax.* ed. Birch, nos. 468–81 was the effect of this. One of them (470–1) gives land to
the abbey at Purton, Lacock, Crudwell, Kemble, &c., but its character does not
inspire confidence.

44 *Gest. Pont.* 406.

45 The date is wrongly given as 972 in *Gest. Pont.* 411, but 982 is correct: *Cod. Dipl.* ed.
Kemble, no. 632; *Reg. Malm.* i, 318–20. But the charter appears to have been
retouched at a later date.

46 A. Robinson, *Saxon Bps. of Wells,* 67.

47 *Cod. Dipl.* ed. Kemble, nos. 684, 698. Regarded as genuine by Stenton: *Anglo-Saxon
Engl.* 449.

referring vaguely, and confessedly obscurely, to a predecessor of Abbot Wulsin of Westminster, who was himself appointed in 958.

In the Cottonian list the name of Cynebertus follows that of Brihtwold, but no other mention is made of this abbot.[48]

Finally, we come to Robert Foliot, who was supposed to have succeeded Osbert Foliot in 1182. For his existence we have one reference alone, that of the early 13th-century annalist who states that at Osbert's death another Prior of Gloucester, called Robert Foliot, succeeded him.[49] There is no reason to believe that there was ever an Abbot of Malmesbury of this name,[50] and it seems reasonable to suppose that the annalist has simply transposed the name Osbert for Robert, and that he is merely recording the accession of Osbert on the death of the previous Abbot Robert.

> Mailduib, c. 637.[51]
> Aldhelm, probably appointed ? 675.[52]
> Eaba, occurs c. 730.[53]
> Aethelheard, occurs before and in 749.[54]
> Cuthbert, appointed 766.[55]
> ——
> Aelfric, occurs before 974.[56]
> Aethelweard I, occurs after 977.[57]
> Cyneweard.[58]

48 The name may have come from *Cuniberctus abbas* who witnesses *Cart. Sax.* ed. Birch, no. 37; see Ehwald, *Aldhelmi Opera,* 509.

49 This is a correction of the original text which records the election in 1180 of Osbert Foliot: B.M., Cott. MS. Faust. B. I, f. 22b.

50 No other reference to this supposed abbot is known, although a document in the Register refers to Robert II as abbot on 7 Mar. of an unspecified year; this must, however, refer to Robert of Melûn; *Reg. Malm.* i, 443–4.

51 *Eulog. Hist.* (Rolls Ser.), iii, 279. Plummer, *Baedae Op. Hist.* ii, 149, says possibly earlier than 640.

52 *Gest. Pont.* 385; cf. Plummer, *Baedae Op. Hist.* ii, 309. Aldhelm died 25 May 709: *Gest. Pont.* 382, 385.

53 *Epist. Merow.* ed. Dümmler, i, 421.

54 *Gest. Pont.* 389; *Flor. Wig.* (Engl. Hist. Soc.), i, 62, n. 2; *Cart. Sax.* ed. Birch, no. 179.

55 *Gest. Pont.* 389. He was alive in 803: *Cart. Sax.* ed. Birch, no. 312.

56 *Gest. Pont.* 404–5; *Cart. Rameseia* (Rolls Ser.), ii, 59. He probably became Bp. of Crediton in 977: *Gest. Pont.* 406.

57 *Gest. Pont.* 411.

58 Ibid.

Beorhtelm.[59]
Beorhtwold I.[60]
Eadric, occurs before and in 1012.[61]
Wulfsine, occurs *c.* 1023–4.[62]
Aethelweard II, occurs *c.* 1033–4.[63]
Aelfwine, occurs *c.* 1043–4.[64]
Beorhtwold II, occurs *c.* 1045–6.[65]
Beorhtric, occurs 1052–3.[66]
Turold, appointed 1066–7.[67]
Warin, appointed 1070.[68]
Godfrey, appointed ? 1090.[69]
Eadwulf, appointed 1105–6.[70]
[Roger, Bp. of Salisbury, seized the abbey 1118.[71]]
John, appointed 1139.[72]
Peter Moraunt, appointed 1141.[73]
Gregory, appointed ? 1158.[74]
Robert de Veneys, appointed 1171–2.[75]
Osbert Foliot, appointed 1176–7.[76]

59 Ibid.
60 Ibid.
61 *Cod. Dipl.* ed. Kemble, no. 719.
62 See above, p. 155.
63 Ibid.
64 Aethelweard II was abbot for 10 years: *Gest. Pont.* 411.
65 Aelfwine was abbot for 1½ years: ibid.
66 Ibid. 182–3 and above, pp. 156–7. Beorhtwold II was abbot for 7 years.
67 Beorhtric was translated to Burton soon after death of Leofric of Peterborough, 1 Nov. 1066: *Chron. Hugh Candidus,* ed. Mellows, 75; *Two Sax. Chrons.* ed. Plummer, i, 198.
68 *Gest. Pont.* 420; *Chron. Hugh Candidus,* ed. Mellows, 161.
69 B.M., Cott. MS. Vit. A. X, ff. 158–60.
70 *Ann. Mon.* (Rolls Ser.), ii, 42.
71 Ibid. Roger died 11 Dec. 1139: *Gest. Regum,* ii, 557.
72 *Gest. Regum,* ii, 557.
73 John died 19 Aug. 1140: *Flor. Wig.* (Engl. Hist. Soc.), ii, 122. Peter was abbot by Mar. or Apr. 1141: *Gest. Regum,* ii, 573.
74 Peter died 5 Feb. 1159 according to *Chron. Edw. I and Edw. II* (Rolls Ser.), ii, cxix, but see above, p. 164.
75 Gregory died 1168: *Pipe R.* 1169 (P.R.S. xiii), 22. For Robert's succession see ibid. 1172 (xviii), 128.
76 Haddan and Stubbs, *Councils,* i, 385; *Reg. Malm.* i, 370. He died 17 Mar. 1182: B.M., Cott. MS. Tib. E. IV, *sub anno* 1181. Cf. *Pipe R.* 1182 (P.R.S. xxxi), 88.

Nicholas, appointed 1183.[77]

Robert of Melûn, appointed 1189–90.[78]

Walter Loring, mentioned as abbot-elect 1208.[79]

John Walsh, assent to election 1222.[80]

Geoffrey, assent to election 1246.[81]

William of Colerne, assent to election 1260.[82]

William of Badminton, assent to election 1296.[83]

Adam de la (atte) Hoke, assent to election 1324.[84]

John of Tintern, assent to election 1340.[85]

Simon de Aumeney, assent to election 1349.[86]

Walter de Camme, assent to election 1362.[87]

Thomas Chel(es)worth, assent to election 1396.[88]

Roger Pershore, assent to election 1424.[89]

Thomas Bristow, elected 1434.[90]

John Andever S.T.P., elected 1456.[91]

John Ayly, elected 1469.[92]

Thomas Olveston, temporalities restored 1480.[93]

Richard Frampton, elected 1510.[94]

Richard Camme, assent to election 1515.[95]

Robert Frampton, assent to election 1533.[96]

---

77 *Ann. Mon.* (Rolls Ser.), i, 53; ibid. ii, 243. Deposed 1187: *Pipe R.* 1188 (P.R.S. xxxviii), 139.
78 Robert followed between 1189 and 1190: *Pipe R.* 1190 (P. R. S. N.S. i), 120, 123. He died 24 May 1206: ibid. 1208 (P.R.S. N.S. xxiii), 201.
79 Ibid. 1208 (P.R.S. N.S. xxiii), 195. He died 1222: *Ann. Mon.* (Rolls Ser.), iii, 77.
80 *Cal. Pat.* 1216–25, 351.
81 Ibid. 1232–47, 476.
82 Ibid. 1258–66, 122.
83 Ibid. 1292–1301, 208.
84 Ibid. 1321–4, 423.
85 *Eulog. Hist.* (Rolls Ser.), iii, 452.
86 *Cal. Pat.* 1348–50, 366.
87 *Eulog. Hist.* (Rolls Ser.), iii, 313.
88 *Cal. Pat.* 1392–6, 684.
89 Ibid. 1422–9, 194.
90 Sar. Reg. Neville, f. 16*a*.
91 Sar. Reg. Beauchamp, ff. 26*b*–27*a*.
92 Ibid. f. 112*a*.
93 *Cal. Pat.* 1476–85, 202.
94 Sar. Reg. Audley, ff. 135*a*–136*a*. Formal confirmation 22 July 1511: ibid.
95 *L. & P. Hen. VIII*, ii, p. 91.
96 Ibid. vi, p. 404.

A conventual seal, appended to a document of 1231, is vesica-shaped (2½ by 1¾ in.), and shows a figure in pontificals, probably St. Aldhelm, wearing a mitre and holding a crosier in his left hand. The right hand is broken off, but was probably raised in blessing. On either side is a small trefoil-headed niche; that to the left is damaged, but the other shows a tonsured head. These probably represent the apostles Peter and Paul. The inscription has perished.

The seal of Abbot John Walsh is appended to the same document. It is identical in size and shape and very similar in design, showing a tonsured figure in a chasuble, with a crosier in the right hand and a book in the left. The legend is:

SIGI . . . IS ABBATIS MALMESBIR

On each seal the figure stands on a similar platform and has a cross within a crescent over the head. The counter-seals are identical (2.125 by 0.875 in.) and are apparently impressions from a Roman intaglio jewel showing the profile and shoulders of a classical figure with a strongly aquiline nose. The inscription reads:

+ SIGNO CREDATIS ET LITTERE[97]

Another seal,[98] of unknown date, is a pointed oval, 2.875 by 1.75 in. Beneath a triple panelled canopy the Virgin is seated crowned, with the Child on her right knee, and a sceptre in her left hand. On either side stand St. Peter with the keys and St. Paul with a sword. In the base, under an arch, is the abbot praying between two shields of arms: one, *France modern and England quarterly* and the other *a griffin*. The inscription is:

SIGI . . . MONAST . . . O BE MRIE DE MALMESBU . . .

A badly damaged circular seal[99] used in 1380 shows a seated figure between two plants. The legend is:

SOLUCI . . . IME . . . EG . . .

---

97 E 40/4850; also C 147/137.
98 SC 13/O 61; C 146/1634.
99 E 213/32.

St. John's bridge and St. John's almshouse in 1809

HOSPITALS

THE HOSPITAL OF ST. JOHN THE BAPTIST

The date of the foundation of this hospital is unknown, but it apparently incorporated an ancient chapel said, according to tradition in 1389, to have been established and endowed by the citizens of Malmesbury in recognition of King Athelstan's charter.[1] In a late 13th- or early 14th-century rental of Malmesbury Abbey the hospital of St. John was said to lie in 'Nethwalle', and to pay 2s. 8¾d. for its site, which comprised lands apparently formerly belonging to William Aldune and Thomas Purs and a parcel called *De Profundis*.[2] In 1247 the master, brethren, and sisters acquired 2 messuages in Malmesbury from Walter and Emma Bodmin, and received the donors and their heirs into all spiritual benefits of the house.[3]

In the mid 13th century the Vicar of St. Paul's, Malmesbury, whose parish included the hospital, accused the master and brethren of encroaching upon his rights. Bishop Walter of Salisbury (probably Walter de la Wyle, 1263–71) referred the complaint to his official, Constantine of Mildenhall, and later confirmed Constantine's award: the hospital was to remain subject to the vicar and the members of its unhabited household (*familia*) were to be in the same position as other parishioners; no parishioner was to be admitted to the sacraments at the hospital; the prior, brethren, and sisters, wearing their habit and 'signs', might worship in their chapel, but they were to pay their oblations and lesser tithes to the church, and 3s. 4d. and ½ pound of wax yearly to the vicar; the

---

1 C 47/46/443; *W.A.M.* xxix, 122; R. H. Luce, 'St. John's Almshouse, Malmesbury', *W.A.M.* liii, 119. Athelstan's charter twice confirmed and twice recited was probably itself a forgery: *Wilts. Borough Records* (W.A.S. Rec. Brch.), 29.
2 *Reg. Malmesburiense* (Rolls Ser.), i, 119.
3 CP 25(1) 251/15/42.

priors were to swear in the vicar's presence to observe this award within eight days of institution.[4]

The king granted the 'chapel' in 1344 to one of his clerks (already incumbent of a church in Dorset), and in 1345 he granted it to Robert of Frome.[5]

In June 1410 the Bishop of Salisbury gave an indulgence of forty days in favour of the hospital.[6]

Leland, in 1540–2, found a 'poore hospitale' outside the town on the road to Chippenham;[7] the chantry commissioners of 1545 and 1547 did not mention any hospitals at Malmesbury. It is recorded that the property was confiscated; that during Elizabeth's reign John and William Marsh of London gave their share to John Stump, who bought the rest from John Herbert and Andrew Palmer of London and transferred the whole to the corporation in 1580 for £26 13s. 4d.[8] In 1616 a meeting of the borough court was held for the first time at the hospital, where it continued thereafter to meet.[9]

The hospital existed, as an almshouse, in 1622; in 1623 the aldermen and burgesses accepted responsibility for repairs and maintenance, and in 1629 they allocated individual payments amounting to £20 to a schoolmaster and the 'five poor pepell' at St. John's.[10] By Letters Patent of 1697[11] the 'Hospital or Almshouse' was confirmed to the aldermen and capital burgesses, with a direction to pay £10 to the schoolmaster and £10 to the five poor persons 'according to ancient custom'. Mr. Moffatt wrote in 1805 that the site of the priory was then charged with £20 a year towards the support of a free school and an almshouse, perhaps established in 1629.[12] The Charity Commissioners found in 1834 that the property had been held from time immemorial

---

4 Reg. Malm. (Rolls Ser.), ii, 75–78. The document is followed in the register by one dated 1261. Constantine was a member of the chapter in 1271, and apparently Archdeacon of Sudbury in 1268 and 1273: John Le Neve and T. D. Hardy, Fasti Ecclesiae Anglicanae, ii, 490. His name does not appear in Fasti Eccl. Sar. ed. Jones.
5 Cal. Pat. 1343–5, 214, 259, 476.
6 W.A.M. xxxviii, 31.
7 Leland, Itin. ed. L. Toulmin Smith, i, 133.
8 J. M. Moffatt, History of Malmesbury, 122.
9 W.A.M. liii, 123.
10 Ibid.
11 C 66/3382/11.
12 Moffatt, Hist. of Malmesbury, 122.

by the aldermen and capital burgesses as an almshouse, and in 1904 that six widows of freemen were in residence.[13] The widows remained in occupation until 1948.[14]

The Court House, the almshouse, some cottages, and the gasworks lying at the foot of the hill on the road from Malmesbury to Chippenham now occupy the hospital site; and a blocked doorway, of perhaps about 1200,[15] reset, with a tympanum and lower jambs, survives from the medieval frontage. Above it is an arch of medieval stones framing an inscription which records that in 1694 Michael Weekes gave an additional endowment of £10 a year.

MASTERS

Walter, occurs 1247.[16]

William of Tauton, appointed 1344, resigned 1345.[17]

Robert of Frome, appointed 1345.[18]

THE HOSPITAL OF ST. MARY MAGDALENE

This hospital is mentioned in an undated charter commemorating the deeds of Walter Loring, Abbot of Malmesbury (1208–22).[19] During Walter's abbacy a 'monk's corrody' had been granted in perpetuity to the infirm brethren of the hospital.[20] The lepers of Malmesbury, possibly the inmates of this hospital, were granted protection with clause *rogamus* in 1235.[21] In 1281 the chaplain of the hospital was in receipt of a quarterly pittance of 16s. 8d. for broth granted by the Abbot and Convent of Malmesbury.[22] Late in the 13th century 10d. a year was paid by the hospital to the town for the tenement of Juliana Sewaker.[23]

13 *Endowed Char. Wilts.* H.C. 273, pp. 672, 683 (1908), lxxx.
14 Ex inf. High Steward's office; cf. *W.A.M.* liii, 124.
15 Checked with Min. of Works (Anc. Mon. Dept.). The doorway was illustrated by Canon Jackson in 1854 (*W.A.M.* i, 142) and by R. H. Luce (*W.A.M.* liii, 120), who suggests a date about 1185. Above, illus. on p. 200.
16 CP 25(1) 251/15/42.
17 *Cal. Pat.* 1343–5, 259, 476.
18 Ibid. 476.   19 See article on Malmesbury Abbey.
20 *Reg. Malmesburiense* (Rolls Ser.), ii, 80.
21 *Cal. Pat.* 1232–47, 115.   22 *Reg. Malm.* (Rolls Ser.), ii, 217.
23 Ibid. i, 119.

John London, clerk of the king's chapel, was appointed to the hospital of St. Mary Magdalene, Burton (Malmesbury), in 1439.[24] He was an executor of the will of Edward, Duke of York, who fell at Agincourt,[25] and for four years he had drawn a pension from Abingdon Abbey.[26] His appointment was apparently contested by the Abbot of Malmesbury, whom he sued in Chancery. London maintained that the house belonged to the king's ancestors of the Earldom of Hereford, and that the patronage had passed to the Duchy of Lancaster.[27]

No later record of this hospital seems to exist. It lay south of Malmesbury on the hill leading to Burton.[28] Burton Hill Chapel, a small medieval building on the east side of the Chippenham road, was pulled down about 1860.[29]

24 Ex inf. Duchy of Lancaster Office; *Bull. Inst. Hist. Res.* xviii, 74.
25 *Cal. Pat.* 1436–41, 324; John Nichols, *Royal Wills,* 222.
26 *Cal. Close,* 1435–41, 56.
27 C 1/16/316.
28 R. H. Luce, *Pages from History of Malmesbury,* 38.
29 *W.A.M.* x, 293; illus. in Aubrey, *Topog. Coll.* ed. Jackson, pl. xxvi.

INDEX

NOTE. Page numbers in bold face are those of a chapter. A page number in italics refers to a map or illustration on that page. A number followed by *n* is a reference only to the footnotes on that page.

pet food wholesalers, 56
Peterborough (Northants.):
  abbey, 158
  abbot, see Leofric
Petre, Wm., 186
Petty:
  Anne, see Ashe
  Thos., 40
Pilton (Devon), 179, 183
  prior, 183 *n*
Pinn:
  Anne, see Ridler
  Wm., 37
pipe making, 112
plague, 73
Plantagenet, Geo., duke of Clarence, 183
Player's, see Foxley: man.
Pleydell-Bouverie:
  (formerly Bouverie), Jacob, earl of Rad-
    nor (d. 1828), 42, 101
  Jacob, earl of Radnor (d. 1930), 100
  and see Bouverie
police force, see Malmesbury: borough;
  Wiltshire: county police force
police station, see Malmesbury
Pollen:
  C. J., 88
  Sir John, Bt. (d. 1863), 110
  Sir John, Bt. (d. 1959), 110
  Sir John, Bt. (fl. 1987), 110
  Sir Ric., Bt. (d. 1881), 110
  Sir Ric., Bt. (d. 1918), 110
  Sir Ric., Bt. (d. 1930), 110
  fam., 111
Poole:
  Sir Giles, 110
  Sir Hen. (d. 1616), 110
  Hen. (fl. 1642), 110–11
  Jos., 25
  fam., 77
Poole Brothers, 25
poor-law union, see Malmesbury
poor relief, see *under places; and see (for
  cross references)* poorhouse;
  workhouses
Poore, Ric., bp. of Salisbury, 169

poorhouse, see Westport
pope, the, 175, 181; *and see* Adrian IV;
  Alexander III; Anastasius; Celestine III;
  Eugenius III; Honorius II; Honorius
  III; Innocent III; Sergius I; Urban VI
Porter, Wm., 45, 82
Potterne, 171
prehistoric remains, see Malmesbury
Presbyterians, 88–90, 94, 143–4
prison, see Malmesbury
Pritchard, P. J., 38
professions, see *(for cross references)*
  occupations and professions
punishments, see ducking stool; *and see*
  Malmesbury: prison
Purdue, fam., 88
Purs, Thos., 45
Purton, 152, 159, 175, 188–9
  ch., 167–8, 172
Pye-TMC Ltd., 57

Quakers (Society of Friends), 89, 107, 114
quarries and quarrying, 5, 103–4, 112,
  136
quarter sessions, see Wiltshire

R.A.F. station, see Hullavington; *and see*
  hangar
radio, electrical, and electronic equipment
  manufacture, 56–7
Radnor:
  earldom, 100
  earls of, see Bouverie, Wm.; Pleydell-
    Bouverie
railway station, see Malmesbury
railways, see Bristol & South Wales
  Railway; G.W.R.; Malmesbury
  railway
Raleigh, Sir Wal., 125
Ramsbury, 181
  bp., see Heremann
Ratcliffe, Edwin, 55
Reading (Berks.), 162
Ready Animal Foods, 56
Rectory (manors of the name), see
  Malmesbury: man.; Westport: man.